HIGH DESERT

HIGH DESERT

A Journey of Survival and Hope

by Kim Douglas

Bahá'í
PUBLISHING
Wilmette, Illinois

Bahá'í Publishing
415 Linden Avenue, Wilmette, Illinois 60091-2844
Copyright © 2009 by the National Spiritual Assembly
of the Bahá'ís of the United States

12   11   10   09   4   3   2   1

Library of Congress Cataloging-in-Publication Data
Douglas, Kim.
  High desert : a journey of survival and hope / by Kim Douglas.
    p. cm.
  ISBN-13: 978-1-931847-59-9 (alk. paper)
  1. Family violence. 2. Victims of family violence—Psychology. 3. Abused children—
Family relationships. 4. Bahai Faith. I. Title.

  HV6626.2.D72 2009
  362.82'92092—dc22
  [B]
                                2008055042

Cover design by Robert A. Reddy
Book design by Suni D. Hannan

This book is dedicated to those who have lost their lives
to intimate-partner and family violence.

Contents

Acknowledgments

The idea for this book was conceived decades before I was recovered and strong enough to write it. Without divine assistance and the encouragement and support of many wonderful people who have come into my life, I would not have had the courage to write with such transparency.

My intimate partner in life, David, has endured some of the fallout of my violent past. Nonetheless, he has supported and encouraged me to persevere in my healing process. He has modeled to me exceptional parenting skills, though, humble man that he is, he'd be the last to admit it. He has joined me in therapy at times so we can learn together from the marriage mechanic, as I call our therapist, how to better maintain our marriage and family. He has loved and supported me and urged me to write about overcoming the effects of my past.

My lovable and capable daughters—Aleah and Anisa—are gifts from God. I hope and pray that when they begin to build their adult lives they will examine their childhood and repeat the traditions and behaviors worthy of being passed down to their children and grandchildren. I give them my full permission to do better where I have fallen short, to avoid repeating my mistakes, and to strive to create peaceful and loving homes for their families.

My mom and my brothers, Mike and Chuck, deserve acknowledgment for having endured violence that no one deserves. They have willingly agreed to have our family story shared and have offered their emotional support throughout the writing of the book.

Jaco and Michelle Hamman's generosity in providing their cottage on Silver Lake enabled me to make significant progress on the book. Nancy McKenzie, another angel, offered her cottage, which enabled me to set aside the daily challenges to focus on revising the book.

Pat Crum Lubben, Carmelita LaPorte, Robyn Afrik, and Kristen Gray were readers of the manuscript in an earlier form, and their feedback helped me in the revision process. Pat Crum, an advocate of children, an inspiration, a teacher, and a friend, continues to provide a listening ear and astute insights about parenting when I feel challenged in my role as a parent. She appears in the book, as she was one of my teachers for the Nurturing Parenting Program.

My Juice Plus business leaders and team, especially Dr. Candace Corson and Kortney Burgess, offered their understanding, support, and help with my growing business, especially during the final stages of the editing process. Dr. Corson's leadership is a model of integrity, vision, and health that serves me in my personal growth and in my service to others.

And I would not be here, functioning and thriving as I am, without the expertise of numerous therapists who listened, questioned, encouraged, and challenged me. I want to acknowledge the expertise of Denise Hames, Wanda Decker, Sara Shambarger, Ishwara Thomas, Dr. Roger Danchise, and Lois Khan. The workshop I attended with Marion Woodman, author of *Addiction to Perfection,* remains a highlight in my healing process.

Terry Cassiday and Bahhaj Taherzadeh, my editors, have offered their generous and astute insights and helped the manuscript reach its potential through the revision and editing processes. Their belief in the book and its potential to impact readers fuels my own hope that the story can help and inspire those who have been victimized. In this way, what I have suffered will have greater purpose.

I am forever grateful to all of you and the many others—family members, friends, mentors, teachers, and writers—who have listened, tried to understand, and encouraged me to persevere through the challenges of healing and endeavoring to break the cycle of violence.

Note to the Reader

Some of the names of the individuals who appear in the book have been changed to protect their privacy.

Prologue: Lilacs

One Sunday morning around the breakfast table, Dad glanced at Mom and said, "Can't you comb your hair, Carole, put on a little lipstick? You look like shit."

Mom didn't say anything. What could she say?

"You don't care," Dad went on. "You don't give a damn. Just look!" He stood up, pointing at the back of the chair. "There's fucking grease!" Dad picked up his plate and hurled it against the wall. Then he slammed his glass down onto the table. Eggs, juice, and blood splattered. At the sink he turned on the faucet and held his hand under the running water. Wrapping a dish towel around his hand, he stumbled into the living room.

I leaned against the wall in the kitchen, trying to stop myself from trembling. Mom paced. In the kitchen, she looked at my younger brother, Mike, then at me. In the hallway she stole a glance at Dad lying on the sofa, his hand held up. She didn't know what to do. None of us did. There was no way around my Dad, who stood at the center and the opening of this crazy maze in which we were all trapped.

An odd sound broke through the tension. Mom hurried into the living room. I glanced in at my Dad. He was crying. I had never heard or seen him cry. When someone cries you're supposed to comfort them, but how could I possibly do that? I was more accustomed to Dad as tyrant than Dad as a hurt man.

Within minutes, he flew off the sofa, shouting, "Band-Aids! Get me some Band-Aids." Mom raced upstairs.

"Where in the hell are you going?" Dad screamed at her.

"They're upstairs," Mom answered, but then she called down from the bathroom that she couldn't find any.

Dad stormed up the steps, as she was coming back down. "You're blind, Carole. You're fucking blind." We could hear him tossing the contents of the medicine cabinet onto the floor.

Mom, back in the kitchen, grabbed me. "Go next door. Get Mr. Hanson! Tell him we need help!"

Mom had never sent me to get help before. Stunned, I raced across the yard and pounded on the Hansons' door. No one was answering. I rang the bell. Still no one came to the door. What should I do—go home, try another neighbor? I didn't really know, but I couldn't go back. I just couldn't. So I raced down the alley toward the Armstrongs' house. Maybe they could help.

Mrs. Armstrong, in her nightgown, opened the door. Behind her, Mr. Armstrong zipped up his jeans. "Kim, what's wrong?" he asked guiding me into the house.

I broke down but managed to share a few details.

"Has this happened before?" Mrs. Armstrong asked, shocked.

I couldn't answer.

"Has your dad ever done this before?" Mr. Armstrong tried.

I looked at the floor and nodded.

"I think we should get the Wolfes. They're psychologists. They'll know what to do," Mr. Armstrong said, more to Mrs. Armstrong than to me.

More people finding out couldn't be a good thing, but I didn't say "no." I was used to other people making decisions for me, so I didn't protest.

Within minutes, the Wolfes were standing in the Armstrongs' kitchen. "Kim, we need to call the police," Dr. Wolfe said.

"Why?" I asked, horrified by the thought.

"What your dad is doing is against the law."

"Against the law?" I thought to myself, *Murder is against the law, bank robbery, but not what Dad's doing.*

The police arrived, and after asking a few questions, they walked down the street. My mother answered the door, one of the two officers told me later, and she said that nothing was wrong, just a small family spat, now under control. The officers explained to me that nothing more could be done since none of the neighbors had witnessed the violence.

Shortly after the police left, my mother called. Mrs. Armstrong handed me the phone.

"Kimberly, you can come home now," she said in a tone indicating I had done something wrong. *Kimberly* was my name when Mom was mad or disappointed. I should not have gone to the Armstrongs' house. I should not have let the Wolfes call the police.

"Why did you go there?" Mom asked when I arrived home.

"No one was home next door. I didn't know what to do," I responded, and then whispered, "Where's Dad?"

"He and your brother went to the hospital. Your dad needs stitches. The cut wouldn't stop bleeding."

Within an hour Dad returned. I was not to betray the family again, he lectured. What went on in our house was no one's business. "Go to your room and stay there for the rest of the day," he ordered.

I closed my bedroom door and pulled the shades. I lay on my bed and stared at the blue and white wallpaper, the pinstripes jailing me. I closed my eyes, but all I could see was my stupid self running down the alley and through the Armstrongs' yard. Why had I done that? I should have returned home instead. I should have said "no" when they suggested involving the Wolfes and the police.

I paid the Armstrongs back the very next day. I desecrated their beautiful lilacs. I tore one twig off and tossed it across the lawn, then another twig, then a limb. I ripped off the flowers and littered them across the steps. I massacred that bush right down to its core. How else could I, an eight-year-old, express the ineffable frustration and torture inside?

Mrs. Armstrong made comments that indicated she sensed I was the guilty one, though she never directly said so.

"Such a beautiful plant."

"Someone very upset about something."

"Someone who couldn't help themselves."

I heard these comments from her off and on, but I never confessed.

Years—what seems like lifetimes—later, I have a different perspective on that day. If I could speak to the young girl I was, I would say, "You did the right thing. You reached out, shared the secret, wrestled with the part of you that your dad was trying to strangle. This was a turning point. You let a new, freer, stronger individual come into existence, the part of you that would begin to listen to dreams, to flee across the country, to build a life different than the one you were given, not by choice but by birth arrangement. Not so bad the tearing apart of beautiful lilacs you love seeing whole and sturdy today. They were there for you. They took some of the anguish from inside, some of the tumult you were barely surviving. You pruned the bush that year. It did not die. The following year it grew back, blossomed, and doubled in size."

Part 1: Angel in the Graveyard

The Same Cycle

I reached the Arizona Inn at 5:30 a.m. and circled the inner brick walkways along with other early morning joggers attracted to the deep green and vibrant manicured lawns. I stole glances of the native plants I ran past. I loved the slender tinted green branches of the Palo Verde; the silly looking pancake of a cactus, the prickly pear; the spindly and winding ocotillo; and the stately soldier, the saguaro. The scent of creosote intoxicated me.

On my way home I focused on the dark peaks and curves of the Rincon Mountains. I preferred their mystery at this hour—silhouettes without texture, an unexamined profile of peaks, curves, and valleys—the beauty of the earth from a distance, like the view astronauts possess from space, the swirl of our existence. As the sun inched higher, darts of lavender and magenta, swirls of saffron and old gold tangled with one another. Soon the colors of the day's early canvas would evaporate into blinding fumes of dust and light, and I would feel disappointed by what further illumination revealed: wrinkles and folds, weeds and smog.

Back home, as I styled my hair and applied makeup, I felt proud. Another day, another three miles, part of a regimen in my quest to get thin. Both my pride and the release of endorphins—those feel-good brain chemicals—made it worth the agony of getting up before dawn.

After a few prayers, I rode my bike to campus to make an 8:30 class. After physical geography, which frankly bored me, I raced to Modern Grammar and Usage—much more interesting for this English major. Brit Lit was next. However, this was one English class that didn't captivate me. Where were the women writers? It seemed as if every "major" author was named John or William. I struggled to pay attention in that class. And at times I felt guilty for struggling. I should love Lord Byron the way I love Margaret Atwood, right?

When I arrived at Bentley's House of Coffee and Tea, one of the most popular venues near campus, a line of customers stood all the way from the counter to the door, and every seat in the restaurant was taken. Jo, the manager, was preparing lunch orders in the back. "Hey Kim. Glad you're here. We're swamped," she said. "Why don't you help at the counter?" Jo had one eye on the crowd and one eye on the plate in front of her and still managed to sound friendly.

For the next hour and a half, I took and rang up lunch orders for professors, students, nearby storeowners and workers, stay-at-home moms with their kids, and doctors and nurses from the University Medical Center, who knew they couldn't get coffee as good anywhere else. Jo served the best iced and hot mocha and kept secret the prized recipe for these decadent and delicious drinks that drew in the customers.

Bentley's was dreamed into existence by the managers, Jo and Willow. During a vacation several years back, they felt disheartened about returning to their respective jobs. They yearned for fun and meaningful work—not the nine-to-five drudgery that just so happened to pay the bills. "If we could do anything, what would that be?" they asked each other. While exploring possible answers, they gave themselves permission to dream without allowing any financial worries to creep in. They both imagined opening a coffeehouse, and not just any ordinary coffeehouse— the best coffeehouse in town, a coffeehouse that would showcase the art and photography of local artists and would bring in local performers and poets, a coffeehouse where the customers could study and hang out, a coffeehouse that served the best coffees, teas, pastries, and light meals. Excited by their vision, they returned home and started making concrete plans. Family and friends loaned them money. They secured a fabulous space near the University of Arizona's main campus, and within several years they opened a second coffeehouse in downtown Tucson.

Their story gave me hope that perhaps I could dream. Perhaps I could achieve success. Maybe one day my fears about getting married would subside and I'd find that special man, get married, and raise children while progressing in a career involving writing. And . . . perhaps someday I would feel freed of the past.

Settled in the library, I tried my best to do what good students do—study. But I struggled to stay awake. The physical geography textbook bored me. Yes, I loved the desert and learning the names of the remarkable plant life, but I disliked reading about the causes and history of earthquakes, continental drift, and volcanoes. I skimmed the pages, nodded off, wakened, jotted a note, and wakened again. With highlighter in hand, I marked a sentence I hoped was a main point. I drifted off again. When I forced my eyes open a few minutes later, I decided to try finishing "Paradise Lost." Even though my professor boasted that this epic poem was Milton's greatest achievement, that the language was a superb example of rhythm and rhyme, that this work inspired Keats and a writer named Joseph Hayden whom I had never heard of, I found myself drifting and feeling guilty for it. I was an English major after all. I should love Milton. I should be able to read this work and understand what I was reading, but I felt lost. Yes, there was Satan. Yes, there was Adam and Eve. Yes, even Almighty God was present in this work, but the language was stilted and hard, and I was tired. How would I ever get an "A" in this class?

I packed up the very books I had barely absorbed and headed over to the 3HO Sikh Ashram just off campus for my late afternoon yoga and meditation class. I slipped off my Birkenstocks, pulled a beach towel from my backpack, and set up for the hour-long class. This room had come to feel like a kind of home to me. I liked the high ceilings, the tall open windows, the four white walls featuring a photo of Yogi Bhajan and several colorful and dramatic pictures of the gods and goddesses from Hindu scriptures (even though the photo and pictures initially felt a little strange to me). I liked that an altar was set up in front, and some days sandalwood incense burned. Hari Bal Dev sat in full lotus position on a sheepskin mat in front of the altar. Several students on sheepskins or towels, like myself, prepared for the class. Some stretched their legs and wriggled their fingers and toes. Others sat in half- or full-lotus, stretching their necks to the right, then down to their chest, then to the left. Some stood and reached their arms and fingers toward the ceiling. I lay down that day, listened to the doves cooing, the tick of the wind in the magnolias outside, the shrill of the crickets and cicadas.

When I first started taking yoga, the exercises challenged and invigorated me and prepared me to meditate. Often during meditation Aunt Mildred and Fran Scharli—two women who had a great influence on me and had passed away—came to mind. I felt such grief I couldn't hold in the tears. My instructors acknowledged and affirmed my process. They let me know that it was OK to cry and show my emotions, that yoga and meditation sometimes accessed parts of ourselves we had neglected and released emotions we had held in or buried.

I left the ashram and returned to campus for a three-hour creative writing class with Steve Orlen. Though tired, I felt invigorated because of my enthusiasm for writing. The discussions, the reading of poems by well-known poets and us lesser known-wannabes, filled me with the same kind of feelings I had during yoga class and during my own private prayers and community devotions at the Bahá'í Center. I felt as if the very molecules in the air were charged. I was not lost in chaos, not escaping my body and the moment to fantasy, a wine-high, or worry. I was sensing a completeness in the actual moment. There was beauty to the long table cluttered with our open books, beauty to the silence after Steve read Rilke or Neruda to open the class. Though I felt nervous about sharing my poems, I valued discussions of my work and that of other students. Each word on the page became significant, each sound, each rhythm. The possibilities that existed for revising our creative work fueled me. I couldn't wait to get home and revise my poems-in-progress.

By 9:30 I steered down Lee Street past Campbell Avenue toward Tucson Boulevard, where I had a choice to make, but it didn't feel like a choice because I didn't pause to ponder and decide. I turned right, away from my apartment. I turned right and pedaled, pedaled hard. I didn't think. I didn't allow myself to think. I just aimed straight for the 7-11. Junkie-Kim pedaling, parking her bike, not bothering to lock it, pulling out the six dollars and seventy-five cents tip money from Bentley's. I bought five pastries, a quart of chocolate-chip ice cream, and three butterfingers. I paid. I placed the bagged items in my backpack. I thanked the cashier. I left the store and climbed onto my bike and rode under the star-filled sky toward my tiny one-room apartment on Lee Street.

When I arrived home, I emptied the contents of my backpack and sat down to eat. I ate everything I had just purchased. I ate until I had to unbutton my shorts. I ate until I felt sick. It didn't matter that I felt sick because I would do what I always did, each and every night. I would stick my finger down my throat and rid myself of everything I had just taken in. I would feel better. I would clean the toilet and the sink. I would brush my teeth and drink a big glass of water and feel energized enough to work on my poems. Night after night, the same cycle—a stop at the 7-11, tearing into the packages at home and stuffing myself, then relieving myself, then working on a poem, then bed. In the morning I would run again to make sure I stayed thin, and then it was off to another day on campus, the coffeehouse, or the Tucson Bahá'í Center.

Some nights, like that particular night, I cleaned the toilet and sink and paused a moment in front of the mirror. I looked at myself, my eyes a little bloodshot from the trauma I had inflicted. What was I doing to myself? Why? What was wrong with me that I felt so imprisoned by my own tendencies? I had read about the "prison of self" in the Bahá'í writings. 'Abdu'l-Bahá wrote that the prison of self was the greatest of prisons.[1] How would I release myself from that prison? I couldn't imagine my life without the stop at 7-11. No matter how many times I said I would stop, that I wouldn't binge anymore, I continued to do it.

I managed to utter a couple of prayers and fell into bed. The alarm sounded all too soon, and I fumbled out of bed for a repeat performance of the day before. I raced past the glimpse I took of myself in the mirror, the prayers that I uttered as I rushed out the door. I didn't recognize, at the time, that I was engaged in two kinds of processes—some were life-defeating and destructive and the others were life-giving and renewing. The addictive behaviors and excess activity were destructive. New behaviors such as prayer and meditation were sustaining. Studying what I loved at the university and deciding to major in creative writing were affirming choices

---

1. 'Abdu'l-Bahá, *'Abdu'l-Bahá in London,* (London: Bahá'í Publishing Trust, 1982), p. 120.

that showed I was learning to honor myself. Hiking, jogging, biking, and my practice of yoga were renewing activities most of the time. But still I fell back into the binging and purging, day after day after day.

The Long Healing Prayer

One of several hundred, I crossed a stretch of lawn known as the mall, waving to friends and acquaintances. The mall spanned almost a mile of the University of Arizona's campus. I felt at home here, though a few years before, I had stood at the edge of campus looking in. I longed to return to school, but worried. Would I allow parties to distract me from my studies? Would I end up dropping out again, like I had at the University of Missouri? And what about my dream to major in creative writing? Was Dad right, that such an impractical choice would lead nowhere?

New friends urged me to follow my heart. They made comments, like "have faith," or "you don't want to choose a career just for the money you might earn," or "the best careers are where your natural talents and service intersect." I had never received such advice before, and I liked it. Less comfortable were the suggestions that I apply for student loans so I could immediately return to school. Dad had raised me to believe that borrowing money was worse than committing a mortal sin. I tried to believe that my friends were right, that paying for my college education was an investment in my future.

Just as I approached the student commons, Dr. Atefat, a friend from the Bahá'í community and a professor, called out to me. "How are you, dear friend?" he said as he reached out and shook my hand.

"I'm fine," I replied, but my eyes filled with tears.

"What's wrong?" Dr. Atefat asked, pulling me over to a bench so we could sit down and talk.

"I don't know," I said trying to hold in my emotions but not having an easy time of it. "I've been feeling really down lately."

"Maybe it's depression," Dr. Atefat said as if diagnosing me. "A lot of people have trouble with depression. I have struggled with it myself."

"You have?" I asked, surprised because he seemed like one of the most joyful people I knew.

Dr. Atefat shared that he had recently traveled to Georgia to meet with a physician about a few different health challenges including the depression. The doctor prescribed dietary changes, some medicine, and the recitation of the Long Healing Prayer twice a day.

"Twice a day?" I said, surprised, as the prayer was several pages long.

"Twice a day," he affirmed with a nod. "You might give it a try. Don't feel badly if you only say it once a day. That's better than not at all. I've been saying the prayer for a couple of weeks now, and I feel great." Dr. Atefat smiled his warm broad smile and continued, "I humbly offer you that advice. Expect incredible things to happen. It's a very powerful prayer."

That night I arrived home, this time without stopping at the 7-11. After freshening up, I sat on the one chair I owned—a comfy umbrella chair. I crossed my legs, opened the prayer book, and began reciting. The rhythm of the particular combination of words and the repetition of the refrain soothed me. I chanted, "I Call on Thee O Spirit! O Light! O Most Manifest One! Thou the Sufficing, Thou the Healing, Thou the Abiding, O Thou Abiding One . . ."[2]

I had grown up attending St. Athanasius Catholic Church with Mom and my brothers. Dad was a non-practicing Lutheran who studied the world religions, and on many weekends sat at the dining room table typing out his thoughts on the similarities and differences of the major faiths and the connections between religion and theology, ecology, philosophy, and other sciences. He had no desire to attend church and instead practiced his own brand of faith. I, however, didn't mind attending mass. I enjoyed some of the rituals. While kneeling at the pew, I imitated Aunt Lorel. Trembling, tears streaming, she covered her face with her palms to try and make her emotional communion more private. I knew something powerful was going on. I knew that she was close to God in those moments. I thought if I knelt long enough and covered my face and trembled a little, maybe I, too, would have that same kind of connection.

Because our church-going was sporadic, I remembered very few prayers from my Catholic upbringing. The Lord's Prayer came easily, but I could recall little else. Since becoming a Bahá'í, I had come to appreciate the

---

2. Bahá'u'lláh, in *Bahá'í Prayers*, (Wilmette, IL: Bahá'í Publishing Trust, 2002), p. 104.

Bahá'í prayers for how they expressed the innermost sentiments of my heart with words I often couldn't devise on my own.

I resumed chanting, drifting into the music of the prayer, surrendering to supplication. Turning the pages, I switched from chanting to singing. The repetition of particular verses, the alliteration and assonance created a lyrical quality. I could have just uttered the words, but the poet in me resisted such a dry encounter with the language of the prayer

When I came to the ending, I sat with my eyes closed. The quietness contained my heartbeat, my breath, the cooing of the dove outside the window, and the distant *shhhh* of the traffic on Tucson Boulevard. I sat in a state of surrender, for where else could I go with my problems but to God? The words of the prayer inspired and fueled me with hope. I added a few of my own ordinary words: *Heal me, O God. Help me overcome this insanity with food. Help me live like a normal person.*

I wanted an instant cure, but that didn't happen. There was no McDonald's response to the prayers, no easy drive-through here. And so, for days I kept on chanting away, hoping for guidance, for relief. Alone in the privacy of my apartment, I tried to connect with God and find that part of me created in His image.

Grave Digger

I didn't know the man standing among rectangular blocks of cement covered with aluminum squares. He wore a long white robe. A turban covered his head and a silver beard fell to his chest. Scrawled on those squares were letters of an alphabet I had not been taught. I had seen Hebrew and Arabic prayers before and admired the artistic qualities of the letters. I believed these letters were from the Arabic alphabet, but I could not decipher the slants and curves. The man's eyes gleamed in the dark as he waved me toward him.

I hesitated, but he smiled, and I found myself comforted by his grin. I walked over. "Yes?" I said.

"Are you looking for this?" he asked, handing me a shovel.

"Why would I need that?"

"You have some work to do, don't you?"

"Excuse me?" I asked.

"You need to dig yourself out."

"Dig myself out? What are you talking about?" I asked, though I sensed the shovel was mine.

He continued to hold out the shovel—rusted and coated with dirt. He said nothing, but his eyes broke through my resistance. I tried but couldn't look away from his caring gaze.

"So, I'm supposed to take this?"

He nodded. I laughed a nervous laugh. His focus remained unbroken.

"You haven't killed yourself, not yet."

I looked away from those onyx mirrors. What was he talking about? I wasn't killing myself.

"You need to start digging," he repeated with even more authority in his voice. I looked at him. His eyes filled with my image—a young woman paralyzed by fear. Why was I so afraid? He was not my father. His voice was focused and concerned yet transcended itself. It was free. It was angry. It was music. It was Coltrane. It was John Coltrane and a singer endeavoring to climb the scales of music that broke all rules. The words *now* and *start* and *digging* were directed toward me. Who was I to have someone care this much?

"But I'm standing right here," I persisted.

"You can't hide her," he said, heaving the shovel into the dirt so that it remained upright. He placed his hands on my shoulders. "You need her—the wounded, hurt, and angry child—you need her to survive."

"Who are you?" I asked.

"You can't use religion the way you are—uttering prayers and practicing new habits, expecting your life to be transformed. You can't bury your past. You must examine it. You need to love the little girl you blame and label *wild, fat, no good.*"

I looked at the ground—mostly dirt, a little dried grass, a tombstone with no name, no dates. I looked at the shovel and hesitated before picking it up.

"Go ahead," the man urged.

After a few half-hearted attempts, I looked up.

He nodded and cocked his head toward the shovel and ground.

I continued exerting a little more effort, but I didn't want to dig deeper. It was easier this way, trying to move on, build a life and let the past lay to rest. Use religion to bury the past? Why not?

But he called that dishonest. "Face yourself," he said. "Look at what you have endured and suffered."

Tears came to my eyes. What if I couldn't survive looking at the suffering? I closed my eyes and heaved the shovel into the ground, breaking into a sweat. Was I getting anywhere, any closer to some supposed grave where my secrets belonged? I doubted it.

"Need a little help?" he asked. "We can do this together."

I nodded. "I haven't spent much time trying to dig myself out of the ground."

"But too much energy trying to keep yourself there."

I looked at him and realized he knew more about me than I knew about myself.

After a long while, we reached the tomb. We shoveled around it so we could open the box. When we did, I didn't face myself as I had expected. Instead, something like gravity pulled me in and back through the years, a cyclone of images from the past swirling around me.

When I woke up I lay there, stilled and startled. Scatterings of moonlight slipped in through the slits of the bamboo shade. I felt far from the futon I had been sleeping on, far from the single closet in the single room that held the bed that I rolled up into a sofa during the daytime, far from the built-in kitchen counter with one barstool, where I ate, studied, and read. I could almost smell the foreign earth I had been digging. I could almost touch the turban and the beard of the man, some kind of saint trying to help me. I sat up and rolled up the blind to look out onto the yard. The full moon illumined the prickly pear, ocotillo, and the rock garden that the owners of the house across the yard maintained.

There I sat, trying to settle myself, trying to be in Tucson but holding another dream—another clear message. The meaning seemed accurate. I had studied the Bahá'í Faith for several months and realized when I decided to join that I was on a journey of discovery and growth. I did not want to believe that journey involved muddling around with my past. I had seen a counselor here and there and didn't really like digging through my childhood, but apparently I needed to find a new counselor and commit to the weekly sessions for longer than a few months.

By the end of the week I forgot about the dream. I didn't bother to check out counseling. I didn't want to consider my past. I was mostly happy with my life. A little depression never hurt anybody. Besides, I was saying the Long Healing Prayer like Dr. Atefat had suggested.

Intervention

The intense desert light muted the red whirling lights of the ambulances and police cars. Officers approached and asked the bystanders what had happened. "Flew off the bike," "got hit rounding the corner," "conscious but dazed." I couldn't tell who said what, except for the woman with spiked silver hair who had leaned over and taken hold of my hand a few minutes earlier. "They're here, now. Don't you worry; you're going to be fine," she said with such conviction that it penetrated the shock.

Two paramedics replaced her. They knelt down, one taking my pulse, the other asking me what hurt. Palm fronds spun above their concerned faces. I tried to speak, but I felt nauseous and dizzy. I tried to lift my head, but the paramedic with a finger on my wrist held down my shoulder with his other hand.

"Don't move," he said, but he didn't need to. Just that miniscule lift of my head caused a full body spasm. I gasped and choked on a scream. "You may have broken your back," he whispered as if the volume of his voice could sedate me. "If this is a spinal injury, we need to keep you quiet and still. We're going to cut off your backpack with scissors. Then we're going to slide a board under you, and once we stabilize you on the board, we'll lift you to the stretcher. OK?"

I turned my head toward the ground. Stones, shoes, car wheels, and asphalt continued to swirl. As the paramedics lifted me onto the stretcher, the searing pain filled me with dread.

That particular Sunday, Easter Sunday, I had made plans to spend the day with Adam, my boyfriend at the time, and his children, who were visiting him for the weekend. We would play games, swim at the apartment pool, and I could lounge in the sun while catching up on the homework I had put off all weekend. That morning I filled my backpack with all those heavy textbooks, then set out on my bike and began the three-mile trek to his apartment. Pedaling down Lee Street, I made the unusual decision to turn onto typically busy Tucson Boulevard. It was Sunday. It was Easter. Most cars were parked in church lots. I figured it was safe and headed north all the way to Prince Avenue and turned left. Barely a moment had passed, not even a second. In that miniscule sliver, a bang startled me. In that instant, that startle, I felt as if I were about to become the spectator of an accident. Instead, I flew through the air, landed, and rolled. Then cars pulled over, car doors opened, and dozens of people surrounded me. Stunned and immobilized, the only thing I could register was the blue, cloudless sky.

The ambulance driver sped toward Tucson General Hospital, less than a mile from the accident site. Every bump in the road shot through the wheels and shocks of the ambulance and into me. I cried out, unable to restrain myself. "Hang on! We're almost there," the paramedic sitting next to me urged. I closed my eyes and remembered the prayer. Was this the answer? What had I done to deserve this?

Within moments, the medics wheeled me through the entrance of Tucson General's Emergency Department. A couple of nurses led us to a curtained-off makeshift room. One of them consulted with the paramedics and then suggested I contact a loved one. I asked for a phone so I could call my boyfriend, Adam. The other nurse began checking my vitals. She wrapped the blood pressure cuff around my arm. Her finger rested on my wrist. Then she placed a thermometer under my tongue. A doctor entered, exited, and returned with another doctor. They poked and pricked and asked, "Can you feel this? Can you feel that? Can you lift up your right leg? . . . wiggle your left toes?"

Within fifteen minutes, Adam tore into the room, his children Angie and Tyler following close behind. He grabbed hold of my hand and kissed me.

"Hey, guys," I greeted the kids. Tyler's eyes grew wide, and Angie squinted and bit the inside of her lower lip. I managed a smile and said, "Don't worry. I'm going to be OK." But just as I said that, another spasm had me yelping. Two more doctors scurried in and asked Adam and the kids to make themselves comfortable in the waiting area. All three looked panicked. "Try not to worry," I said to them as they slipped through the curtains and out of sight.

That afternoon doctors sent me by ambulance to the University Medical Center because Tucson General didn't have the proper equipment to perform a Magnetic Resonance Imaging (MRI) scan. The driver wheeled me to an elevator and down to the basement where the MRI equipment was located. "The technician should be here soon. She's been called. It's kind of quiet 'cuz it's Easter. You gonna be OK here?"

I nodded.

The driver wished me well and departed.

Beneath a sheet and a cotton blanket in the bowels of the medical center, I peered from my flat-on-the-back spot toward the various office doors, all closed. Pipes painted the same drab beige as the walls ran just below the ceiling. No one walked the halls—not one doctor, nurse, technician, or visitor. I wanted to call the ambulance driver back. I wanted a paramedic, a nurse from the other hospital, anyone. Adam had left to take the kids to their mom's and didn't know yet that I had been sent here. I wanted out, but every tiny movement hurt. I called, "Is anyone there? Anyone? Please! I need help." But I knew my calls were pointless, just as I knew the familiar feelings of hopelessness and isolation represented by the closed doors, the long empty hallway, the drab pipe-covered ceiling, and the absolute and horrifying silence. So this was the answer to my prayers?

Finally, the technician showed up muttering an apology and something about finishing Easter dinner. She spun me into the room that held the huge MRI machine. After a few agonizing moments of transferring me from the stretcher onto the hard table, she explained how the procedure would work. She would leave the room, press a few buttons, and the table would slide into that odd cylindrical tunnel. When I was inside the machine, she would ask me to hold my breath and would begin the imaging.

Once I was settled back at Tucson General, a nurse encouraged me to call my family. "They would want to be here. This is quite serious," she said. I agreed with her in part. Mom would want to be here. Dad, however, would not want the bother. Several years earlier when I studied at the University of Missouri, I was hospitalized for severe abdominal pain. When I called home, Dad responded by saying, "Don't tell your mother. Just call me at work and keep me informed of what the doctors have to say." Did I ask "Why aren't you coming to offer support?" No, of course not. No one argued with Dad. I didn't feel comfortable expressing that I needed support. Why would this hospitalization be any different?

I didn't feel up to explaining the complications of my family to the nurse, so after further encouragement I dialed the number. My youngest brother, Chuck, answered the phone. After saying a brief hello to him, I asked for Mom and Dad. He informed me that they were at the cabin in northern Wisconsin and wouldn't be home for a few days. A part of me felt relieved that they weren't home. I wasn't sure I could take a rejection.

"So, what's up that you need to talk to them?" he asked.

"Nothing major," I said. "A little accident, that's all."

"An accident? What happened?"

"I was riding my bike and got hit by a car. I'm OK though. They're doing a few tests at the hospital."

"A few tests? So what's wrong?"

"Maybe a broken back."

"Shit, Kim! A broken back? Mom and Dad should know about this."

"Well, don't bother them," I said, fearing Dad's reaction.

"What are you talking about? Hell, a broken back is a broken back!"

"Bones break and they heal. It's no big deal."

"I don't know, Kim. A broken back can be serious. I think I should call Mom and Dad."

"Don't bother them. There's nothing they can do anyway. They'll be home soon enough and you can have them call me then."

I gave Chuck the name of the hospital and my phone number and made him promise not to bother Mom and Dad.

I later learned that Chuck called the hospital and asked to speak to a doctor who knew about my situation. Informing Chuck of the critical nature of the injuries, the doctor urged him to contact Mom and Dad. "They should make every effort to get to Tucson as soon as possible," the doctor said. Devastated to learn that I was partially paralyzed, Chuck proceeded to make more phone calls and arranged to have my parents informed of the situation. Mom and Dad telephoned the next morning to let me know that they would arrive in Tucson that night. I apologized for disrupting their vacation, but Dad was not angry. He reassured me and told me to hang in there.

While Mom and Dad journeyed by jet to Tucson, I endured another day of various doctor visits. They came with their instruments and questions. The diagnosis was spinal compression fractures. They mentioned partial paralysis, but I knew they were wrong. I believed that the paralysis was not real but all in my head. I had to will the paralysis away before Dad arrived. Even though he was traveling to Tucson, I felt nervous about his visiting me. He hated illness. He would use the word psychosomatic, just as he had in the past. He would find a way to convey that I had inconvenienced him.

Apparitions

Mom and Dad weaved in and out, in and out. I smiled. They circled my bedside. They could not be real. They could not be here. Yet they were talking, patting my hand, reassuring me, describing snow and Ellery and gas stations opening just for them. They were here. They had been shoveled out, shoveled out! And look, they were bending down to kiss me. They were my parents and they showed up. Showed up? To where in these nowherish moments? And good-night then, good-night, I said, they said, and they were taking off in the car they had rented at the airport for a motel on Miracle Mile. I lay there drifting, drifting, high on morphine and beginning to dream. I was dreaming that I was dreaming.

The next day I consoled Adam, my parents, and even the doctors. "Mind over matter, a little rest, a few pain meds, and I'll be fine," I told them. I accepted the diagnosis of compression fractures, but the paralysis? No, not me, I responded. I would be running in a few months. I didn't need surgery. But after my parents left to get some rest and Adam headed off to work, another doctor entered the room. He offered a brief greeting and then turned his attention to the crew of students who had followed him in. He held up an X-ray toward the window and traced his finger along the image of my spine. He used terminology I didn't understand and stated that the probability was high that surgery could alleviate some or all of the paralysis. As they left the room, one of the students hung back, offered me his hand, and wished me well. The warmth of his hand and his concerned gaze scared me. What if I really was paralyzed?

Over the next few days family members, friends, and professors from the university, members of the Bahá'í community, coworkers from Bentley's coffeehouse, friends from the ashram where I studied yoga, and friends from around the country began calling, sending flowers, and visiting. Balloons marked "Get Well" floated above ivy and miniature rose plants. Daffodils, tiger lilies, hyacinths, tulips, and daisies adorned the windowsill. Dozens of cards with messages of grief and hope arrived each day. The unrelenting phone calls resulted in the decision to have the hospital operator screen calls and only let family members through to the nurses' station. The attention and expressions of love overwhelmed and uplifted me. My local friends came in crying, and I ended up reassuring them that I would be fine.

The fourth afternoon of my hospitalization, Dr. Luke Lukens entered the room. I welcomed him, but his response was less than enthusiastic. "It's time for a serious talk," he began.

"Should we leave?" my dad asked the doctor. "Do you want privacy?"

"No, that's not necessary. I think it would be good for you to hear what I have to say," Dr. Lukens responded. Then he turned his attention to me.

"Kim, this is your fourth day in the hospital. You realize that, don't you?"

I nodded.

"I've been appointed by several doctors to represent them and me. Quite frankly, we're concerned, not just about the nature of your injuries but your attitude."

"My attitude?" I asked, wondering why. I exhibited positive thinking, didn't I? I hadn't allowed myself to accept the ridiculous diagnosis of partial paralysis.

"Yes, your attitude. We're worried that you are not taking your condition seriously and that you're avoiding making decisions about surgery."

I wanted to say that I didn't think surgery was necessary, but I couldn't bring myself to talk. Dr. Lukens's intense, rather punitive tone intimidated me.

"This is serious, Kim. Four days ago you were hit by a car. You have spinal compression fractures, and you are partially paralyzed. Do you realize that you may never walk again? You have lost bowel and bladder control. You might not be able to have a sexual relationship with your future husband. You might not be able to have children. You are in critical condition. Each and every day you continue to lie here and not make a decision, your muscles are atrophying even more. You need to make a decision soon. There's no time to waste. Do you understand?"

Adam sat down on the edge of my bed and held my hand, worry reflected in his eyes. Barbara, another friend, cried. My parents tried to look strong, but my mom teared up and my dad opened and closed his fist. I could barely breathe. This was not a tragic scene in a movie. We were not actors and actresses. This was not some invented drama recreated so that reality and fiction blurred. This was an actual moment in my life.

"Can you make a decision by tomorrow?" Dr. Lukens asked, his eyes softening.

"Yes," I managed to respond.

That night I telephoned a friend who happened to be a local physician to ask her to recommend a doctor. She suggested that I contact Dr. Lawrence Manning. Dr. Manning met with me the following morning and suggested orthopedic surgery. He explained that he would insert Harrington rods into my back to decompress the fractures. Unlike neurosurgery, which would involve direct contact with nerve endings, this approach would allow for a more natural alleviation of the pressure on nerve endings. "I feel confident that you'll walk again and live a mostly normal life. You might have a permanent limp. When you get pregnant someday, the latter months of your pregnancy will be difficult, maybe even excruciating, but you can expect to have a full life."

His optimism tempered with realistic caution appealed to me. I selected Dr. Manning to perform the surgery, though I still doubted the diagnosis.

Pre-Op Talk

A few hours before surgery the next morning, Mom warned, "When you wake up, Kim, it will feel as though a bomb has exploded in your body."

A bomb? What would that feel like? I looked out the window of my new room at St. Joseph Hospital. I had been transferred to St. Joe because Dr. Manning worked there.

"I'll be OK, Mom. Don't worry," I said, trying to reassure both of us. I didn't want to know what my mom knew. She had had surgery on her gall bladder when I was eight. I didn't want to remember visiting her, didn't want to recall seeing her in such pain.

Mom left for a cigarette break, and Dad replaced her, having taken care of his nicotine addiction. He sat down on the chair next to the bed and teased me. "All of Tucson is praying for you this morning. The hospital is thinking about hiring extra operators to handle all the calls. They've never known anyone to have as many friends as you. They've asked if you're famous."

I laughed, feeling flattered. I really had developed a community of good friends in Tucson. People really did care about me.

"Not only are people praying in Tucson, but your brother Chuck bicycled all the way to Wilmette to the Bahá'í Temple to ask the folks there to pray. But they already knew about your accident and, heck, there were hundreds praying already." Dad had a tendency to exaggerate to make a story good. I didn't mind the exaggeration. I laughed some more and Dad continued. "Chuckie boy tells us that Bahá'ís in Africa are praying for you, too. And that the Bahá'ís in Wilmette contacted the Bahá'ís over there in Haifa, and they're praying at your shrines there."

I wasn't surprised to hear that but felt delighted that my brother could experience the connectedness of the Bahá'í community. Though it was the second most widely distributed religion in the world next to Christianity, it was still numerically small and definitely a minority religion. Yet the Bahá'ís remained linked and involved with one another as individuals and communities. I imagined Chuck experiencing some of that intimacy after riding the seven miles from Glenview to Wilmette. I could see him sharing details of the accident with my former coworkers and friends, and those same friends nodding because they already knew. I could picture them leading Chuck into the House of Worship to pray alongside those who were already praying. The Bahá'ís would offer him comfort, for surely worry had motivated him to pedal seven miles beneath the bare branches of elm and maple, through slush and melting snow.

About half an hour before surgery, a couple of technicians wheeled me to the pre-operating room. My parents followed along and were allowed to remain with me for a few minutes. Earlier I had told Mom that I wanted to talk to Dad alone. I wanted to thank him for coming to Tucson to help me through this. He was here. He was trying to comfort me. He was talking with doctors, friends, the Bahá'ís. He was my dad. He had paid to fly to Tucson and didn't mention money, didn't even seem anxious about the cost. That week Dad was concerned about me and my welfare. I wanted to express my gratitude, but sharing how I felt made me nervous. What if he perceived my thanks as an insult?

When Mom excused herself, saying that she was going to have a cigarette before situating herself in the waiting room, Dad remained standing at my side. He smiled and said, "Everything is going to be fine, Kim, just fine. Dr. Manning is a superb doctor. You couldn't be in a better place."

I nodded and looked past him toward the drab white walls, the ordinary institutional clock—white and black with a red second hand pulsing its way around the circle of numbers. The fluorescent lights cast a yellow haze over the sterile room. I moved my gaze toward the window and the Tucson sky and then to my dad's gray eyes, his dark pupils, his gaze on me. He was standing less than a foot away, yet something in his gaze remained remote. No, couldn't be. He was right there, and he was looking at me. He was my concerned dad. My old fears were just getting in the way.

"Dad," I said, taking a deep breath, "it means so much to me that you and Mom came to Tucson."

"It's nothing, Kim," he said.

"Well, it means a lot to me that you are here. I need you right now," I said, tearing up.

"Kim, you're going to be fine. This Dr. Manning, he's right up there at the top. He's a fine surgeon."

I nodded and then took the plunge. "Dad, I know we haven't always had the best relationship. I just want to tell you again how grateful I am that you are here." There, I had said it, the part about us not always having been close.

But Dad interrupted. "Kim. No, no, no. That's nonsense. We have a great relationship. Like father, like daughter. Everything's going to be just fine. Don't even thank me. Naturally I'd be here."

I smiled and nodded but felt disappointed. His denial bothered me. I hungered for an acknowledgment. I wanted Dad to say, "Yeah, it's been hell. I'm sorry, so sorry. Will you ever forgive me?" But he acted like the past I remembered didn't exist, and I wasn't about to try and talk sense into him with surgery only minutes away.

Mom returned, leaned over, and kissed me. Dad brushed my cheek with a kiss. "We'll be in the waiting room along with all your friends, who," he chuckled, "are still praying."

I lay back. The anesthesiologist added a clear liquid to the IV and asked me to start counting backward from a hundred. "One hundred, ninety-nine, ninety-eight, ninety-seven . . ." Within moments, the room went dark.

Intensive Care

I tried to open my eyes but I couldn't. Who was arguing? Who hated who? "Get out!" someone screamed. "Get out of here, I've had enough!" Then there was weeping. The havoc outside me, the cries, the shouts, the voices of people I couldn't identify resembled the brokenness of my own body. Where was I that I felt so shattered and blown apart?

Finally my eyes fluttered open. I detected a clear tube. Was it going into my neck? Was there a hole in my neck? No one told me there would be such a hole! Everywhere I looked there were wires. *It will feel as though a bomb exploded,* Mom had warned about the surgery. Now I understood her warning. Now I was living through what she had described. But who was threatening whom?

"Well, hello there," a nurse said, walking into my view. "My name is Maureen. Glad to see you're waking up. You're in the intensive care unit, Kim. The surgery went well. I'll be assisting you for the next few hours."

I spotted the TV screen up in the corner between the ceiling and the wall. "Turn it off," I tried to say, my voice less than a whisper. "Off. Off," I attempted to say, but my voice seemed to belong to someone else. What happened that words had lost their shape, stretched into a sort of oblivion of grunts, moans, breath?

"I'm sorry. I'm having a hard time understanding," Maureen responded, sensing my distress.

How could I communicate to her that the impact of the domestic war on the TV screen would not serve to heal me? I had visualized waking to music. I had selected Georgia Kelly's "Seapeace." I had had so little control over this whole accident and everything that was happening, but I had planned my waking. I had planned on music, soothing music, healing music, not hell. And I couldn't even speak. I couldn't even express what was inside me.

"Your parents are in the waiting room. I'm sure they will be glad to see you, and maybe they'll have an easier time grasping what you're trying to tell me," Maureen said and exited the room.

Within minutes my parents entered looking eager yet worried. "What is it?" Mom asked. "The nurse says you're asking for something but she can't understand."

"Off, TV off," I repeated.

"What's she saying?" Dad asked Mom.

I repeated the simple words, still stunned that my brain was making the same kind of effort to communicate that it always had, but the words were emerging distorted, crumbled, making no difference whatsoever.

My mom, at last, understood. "Kim doesn't forget a thing. She wants her music, not the TV. Can we turn off the TV?" Mom asked Maureen. The nurse pressed the off-button on the remote, and the soap opera ended.

While Dad returned to my apartment for the tape recorder, Mom shared some of the details of the surgery that would get repeated over and over in the next week for the many visitors who came. The surgery lasted five hours. Afterward Dr. Manning came into the waiting room where my parents sat with many close friends who represented numerous faiths— Buddhists, Sufis, Sikhs, Hindus, Christians, and Bahá'ís.

"Maybe all those prayers helped," Dr. Manning said and laughed. "I normally feel exhausted after a surgery like this, but today I feel refreshed." He reported that the surgery went without any problems.

Later that afternoon I drifted in and out of consciousness to Georgia Kelly's gentle melodies and healing harmonies. Her skill on the harp soothed me the way I had visualized. I had learned from yoga instructors and friends about the power of creating an environment to support the healing process. It made sense that I wouldn't need any additional tension post surgery. My body had experienced enough trauma from the accident and now more from the surgery. Prayers, music, affirmations, and positive reinforcement were what I needed.

The next day while my parents were visiting, two nurses entered the room. "You both can stay," one of them said to Mom and Dad. "We just need to shift the sheets for circulation purposes. One of the nurses grabbed one end of the bed sheets, and the other grabbed the opposite end. They pulled the sheets tight and lifted me off the bed.

"Aaaahhhh!" I screamed.

"We're sorry, Honey. We hate doing this but it's necessary."

Dad left the room in tears, and for the next couple of days every time the nurses came in to shift the sheets he left saying, "too much for me to take." At the time, I was touched by this gesture. I wanted to believe that Dad loved me so much that he couldn't handle seeing me in pain. But later, after I recovered, I wondered. He had inflicted more pain by his own hand and his own mouth than those nurses. And the nurses were doing something that caused initial pain, but it was an essential pain, a pain that I had to endure to prevent worse problems from evolving. My dad had broken my bones and called me names that were so internalized I spent ample time through much of my adult life striving to edit out the negativity he inflicted.

Dad remained for another couple of days until I was released from the intensive care unit. Then he flew back home to take care of Chuck and return to work. Years later Chuck shared the details of an incident that occurred shortly after Dad's return. A night owl, Chuck spotted Dad still up at 2:30 in the morning. Dad, in a chair pulled up to the TV, stared at the screen filled with black-and-white static. Tears streamed down his face. He mouthed words as if talking to someone. "He was so distressed about you, Kim. He really did care," Chuck said. I pictured the scene that Chuck described. Was Dad mouthing words to me? Was he recognizing any similarities between the pain that I had endured from the accident and the pain he had inflicted on me as a child? Was he feeling remorse? Was he confessing? I ached for some acknowledgment, some accountability. I wanted to believe that this private moment might lead to an apology.

Hovering

That first evening out of intensive care my condition deteriorated. I vomited into the bin Mom held. My fever raged over 102 degrees. When Adam relieved my mom, he spent the next hour wiping up the vomit that didn't make the bin, holding a cool washcloth to my head, and massaging my legs. Because of the fractures and the length of the incision, I couldn't turn onto my side without help. Adam maneuvered me against a body roll the hospital provided. A part of me hovered between my devastated body and elsewhere—where exactly, I couldn't contemplate at the time. Perhaps the combination of an intense bodily experience and morphine had me wavering between the realms of consciousness and unconsciousness.

Two days later Dr. Manning entered my room carrying a plaster brace. "Here's your spine for the next few months," he announced. "You're now ready to try this on. Let me show you how it opens and closes with these Velcro straps." He fiddled with the straps and showed how the brace was comprised of front and back components that were held together by inserting the Velcro straps through clips that brought the two pieces together. "This will enable you to walk until your spine heals. Later today the nurses will help you into this, and you can practice sitting on the edge of your bed. Within a couple of days you'll be walking down the hall."

That's what he thought. The brace was as long as my torso. How would I ever get into it? I couldn't sit up. I could barely roll over. I had never had surgery before, never had the length of my back cut open, vertebrae fused, and a metal rod wired to my spine. The pain was more than I had contemplated. The thought of running the 5-K race I had told the doctors I would run had vanished. I had no desire to retrieve that thought. I just wanted to rest. I wanted to become invisible. The doctors and nurses could take care of others. Later today would become tomorrow. And tomorrow—that day would just get bumped up.

For the next day and a half, each time one of the nurses suggested I try on the brace, I complained: *I'm tired. I'm nauseated right now. Maybe in an hour; the pain is too much right now.* The result of my efforts to delay wearing the brace was a behind-the-scenes meeting involving Dr. Manning, the nurses, and my mom. Mom nicknamed Dr. Manning "General Patton" and ordered him to take charge.

The next morning General Patton arrived in my room and said, "We're going to get you into the brace today, Kim. We can't wait or your poor muscles will atrophy beyond repair."

"One more day," I responded. "Just one more day."

"No, we can't wait. The nurse is going to help me roll you onto your side. While you're on your side I'm going to insert the brace beneath you. Then I'll roll you back onto the brace and clip on the front of the brace."

This summary of events sounded easy to all of them. They acted the part of the nerdy students prepared for the exam. I, however, panicked. Breathing? With what lungs? What air could get down my closing-down trachea? If I had power, I would have fought. Instead, I trembled and gasped as they rolled me onto my side and placed that hard, nasty brace beneath my spine. They maneuvered me back into a prone position, placed the top of the brace over my stomach, and began strapping me in. They didn't stop, didn't miss a move. They rolled me back onto my side and then swiveled me into a seated position.

You've done it!" Dr. Manning exclaimed as if I had scored a touchdown. "The nurses will be doing this three times a day. See how the brace serves as your spine? You can sit. Without it, you wouldn't be able to."

"I'm dizzy," I complained.

"Well, yes. You've been lying down for the past week. Now you can sit, and tomorrow you'll be using a walker and taking a few steps."

"No," I cried.

"Yes. You'll be amazed at how quickly you make progress. We're behind in this part of your recovery."

After helping me back out of the brace, Dr. Manning said good-bye and left the room winking at Mom on his way out.

"Thank you, General Patton," Mom said. She turned her attention to me and explained, "We had to do this, Kim. I hate to see you suffering like this, but you can't just lie here. The only way to get well is to get into that brace."

The tendency to retreat when facing challenges typified my reaction to almost all tests and difficulties. In this situation, a diverse team of family, friends, and health care providers prevented that kind of withdrawal. Throughout the remaining three days in the hospital, the nurses placed me in and out of the brace and helped me to sit up and dangle my feet over the bed. With the help of Mom and Dr. Manning I stood up for the first time. Holding onto Dr. Manning's shoulder, I managed a few steps. A walker enabled me to cross the room. The night before I was released, my friend Randy brought several of his friends to the hospital, people I didn't even know, and they cheered me down the hallway. By the time I left the hospital I was walking without the walker, my *body buddy* serving as my spine.

Saint Mom

Before I arrived home, Mom had prepared my apartment. She set up a twin bed Adam had contributed to replace the futon. Maneuvering onto the futon would be too difficult for me, and I needed an extra bed for Mom and my friends who would volunteer to help after she left. Mom bought a small kitchen table and chairs since I didn't have any. So that I could more easily use the bathroom, she rented a booster seat for the toilet. And she also rented what she called a "donut," which was a contraption to place beneath my head so she could wash my hair with a hose attachment that connected to the sink. Mom purchased clothes that I could wear under and over the brace. I needed to wear cotton tank tops under the brace. Drawstring shorts, loose dresses, and large blouses would serve me through the coming hot summer months. She filled my cabinets with canned goods, knowing the food stamps would not cover what I needed.

Mom worked hard to help me receive state aid. Her history of volunteering at a hospital and assisting elderly friends benefited me. She knew I needed to apply for disability and food stamps, and she picked up the appropriate forms. The combination of persistent pain and the effects of the medications made it impossible for me to comprehend the complicated forms. Mom helped. Pen in hand, she filled out one form after another, asking me questions along the way. I hated the thought of going on food stamps and disability. Dad had made disparaging remarks about lazy people on welfare.

"This is different, Kim," Mom counseled me when I shared my concerns about being dependent on the state. "You can't work. You're disabled. You don't make enough money, and even with this money, you're barely going to make it."

"I hate that damn woman who hit me! I hate going through all this pain and all these forms."

"I wondered if you were going to get upset with her," Mom said. At the time, I didn't find her comment strange. I didn't consider that the real question I needed my mom to ask was: *I wondered when you were going to get upset with your dad, with me, with the impact of how we hurt you?* I was focused on the moment and the pain from the accident. Before surgery I believed and expressed the idea that the woman who had hit me had to be suffering. Imagine hurting someone as she had hurt me. How could she live with herself knowing that she might have paralyzed me? I agonized over these thoughts and questions, not realizing at the time that the emotional intensity of my reaction was connected with the past. Would I ever ask my dad, "How can you live with yourself knowing how you hurt and paralyzed us?"

Expressing how I felt about this woman—someone I didn't know and with whom I had no interaction—was safer. Before surgery, I worried about and even felt sorry for her because if I were in her shoes, I would have felt agony if I had partially paralyzed someone. I assumed she would have the same reaction. After surgery, however, my feelings changed. Sometimes the physical pain caused me to express anger toward her. Sometimes the frustration of trying to figure out how I would finish the semester, how I would work, how I would pay my bills, how I would eat, how I would even take care of myself, took its toll. I couldn't even shower or wash my hair. The reality of how this particular injury was going to affect my daily life made me less compassionate and understanding. While I wrestled with the impact of this accident, I had not allowed myself the same contemplation and range of emotions in response to the eighteen years of violence I had endured during my childhood. I had barely considered how that violence had affected me.

Mom kept busy, driving me to and from the doctor, lawyer, and caseworkers working for the department of economic security. She cooked all my meals. She cleaned. She took my clothes to the laundromat. She fielded phone calls when I needed to rest. She took me and my closer friends out for lunch or dinner. She spent two weeks getting to know my friends, the Bahá'í community, and the beautiful Sonoran Desert.

Then Dad called one night. "You're doing better now, aren't you?" he asked.

"Yes, I guess," I said, sensing tension in his voice.

"Well, your mom's been gone a long time, and I'm sure you don't need her to stay much longer." He was silent, waiting for me to say something.

"I don't know. I guess not," I responded, though the exact opposite was true. The aftermath of surgery had overwhelmed and humbled me. While early on in my hospital stay I minimized the extent of my injuries, I was shocked after surgery. Everything was so much harder.

"Well, good, then. Let me talk to your mom."

I handed over the phone, knowing that Dad was going to order Mom to return home and nothing we said would make any difference. I felt devastated because a part of me felt hopeful when my parents showed up to care for me. I toyed with the idea that Dad had changed and would continue to change even more as he reconsidered how he related to me. I loved that Mom had stayed on to help me out, meet my friends, and spend some special time with me. I loved how Dad had not objected. We were almost like a normal family whose members cared for one another and sacrificed their own wants and needs once in a while for the sake of another in need. *This is the answer to the long prayer,* I had thought. But I realized the notion—that transformation could magically occur—was a fantasy.

Mom didn't have to tell me that she would be calling the airlines when she finished her conversation with Dad. I already knew.

One night before Mom left, we decided to find 143 Linden Street. When we turned onto Linden, Mom sighed. "Nice homes, Kim. She could be rich."

"Mom, this is the 1100 block, and in Tucson, blink your eyes, and the scenery can change."

"We'll see."

We had learned from my attorney that the woman who had hit me carried only the minimum amount of car insurance, all of thirty thousand dollars, not even enough to cover my current medical expenses. My injuries would require follow-up appointments, physical therapy, and possible future surgeries. Any new insurance I might purchase would be unlikely to cover preexisting conditions such as the injuries sustained in this accident. My attorney had suggested that we go after other assets she might have to cover my expenses.

Mom drove past some beautiful adobe homes, then some smaller ones, and then apartments and duplexes. "There, that's it," she said.

We parked the car and stared at the red brick duplex. Again, I wondered about the woman inside. What was it like for her? She had struck and hurt someone she didn't know. I bet she couldn't get the accident out of her mind and felt traumatized. Perhaps she wanted to call and apologize but was advised by her attorney not to initiate any contact. I thought it was odd that two lives could come together in such a tragic way and yet no communication would occur. Surely she wanted to talk, just as I wanted to talk. Surely she was enduring the same emotional pain that I was enduring. Which was worse, being the victim or being the perpetrator of such an accident? I couldn't answer that question. Perhaps it was a ridiculous question, but it was one that I began to obsess over nonetheless. I knew I wouldn't want to live with the feelings of having inflicted such pain on anyone else. But then, I could live without the pain I had sustained. Why would she have so little insurance? Wasn't that irresponsible? But then I had forgotten to put the "X" in the tiny square box indicating that I wanted health insurance on the University of Arizona registration form. I thought I had done so and was stunned when a representative from the business office at Tucson General had informed me that I didn't have the student insurance.

After Mom returned to Chicago I continued to look everywhere for that unmistakable odd blue Toyota station wagon that had two brown stripes on each side. Sometimes, just out of the blue, I would wonder how the woman was feeling about hitting me. On one rare occasion when I was back on the road, about a year into my recovery, I spotted her car at a traffic light. She was putting on lipstick. *Imagine that,* I thought. *She drove away from the light paying more attention to her image in the mirror and her burgundy lips than to anything else. Was she putting on lipstick the day she hit me? Was she talking to her boyfriend? Was she paying attention to the road?*

I wavered back and forth from anger to concern for her. How could she live with herself? How could she put on lipstick while driving? One day, after leaving the office of Disabled Student Services, where I received my physical therapy treatments, I cut through a parking lot on campus to head home and saw the unmistakable car. I looked around. I didn't see anyone resembling the woman who had hit me, the woman putting on lipstick at stoplights. I waited. I walked around the parking lot. I climbed up and down the steps of the administration building and continued to circle the lot while scanning the area for the owner of that car. About twenty minutes later I spotted her. She appeared tired and depressed. Perhaps she couldn't get the accident out of her mind. Should I say something, call out, introduce myself? I waited until she was opening her car door and then called out her name. She looked over at me with questioning eyes. I introduced myself.

"Oh, my!" she said, looking surprised. "I just learned from the insurance company that you had the surgery, that the accident was so severe. I had no idea."

"No idea?"

"No. I was shocked. Are you all right?"

"It's been hard. But we can be glad I wasn't paralyzed. I came very close. The doctors told my parents I came a quarter of an inch away from being paraplegic. Though it's been painful, I'm walking, thank God."

The woman shook her head, her lips trembling. "This has been the hardest time. I was just in another accident. The stress of everything has been so severe . . ."

"I'm sorry for your stress," I responded. We shared a few additional words, and before parting I hugged her.

Later, I questioned my warm interaction with her. Why hadn't she checked to see how I was doing the day she hit me? How could she just go on with her life as if nothing had happened? She was under stress? How about me? And why had I apologized for her stress and offered a hug, only to learn later from my attorney that she had claimed I weaved my bike in and out of traffic?

Like my father, the woman who hit me shrugged off responsibility for the injuries she had inflicted, but in this situation I had legal representation and justice was delivered. I received a small settlement that enabled me to pay off some bills, buy a used Volkswagen, and later travel to Israel as part of my Bahá'í pilgrimage. The lawyers said that I deserved a larger settlement considering the extent of my injuries, but I didn't remain hung up on the issue of money. A year or so later, when I was in therapy to deal with my past in a more in-depth way than I had before, there were times when I wanted to settle with my dad. I wanted justice delivered. I wanted a lawyer to represent me. But that would never happen. I would have to discover other ways to come to acceptance and a sense of inner peace.

Making Up Incompletes

Why had I believed my friends who told me botany was easier and more fun to take in the summer? Halfway across campus, I removed my blouse. Who cared that the body brace showed? Once the temperature rose over the one hundred-degree mark, lately by 9:30 or 10:00 in the morning, comfort outweighed vanity. The air that felt as therapeutic as a sauna an hour before felt like fire now. What was my professor thinking when he planned classes outside on days like this?

After class, I headed toward the library to work on making up the incompletes. I also had to finish my botany homework for that particular day. I didn't get far. The intense heat slowed me down, but worse than the heat were the effects of the bone graft removed from my hip to fuse my spine. Each step felt as if someone were thrusting a knife up and into my hip. I collapsed on a bench near the bookstore to catch my breath.

Within minutes a young man with long brown hair wheeled in my direction. I sensed he was heading straight for me but hoped not. Fury rolled off him. He drove that chair with an intensity I had not seen in other students I met over at Disabled Student Services when I went for my physical therapy treatments. His eyes were wild, his frown deep. Two clear plastic bags hung over the wheelchair. Inside those bags were feces and urine—for everyone to see. Sure enough, he stopped right in front of me. I tried not to stare at the bags, tried to look him in the eye and say "hello."

"So what in the hell happened to you?" he snapped at me.

I knew that no matter what I would say, no matter how I responded, nothing was going to change that man's demeanor, at least not that day. Nonetheless, I regarded him. I looked him in the eye. Beneath his rage I saw a grief so vast that only time and listening ears and the grace of God could reduce its size. I explained to him the details of the accident and told him I had sustained spinal compression fractures. I included details of the orthopedic surgery and the insertion of Harrington rods to decompress the fractures.

And then there was nothing more to say. A temporary silence hung between us.

"Well, take a good damn look at me," he scowled. "Take a good look. The same thing that happened to you happened to me. And I'm here in this chair for life. And you? You walked away."

What could I say? What explanation could I present? None. I had nothing but a meager "I'm sorry" to offer. All he could do was glare at me and wheel off with the same fury and grief he had directed toward me. I watched him until he was out of sight. We both represented possible outcomes to each other. What if he were sweating, wearing a brace, tired of walking across campus? What if I were storming off in a wheelchair? We were both grieving, but his losses were more extensive. I had felt anger at the woman who hit me, anger that I forgot to take out insurance, anger about the incompletes, anger over the pain. But in that moment, I contemplated the range of anger. I contemplated those plastic bags making visible to everyone who crossed this man's path the excrement he could no longer release from his body on his own. Those bags screamed for him. What would my own screams look like if I had been paralyzed?

That fall and throughout the year, I thought about that man, but I never ran into him again. I thought about him with a sense of hope, for I had begun to meet dozens of disabled students. A population of people I had mostly ignored before my accident had now become acquaintances and even friends. Many of them had come to believe their accidents were predestined. A friend named Jennifer shared with me that she had been living a wild life of partying and not taking herself seriously. The accident halted everything and caused her to reevaluate her life. She was now happy and more productive than when she was supposedly an able-bodied person. Another friend, Mark, confided in me that he had been getting more and more addicted to alcohol. He thanked God that he was not the driver in the car accident that paralyzed him. He had driven drunk a number of times and could have hurt or killed someone. Becoming paraplegic caused him to look deep within. Though he grieved and raged for the first year, with the help of counseling and AA he began to reconstruct his life. Now he was in law school, and he had a girlfriend and dreams of a future he couldn't have even fathomed before. Yet another friend, Cheryl, was a victim of a ceiling collapse in a hotel ballroom. No alcoholism or drug addiction prevented her from living to her potential. She had been in law school at the time of her accident, dating an attorney. While law school was put on hold and the relationship with the attorney did not survive her paralysis, she processed her losses with the help of a counselor and made decisions about her future. She decided to move to Tucson because the climate made it easier to wheel around and the university had a great law school. She could still become an attorney and still work toward achieving her dreams.

That the accident had occurred while I was saying the Long Healing Prayer twice a day had caught my attention. If the accident was not an accident but a sign of God's intervention, just as my new friends regarded their own accidents, what was I to learn from this situation?

Sometimes I believed that God was punishing me because, as a result of my background, I interpreted almost anything negative as punishment. At other times I thought God had provided an opportunity for my family to come together and heal by creating something so traumatic that everyone had to show their support.

For years to come, in fact, the accident would be a part of our family lore. We all learned from Chuck that when I called home that night from the hospital, he was having a huge party, beer kegs and all, while Mom and Dad were away. He snuck his friends in the back door because my parents had asked the neighbors who lived across the street to keep an eye on Chuck and the house. When the phone rang, he turned off the stereo and ordered every one of his high school friends to remain quiet. Since my parents didn't have a phone in their cabin, he had telephoned the sheriff. A blizzard had swept the northern Wisconsin region, but that didn't stop Ellery Coons, a family friend who worked for the sheriff's department, from hiking to my parents' property. My parents, snowed in, would remember forever that knock and the doom they sensed. That night Ellery helped to shovel out my parents and arranged to have a gas station opened so they could drive through the night to get back to their home in Chicago and make arrangements to fly to Tucson. In the meantime Chuck and his friends picked up around the house. No speck of dust, no cigarette butts, and no empty beer cups remained. Chuck's party didn't make it into the letter to the editor that Dad wrote months after the incident, but Dad shared the other vital details of what had happened and praised Ellery Coons for his assistance. For years the story of my accident was shared with old friends, relatives, and new acquaintances. I loved the story. Sometimes that story made it seem like my memories of the violence from the past couldn't possibly be real.

While I had received extraordinary help to deal with the trauma of the accident, I realized I needed similar help to deal with the effects of the past. The dream of the man in the graveyard haunted me. He said that I needed to unbury myself. I was not sure I had the energy for that kind of effort, but I made a start by beginning to work with a therapist. I hoped that I would stick it out. In the past I had quit counseling as soon as it started to get too painful.

Dr. Juliet Emerson smiled when I asked how long she thought it would take to deal with everything. I was eager to get through this counseling business in record time, graduate, and have it all over and done with. "I've got all these incompletes to make up, and grad school is right around the corner. My goal is to learn what I have to do so when I'm out of this brace, I don't fall back into the eating disorder," I shared during the second session.

"From the tiny bit you've shared about your past, we're going to need more time, Kim. Healing from trauma is a process, just as personal growth is. It sounds to me as though you've been in and out of counseling and that maybe what's incomplete is your healing work."

"Hmmm," I said, startled by her insight.

"Let's see what we can do," Dr. Emerson said. "Perhaps you'll discover that you're worth this kind of work."

I spent the first three months not wanting to remember anything. One day, rather than asking about my childhood, she asked about the years right after I left home.

"I'd rather not talk about that," I responded. "I'd much rather talk about my childhood."

"Why do you think it would be valuable to talk about your childhood?"

"I want to get well. I want to feel good about myself. I had that dream I told you about, but going back there is like descending into hell. I just don't want to recreate the past. And it's not just my childhood I'm talking about. I left home and made a huge mess of things. What are you going to think of me when you learn about some of the horrible mistakes I've made?"

Though I couldn't see a connection between the past and my inability to create a mature and independent life, Dr. Emerson could. I was starting to see that there was a possibility that some of the awful choices I made were connected to my upbringing, but I could just hear my dad saying that blaming the past was a cop-out. I tried to push his voice out of my head and trust Dr. Emerson's perceptions instead.

Dr. Emerson also proposed an intelligent and creative way to deal with my resistance to exploring my upbringing. She shared that our own brains don't know the difference between what we imagine and what is real. They process our imaginings the same way they process what we experience. To prevent me from being re-traumatized or becoming more ashamed through retelling, we would work together to find a way for me to examine my past as if from a distance, in a way that would enable me to feel safe and in control. The work we would do together would be about healing rather than re-harming and disgracing me.

I imagined myself leaning against a boulder at an overlook more than halfway up the road to Mount Lemmon. During each session I imagined my past was thousands of feet below in the desert valley. I took a snapshot of some moment, some traumatic event, but I remained safe in the high desert where I gained perspective with the help of Dr. Emerson. Though I appeared in those snapshots, I felt detached and distant from them, able to tell Dr. Emerson what had occurred without reliving all the particular details. Sometimes all I could do was unearth a memory; other times we pondered the details and discovered significant meanings. As we worked together, even after sessions filled with grief, anger, or shame, we gave words to what my family and I had kept silent.

Part 2: Snapshots

Still

The Amtrak train wound up and down the same California mountain. How would we ever get to Chicago this way—up and down, up and down the same mountain, clacking and rattling the entire way? My view consisted of rocks, cacti, and a sky smeared because the window I looked out from had not been cleaned. I pressed my nose against it anyway and tried not to ask again, "When will we get there?" Mom said she didn't want to answer that question one more time. So I asked instead, "When will the mountains disappear?" Mom had said there were no mountains in Chicago. "Soon, the mountains will disappear soon," Mom answered.

A man wearing a uniform, hat, and shiny shoes sat across the aisle. He and mom chatted off and on. Mom told him Dad was in the Air Force too, fought fires too, went to officer school too. "I've got a present for you," the man said to me. He smiled, but I curled into Mom's side.

Mike said, "I'll take it."

"Well, then, here you go little man! Here's a quarter. You can buy yourself a soda or a candy bar. And here's one for your sister. Can you give it to her?"

I wanted that quarter for sure. I wanted a Milky Way, but I didn't like the dining car. To get there we had to open the door to the wind and heat and jump across the empty space surrounding only thin strips of metal. What if I fell? Then I would be smashed to smithereens by the very train taking us away from California.

My mom thanked the soldier, one of many who offered shiny quarters or entertained us. One soldier was a magician. He could guess which card was at the top of the deck without looking at the card—ace of hearts, three of diamonds, five of spades, queen of hearts, seven of clubs. He guessed the right card every time. "How do you do that?" Mike asked, grinning. "I want to do that."

One soldier invited us to join him in the dining car and Mom accepted. He led the way, and when he opened that half-metal, half-glass door to let us through, he saw how I froze. Stooping down to my level, he whispered, "Kind of scary, huh?"

I nodded.

"Would you like me to pick you up and carry you across?"

"OK," I mumbled.

He swooped me up and we went through together, my head buried in his coat to avoid seeing the few feet of space that spooked me.

Later, back in our regular seats, the soldier sat across from us, his head tipped into his chest. He snored softly. I curled into Mom's side and drifted off to sleep. When I woke, the soldier was gone. I craned my head and looked up and down the aisle. I tugged at Mom's arm and asked her, "Where did the soldier go, that nice one?" Mom explained that he didn't want to wake me and had asked her to say good-bye. She said that he was visiting his family in Lincoln, Nebraska. I looked at his empty seat. I wished he were still there, wished he would carry me back to the dining car again. I liked feeling safe.

In Chicago's Union Station people swarmed to a train, from a train, toward an exit to hail a taxi, into the arms of waiting relatives. The air was cold. No more mountains and sky, no sunlight. Instead, gray cement, tunnels, dozens of tracks, dozens of trains, voices over loudspeakers announcing cities and arrival and departure times. Mom cried out, "There they are!"

Scrambling toward us were Grandpa Max and Grandma Esther. Everyone embraced, and then Grandpa lifted me up and pecked me with a kiss on my cheek. "Just look at you. My, you've grown. How precious. How very precious you are," he said, tightening his tender arms around me.

We remained with Grandma and Grandpa for ten days in a home that was so peaceful I did everything possible to prevent the calm from shattering. I helped Grandma set the table. I swept the floors with the little broom given to me as a welcome gift. I swept the stairs. I swept and swept and then swept some more. Back home, Dad liked a clean house and yelled when it was messy. *Do everything possible to keep the house clean* was the commandment instilled in me, an order I projected onto every environment, including a home clear across the country, the home where my mother was raised. My four-year-old mind didn't realize that my father's behavior didn't typify the behavior of all men and that not all men flew into rages over a little disorder in their homes.

A photograph from that visit captures me sitting on a simple sofa. Wood floors catch the light from the window behind the sofa. There's little sense of the world outside that window—just a blur of light and haze. My lips come together in neither a frown nor a smile, though I suppose there's a hint of a smile, a sense that *everything's just fine.* I was taught to project *fine,* taught to answer questions affirmatively, taught to keep secret what was really going on. I sat for Grandpa's camera. I sat on his sofa, my skinny four-year-old legs straight out, not yet long enough to bend over the sofa's edge. My hair was cut below the ear in a bob. My straight bangs hung well above my eyebrows. Everything was just so. I wore an ironed dress with a white collar and pleats, saddle shoes laced and tied. My lips were sealed. I was to be seen and not heard, though Aunt Joyce mentioned to Mom that the stillness, the silence, the impeccable behavior seemed so unusual for a child. Mom's sister had five kids of her own, and their home was loud and chaotic. Aunt Joyce wondered how a child could just sit and clean and smile.

The Back Steps

How many days had it been since we returned that I lay on the floor wanting to dissolve into dust particles rising toward the light coming in from the window?

"Get the hell up!" Dad hollered.

I couldn't move. I trembled, trying my best to hold in the cries. He hated it when I cried. So I held my breath.

He came at me with his foot. "I said 'get the hell up.'"

I shut my eyes.

He kicked, but it didn't matter. I couldn't hurt any more than I already did.

The day I was shoved across my parents' room was not the first time I had been hit or shoved by my father, nor would it be the last. While I remember that hard floor, the sling that later held my arm close to my body to allow the broken collarbone to heal, and the back steps that my family and I blamed for the break, I don't remember much more than that. I don't remember the trip to the emergency room, the interactions with doctors and nurses, the X-rays, the bandaging of my arm.

I remember the floor.

I remember my wet underpants.

I remember being advised, "If anyone asks, just tell them you fell down the back steps."

And that's precisely what I did.

Jeep Ride

A year later, Grandpa Max and Grandma Esther moved from Chicago and bought a small bungalow a block away from our house in California. They both wanted a new start and warmer weather. Grandpa found a job as a meat cutter in a butcher shop, and Grandma worked at a dime store. Grandpa appreciated having more unscheduled time than he had had in Chicago as a restaurant manager. Soon he purchased a jeep for adventures in the mountains. He joined us on daylong Saturday trips to Lake Arrowhead. On other weekends, he fished for trout in the streams and boasted about spotting rattlesnakes. When he returned, his cooler filled, he filleted and fried the trout and bass he caught and then invited us over for the feast.

I remember occasions when he pulled up in his jeep and parked in our driveway. He rapped on the door and Mom welcomed him. Often he leaned down toward me so we were eye to eye and asked: *Do you want to come with me to the store? Do you want to ride up front in the jeep with me, then go to the park?* Though I felt like spinning and screaming yes, I held in that excitement, almost as keen as during those hours before Santa Claus visited our house on Christmas Eve, the very Santa Claus I would learn years later was Grandpa Max. Though I was timid, I placed my hand in his and off we went.

Grandpa lifted me into the jeep and handed me a stick of Wrigley's from his pocket. I opened the wrapper and stuck the whole piece of gum in my mouth, enjoying the burst of mint. We wore no seatbelts in those days, and I sat up front right next to my Grandpa, leaning into his soft plumpness. His hands were steady on the wheel. His balding head shone in the bright sun. His smile was for free and for everyone. All through the grocery aisles I held his hand, firm yet gentle. These were the same hands that had held butcher knives, that trimmed the fat off meat and the meat away from bone, but his touch was light and respectful. On the way home we stopped at the park and he pushed me on the swings, so high I felt as if I were flying. For those few hours, my home was not 243 Jefferson. My home was in the care of Max Widtmann.

When my grandparents invited Mike and me to spend the night, I crossed my fingers and hoped Dad would say *yes*. Sometimes he did, especially when he had just been paid and there was a little extra money for the drive-in. He and Mom could enjoy themselves without having to pay a babysitter. But often he didn't want us to go, and he didn't like the fact that Mom's parents had moved to a house that was just a block away. He felt it prevented him from having any kind of private life.

Years later, as an adult, I thought back to the miracle of having Grandma and Grandpa just a block away. Their living in such close proximity to our house had to cause Dad to watch his behavior. Dad wouldn't have wanted his in-laws hearing how explosive he could become. I shared this musing with Mom, but she shook her head. "Your Grandma told me that one time after church Grandpa decided to walk over for a visit. About a half a block away, he heard screams and realized that they were coming from our house. Though he was saddened to hear that fighting was going on, he turned around and went back home."

I pictured my Grandpa on the road, how he stopped when he heard the shouts. What was he thinking when he paused like that? How could he turn back? If only he had realized that what he heard was no ordinary marital fight. If only he understood that Dad's behavior was abusive, that Dad was committing domestic violence. But back then, in the late fifties and early sixties, little information was made public about domestic violence. Grandpa didn't understand Dad was a perpetrator of what today is considered a crime.

Within a year, Dad decided not to reenlist in civil service. His dad offered him a position as a systems analyst in the family business, which made payroll charts for other businesses. Since the military was experiencing cutbacks, he accepted the offer. My grandparents would stay in California, preferring the climate and the mountainous region, while we moved half a continent away to Illinois.

Loss

On March 19, 1961, Dad returned from the Air Force hospital where he had taken Mom the night before. In a matter-of-fact way he said, "The baby is dead. When your mom comes home I don't want you crying and giving her trouble the way you always do. Understand?"

Later that day Grandma, crying, told us about a place called heaven. "The little baby went to heaven. She's with God."

"Where's heaven?" I asked.

"It's far away but it's also close."

"I want to go see the baby," I said.

Grandma shook her head and wiped the tears away with a Kleenex. "We can't go there until it's our time. We have to wait to see the baby. But she's with God."

I didn't understand what *dead* meant, and God was invisible. So I guessed the baby wasn't coming home, that she had somehow disappeared and was invisible, too.

While Grandma was making dinner, I plopped down by the back door to wait for Mom to come home. Although I had been potty-trained for over a year, I wet my pants. I didn't mean to. I just sat there because I wanted that baby. We had a crib and toys for the baby.

Grandma walked over to check on me and realized the accident. "Can't you remember to use the potty? Can't you?" she scolded.

About twelve years later, during a separation from Dad, Mom shared that my sister, whose name would have been Karen, was stillborn. "She would have been mentally retarded, and she had a cleft palate," Mom said. "Maybe it was God's way. Your dad couldn't have handled a child with special needs."

"What's a cleft palate?" I asked.

Mom explained it to me and then added, "I never got to see her. The doctors took her away before I came to. It didn't even feel real. For nine months she moved and squirmed inside me. I knew something was wrong when I stopped feeling all movement."

"You're right. Dad couldn't have handled having a baby with those challenges," I said.

"It was terrible. Not only that, but your Dad didn't offer any support during that time." Mom continued to explain that after the stillbirth, Dad was furious for weeks, especially when Mom broke down and cried. He swore at her and yelled, "Can't you even think of anyone but yourself? Just look at you. How do you think I'm feeling?" But even when Mom attempted to inquire about his feelings, he yelled at her to shut up.

"One day I drove you and Mike to the grocery store. You were doing OK, but Mike threw himself on the tile floor in the baby food section at the grocery store and screamed at me to buy food for the new baby."

I pictured that scene in my mind, a scene that would return to me, especially when I witnessed Dad not supporting any of us for having an emotional response to a challenge or a loss. Emotions drove him crazy, so I did my best not to express any. Better yet, I tried not to feel any.

When I considered this sad time and how my family dealt with loss, I hoped that if I ever married and had children that we would know how to give space for the practice of healthy grieving and the authentic sharing of emotions. I wanted to raise my children in a healthier manner. I didn't want to stifle their emotions. I wanted them to learn how to express themselves. Dr. Emerson reminded me that my own practice of accessing my emotions and learning to feel them rather than stuff them down with food was an excellent beginning in achieving that goal.

Danny Thomas

Instead of asking what we'd like, the butcher at the corner grocery gazed into Mom's eyes and said, "You are very beautiful, really one of the most beautiful women I have ever seen." My eyes dropped, and I stared at the scuff marks on my saddle shoes.

"How about a date?" he continued.

"But I'm married," my mother responded.

"All the beautiful women are taken. What's a lonely guy like me to do?" he asked.

I wondered why he was so lonely since he looked like Danny Thomas.

"You're happy, then?" he asked my mom, "treated like a queen, the way you should be treated, a beautiful woman like you?"

"Well . . ." my mom stammered, "yes."

She looked down at the top of my head. I could feel her eyes there, but I would not look up at her. I could not look at her or Danny Thomas because the piece of steak looked good. That was what my six-year-old self thought to avoid sensing what I was sensing—that the butcher was misbehaving. But then I found myself wondering, "What if my mother was married to this butcher instead of my dad? We might get steak for free . . . or roast beef, or turkey. And he might play chutes and ladders with me."

The butcher handed the package to my mom. He pulled a sucker out of the pocket of his white smock. That smock had blood stains on it that looked like a map of Africa, where Elsa, the lion from "Born Free," learned how to live free.

"Would you like a lollipop?" he asked.

I couldn't say *yes* out loud. *Yes* was stuck in my throat.

"Thank you," my mom said for me. She took the sucker from him, and he winked at her. She handed the lollipop to me. "Say *thank you*," she said.

Somehow I managed to mumble and smile, but I couldn't look at him when he looked at me. I could imagine, though, imagine that Dad died in a car accident on his way home from work, that Danny married my mom and became my dad, and we would all live happily ever after. And I did imagine variations of that story all throughout childhood and felt both relief and shame.

The relief was extraordinary and rescued me many times from the hell of a particular day. How tantalizing! A new life, a new father, a new relationship for my mother! The stories born from my imagination back then, like most fairy tales, solved my problems. Danny Thomas, our butcher who behaved like a prince, rescued my mom, the young maiden, from my dad, the villain. Of course, as a child, I didn't consider the difference between public and private behavior, didn't ponder the possibility that the butcher was not at all like Danny Thomas and that I needed to evaluate him in a number of situations before I labeled him a prince. I couldn't fathom that my mother might create her own happiness and not wait for a prince to come rescue her from a villain. I repeated variations of themes, the themes of fairy tales and soap operas reflecting old and patriarchal patterns.

I felt great shame in moments when I found myself imagining my father dying in a car accident. Even though my father was violent, even though I was terrified of him, even though a part of me understood I deserved better, my dad was a human being. He wasn't all bad. He didn't yell every single day. He didn't beat us and break our bones all the time. He smiled, he joked around, and he played board games with us once in a while. He was a lot of fun in public. People liked my dad. How could I dream him dead? What kind of person would dream her own father dead?

Perhaps it was that very shame that caused me to look away that day in the grocery store, to refuse to make eye contact with the real man behind the slabs of meat.

"Let me know if anything changes," he said to Mom. "A beautiful woman like you needs to be treated like a queen."

"You're very kind," my mom said.

"So you promise, then, that you'll let me know?"

My mom's sigh was loud enough so that I could hear, but when she sighed at home she was more careful.

"Well?" the Danny Thomas butcher pressed.

"Sure," Mom said and laughed, "but don't get your hopes up."

"I can wish, can't I?"

Mom laughed again. It was then that I looked up. The butcher winked at me. He smiled and said, "You're a very cute girl, did you know that?"

I smiled and looked back down at my saddle shoes. He was my Danny Thomas. I loved Danny Thomas. He helped children in hospitals. He hugged his wife and daughter sometimes on TV specials. He was my handsome hero.

Mom said good-bye and then we walked through the aisles to get the week's groceries. She compared prices and checked items off her list. Our cart filled up with Wonder Bread, Blue Bonnet margarine, Cheerios and Raisin Bran, and some Oreos because Chips Ahoy cost twenty-five cents more, Mom said.

"How about a root beer float?" Mom asked.

I nodded. I loved root beer floats. I loved the puffy fizz on top and the ice cream flavored by the root beer. We would have that for dessert, and Dad would be happy because after we shopped Mom always made a great dinner. That was important because my dad had to drive on the Edens Expressway all the way home with a billion cars. "It's the traffic that makes him so miserable," Mom always said. She thought that we'd feel crabby, too, having to drive home like that every day.

And for years I believed that Chicago's rush hour traffic, dirty floors, and uncombed hair were the things that made Dad crabby. In my imaginings of Danny and Mom, we didn't live in Chicago, our house never needed cleaning, and everyone's hair was always combed in place. On days that I experienced my dad's verbal or physical violence, I also experienced Danny's hugs and gifts and saw his arm around my mother's waist.

Dr. Emerson and I began to acknowledge that the ways in which my imagination assisted me as a child could not serve me as an adult. The medicinal power of imagination enabled me to escape the intense pain of my day-to-day existence during childhood. I fled my life through fantasy, and this form of escape became as addictive as taking drugs and prevented me from building an actual life and developing real relationships. When I started dating as a young adult, I sought the ideals of my fantasies and was disappointed when the people I dated fell short of my unrealistic expectations.

Forbidden Dress

Attending first grade exposed me to dresses, stockings, and braids wrapped around the small, round heads of other girls with blue and brown eyes and varying shades of skin color. First grade meant reading *Dick and Jane*, counting and performing simple addition, drawing, and climbing the monkey bars during recess on the playground. I envied some of the girls like Nancy and Kaya, who wore different dresses every day of the week. I wanted dresses. I wanted dresses with pleats, collars, no collars, sashes. I wanted colorful dresses—red, pink, blue, green, or lavender. Couldn't I please have a new dress? I asked my mother.

"I'm sorry. There's just not enough money," she said. I sensed that if she could she would love nothing more than to take me shopping for dresses and shoes.

One afternoon I returned home from school, and lying across my bed was a new melon-colored dress with a white collar.

"Where did you get it?" I asked my mom.

She helped me slip into the dress, explaining that she had managed to save a few pennies here and there, but I shouldn't tell Dad.

I loved the dress. I spun around in my secret dress. I couldn't wait to wear it to school the next day. I didn't want to take it off, ever. But Dad would be home for dinner by five o'clock, and I didn't want to get my mother or myself into trouble. The new dress had to be kept secret. Secrets were like family members living in our house, present but ignored. At some point I wore the dress in front of Dad, who never asked about it. He either didn't notice or regarded the dress, worn enough by then, as old.

There were other secrets. Mom used to hide charge card bills underneath her underwear, bras, and nightgowns. As a child I didn't understand charge cards, and for a number of years I made no connection between them and the bills that arrived after my brothers or I received new clothes or shoes. All I understood was that some mail went on the desk and some went into Mom's top dresser drawer.

Who could blame Mom? Dad screamed about money. There was never enough, he claimed, because of Mom's irresponsibility. She spent way too much on food. She spent too much on herself. She was selfish, and they would suffer in their retirement all because of her. Mom claimed that she couldn't feed the family on the twenty-five dollars a week that he gave her. She couldn't clothe us. Sometimes pushing and shoving or a punch or two accompanied Dad's screaming. Mom covered up her black eyes with pancake makeup and sunglasses. Better to keep hiding the credit card bills rather than request extra funds.

How Dad discovered the charge cards, I haven't a clue. Maybe Mom became desperate and showed them to him. Maybe she explained that my brothers and I needed clothes, that we grew so fast that new clothes needed to replace the old ones. Maybe Dad found the bills by snooping through her drawers. I was too young to know. I didn't understand the actual process that led up to his raging, and often I interpreted his behavior in very concise ways. Grease on a chair, an unpaid bill, lack of money, an empty gas tank, a traffic jam on the highway, a shirt not ironed, Mom frowning while making his breakfast—all of these things were triggers. My child mind created rules: Wipe all grease off chairs, pay all bills on time, don't ever run out of money, fill up the gas tank and don't let it get close to empty, and smile a lot.

Dr. Emerson helped me to realize that following the rules I had created in my mind as a child never stopped the violence. I began to understand that the violence had nothing to do with our behavior but stemmed from my father's lack of skills in managing a home, a family, and his own emotions. He made a choice, Dr. Emerson said, to react to the hundreds of daily upheavals and stresses by blaming others and using power, force, and violence to control us.

No Return

We rode the city bus to the station and climbed the cement steps to wait for the elevated train that would take us from Evanston to the North Side of Chicago, where Mom's sister, Aunt Joyce, and her family lived. I counted the steps—one, two, three . . . I noticed dandelions and pigeons and the variety of people Mom and Dad called *strangers*. I was not to talk to them, ever. On the platform, I kept my eyes low. The long tracks vanished into the distance we would travel.

The squeaking and clacking of the train alerted us. "This is the one," Mom said, reading the schedule she had already studied on the bus. The green and white shoe-box of a train halted and the doors folded open. Once seated, I didn't mind the ride. I sat next to Mom, taking in the deep summer green of maple and elms, the yellow and red brick apartment buildings, billboards, telephone wires, and city streets. The train stopped, and people—those strangers—exited and entered. I wondered about some of them. What caused that old man on the Addison platform to scowl so? And then there was a mom, grabbing at her son's wrist and spanking him. Why would that couple kiss in public when the woman next to them kept rolling her eyes?

"Only a four-block walk from here," Mom informed Mike and me as we exited the train station and found ourselves on a busy street near a park.

"Is that the park where we're going swimming?" Mike asked.

"I think so," Mom said and took our hands to cross the street.

The four-block walk stretched into seven. At last Mom pointed to the red brick house. Upon seeing us, Aunt Joyce, who had been sitting on the sofa by the window, sprung out of her seat and raced to the door. She opened the screen, and before we even made it up the steps, sobbed, "Dad's dead!"

"What?" Mom said.

"He's dead. He died in his sleep last night."

Mom broke down and the two women—sisters, young mothers—held each other and wept.

For the remainder of that day the adults stayed in one part of the house greeting relatives, making phone calls, and making the decisions death demands. The children gathered in the family room in the basement and talked about our Grandpa's passing. We repeated to each other some of the details we gained from the adult conversations. Grandpa's heart had stopped. He, Grandma, and our great-grandma Nonnie were at a hotel in Las Vegas after traveling to Barstow the day before. He had had a job interview in Barstow, and it went so well that they had decided to travel to Vegas for some fun. Nonnie, as usual, won at the slot machines. She always won, and it was always big money—two hundred dollars here, three hundred dollars there. That night she won five hundred dollars, and they had all enjoyed a fabulous dinner. They went to bed happy and hopeful. But Grandma knew when she woke up before Grandpa, always an early riser. She knew. Still, she tugged at his arm and called out his name. And Nonnie knew, too. We could picture in our minds Grandma's trembling fingers dialing the operator of the hotel. We could hear her cries for help. We could see the ambulance arrive, the stretcher holding Grandpa Max, the sheet covering his face.

A week later I held Mom's hand and stood in front of the casket Uncle Ed had helped Grandma purchase. Grandpa's body, the body that had held me in the train station, picked me up for rides to the mountains and to the corner store, was empty. He lay in the casket, his eyes closed, his hands folded, his body stilled. He was gone. Forever gone. I understood that. But I didn't dare touch the emotions attached to that realization. Aunts, uncles, and distant cousins I didn't know that well shook their heads. They shed tears. They rehashed all the details of the prior week to help themselves accept that our young fifty-four-year-old beloved Max had died of a heart attack.

Though I was only six, I knew death meant no return. I knew this was not sleep, not a vacation, not an absence that could be undone. But adults often don't realize the ability of a child to comprehend major events such as death. So it was with Grandma. She assured me that Grandpa was just sleeping. "Not to worry, Honey. His is a nice and peaceful sleep," she said, attempting to look at me, to care for me, though loss etched her clear blue eyes that reflected not me in front of her, but her beloved husband not waking up in that hotel room.

When I remembered certain moments with Grandpa—in Union Station, in his jeep, in the store, I explained to Dr. Emerson how I felt safe, secure, cared for, how silences were comfortable, and how Grandpa's love was manifest in small yet powerful gestures.

"You would not have survived without him," she responded. "You would not have survived."

Single Blade

Children swirled in a dizzying zigzag motion like moths around me. Each Monday afternoon for five weeks we followed the guide our parents paid to teach us about the natural world around us. Our leader, a young man wearing khaki shorts, a sun hat, and binoculars, pointed at the sky, the clouds, and the grasses. He said, "Listen, listen to the shrill and buzzing, the chirps of this great wide world."

I loved this great wide world. I loved that I could roam. There were no straight lines, no solid paths. We explored and repeated the names of flowers—violet, lily of the valley, lilac, morning glory, and lupine. Vines grew up the bark of trees and picket or chain-link fences. We repeated—ivy, honeysuckle, clematis, and wisteria. I felt safe repeating those names. I felt safe in the grasses, some luxurious as silk, some a little prickly. I wanted to stay there on the grounds of Lighthouse Nature Center and wrap myself up in those grasses and flowers, build a cocoon where I could grow and sleep in safety. I wanted to remain in this house with the grass serving as the carpet, the trees and shrubs as the walls, the sky and vast heavens as the ceiling. I wanted to follow our leader deeper and deeper into the mysteries of the natural world that he continued to name until his words began to rise above me, helium balloons sailing for the ether and vanishing. I didn't need words that day. I needed the experience to last, the experience of following a leader who informed and guided and allowed room for exploration and for my natural curiosity to also steer him. I remember how his glistening eyes acknowledged me.

Birthday Party

Tawny Anderson hung posters of Micky Dolenz of the Monkees on the back of her desk at school. Each morning she skipped into class, bent over and kissed him, and announced that she was in love and that he was the absolute cutest Monkee. She sang all of the Monkees' songs by heart, even my favorite, "Daydream Believer." I preferred Davy Jones but wouldn't admit to any crush. I was too shy. I admired Tawny, though. Full of laughter, outspoken in class, she possessed buoyancy and pizzazz. I envied her long blond hair that hung all the way down her back and bounced with her.

I received an invitation to Tawny's tenth birthday party. The invitation said we would watch the movie "Gigi." I couldn't believe her parents had a movie projector and movie screen. Her birthday party equaled going to a movie theater, and so the thought of missing the party devastated me. I doubted that I could go since the party was being held on a Saturday. Dad didn't work on the weekends, and he liked to have us home with him. Receiving permission to leave, even for a few hours, would not happen.

But Mom said, "Don't worry. You can go. Things are busy at work for your dad, and he has to work on Saturdays for a while." She encouraged me not to mention the party to my father, though. And I didn't.

Somehow Mom bought a present—with what money I don't know. After walking me the five or six blocks to the party, she interacted with Tawny's parents as if I went to birthday parties all the time, as if I were a normal child and she a normal parent and this a normal activity. Though I felt a little awkward, I joined in and played musical chairs and pin-the-tail-on-the-donkey. We ate hotdogs and potato chips, drank Pepsi, and ate a cake in the Andersons' dining room decorated with helium balloons and streamers. After Tawny opened more than a dozen presents, we moved into the living room to watch the movie, which I barely absorbed. I watched the screen for a few minutes. Then I watched Tawny, who loved Gigi as much as she loved Mickey Dolenz. She even knew some of the lines of the movie. I glanced at the other girls mesmerized by the large screen. Even after the movie, I soaked in the atmosphere—the laughter, the hugs that Tawny's parents bestowed upon her, the warm interactions.

Since the movie started later than expected, I arrived home to discover Dad had already returned from work. What would he do? Forbid me to go out at all, even in the neighborhood? Hit me? Yell at Mom for sneaking me out? Mrs. Anderson walked me to the door. Mom thanked her for driving me home, but Mom's jitteriness was palpable even though she smiled, even though she asked me as I entered the kitchen if I had had a good time. I don't remember the interactions with my father. I remember the feeling in me—I had done something wrong. I had gone to a birthday party without his knowing. His knowing would have meant that I couldn't go. When I might have returned home excited as a young girl should be, I returned home filled with guilt and the knowledge that fun equaled secrets and shame and then an outburst. Dad yelled at Mom for allowing me to go without consulting him.

Still, images from the birthday party fueled my imagination. In my imagination I attended more parties and hosted them as well. My home was not my home, though. I had another home, like Tawny's two-story red brick home with an attic. My dad did not exist there. I had another father. Every time I imagined a birthday party, that father grilled hamburgers and hot dogs, and he looked on while I opened presents—new clothes, a bicycle, Barbies, a stereo. He set up the projector so we could watch a movie. I was a child, a happy-go-lucky nine-year-old breaking into smiles as a dozen other nine-year-olds sang happy birthday to me.

Ballerina

She always appeared late at night, twirling in exaggerated slow motion. Had I fallen asleep and awakened, or was I asleep and dreaming? Or had I never fallen asleep and instead slipped into this odd state of being, this hallucination of sorts? It was impossible. There couldn't be a ballerina in my room, but she was there, dancing without music. She pirouetted and spun as if on depleted batteries—slow, slow, heavy, slow. She reminded me of the ballerina inside Grandma Esther's jewelry box. When I opened the box, the ballerina sprung up and twirled to a melody I can't recall. My thoughts mimed her sluggish movements. She was thinking—or was I thinking?—go away, go away. I willed my brain to speed up the languid words, words that took forever for my mind to express—go away, go away. My words and my thinking matched her diminishing speed. I tried to will her movement to pick up speed, thinking if she moved faster I would think faster, but nothing worked. I could not speed her up. I could not imagine her away. I could not will her thoughts—my thoughts—not to sound like a tape recorder at the wrong speed. I panicked. My will didn't matter. My effort to increase the speed, to make what sounded and felt abnormal to become normal, made no difference. I thought I might die having to endure this torture. I didn't want this dancer here. I wanted her out. I wanted to prevent my own demise.

Years later in a sociology class, a professor explained that extreme isolation can produce hallucinations. Immediately the ballerina came to mind. Was she the result of the isolation I experienced as a child? Was she a consequence of the abuse, a symbol produced by the complexity of my own human nature? Was she a shoot sprung out of my own soil, a shoot almost stillborn, unable to thrive in a violent environment?

I read and reread those pages on hallucinations. I was becoming conscious of the reasons for my experiences. That consciousness, those steps toward understanding my past and my responses to it, helped me feel something like power for the first time. I had heard professors say "Knowledge is power." Now I understood that phrase not as some mere intellectual sentiment but as a feeling taking root inside and edifying me.

Twisted Truths

Mulberry bushes or picket fences separated the dozens of two-story stucco bungalows lining the street. Elm trees towered high—always a few chain-sawed down each summer as a result of Dutch elm disease. Backyards filled with swing sets and sandboxes entertained the children in our neighborhood, as did the alleyway, the el-tracks, and a school playground at the north end of our block. Just a block away, a small grocery store and a drugstore provided us kids with ten-cent candy bars and even cheaper bubblegum. Our parents appreciated the close proximity to the grocer for those last-minute ingredients for a recipe or needed laundry detergent.

Late one morning, several women on the block stood chatting on the Essenburgs' lawn. Mom and I, on our way to the grocery, walked toward them. "Good morning. How are you?" Mom called out.

"Fine, but what about you?" Mrs. Herron asked, shaking her head.

"Covering up that black eye, huh?" Mrs. West asked.

"Ron has to stop hitting you, Carole," Mrs. Brower said in a singsong manner.

I was horrified. How did they know Dad had beaten Mom? And why were they joking with Mom about this?

Mom removed her glasses, saying, "Yep, gotta cover up these things."

"That's quite a bruiser," Mrs. Jones said. "So what actually happened?"

"Well, Ron hit me, of course," Mom responded and laughed.

What was going on? Why were all the neighbors joking around like this? Why did Mom admit that Dad had given her a black eye? We weren't supposed to betray him like this.

"Yeah, my husband beats me all the time," Mrs. Brower said, "a bruise here, a bruise there. And you, Allison, how about you? Does Ted carry on that way?"

Mrs. Jones, or Allison, as the women referred to her, rolled her eyes. "Come on, now, Barb." And then addressing my mom, she asked, "So what really happened, Carole?"

"I was vacuuming and not paying much attention and hit my eye with the hose attachment."

I was relieved until Mrs. West said, "Sure, Carole, excuses, excuses."

My mom laughed. "If you want to know the truth, Ron just attacked me and went wild."

What was I to do? How was I to play this game I didn't get? Poker-faced, I showed no emotion—at least I tried to show no emotion. Underneath that blank face I felt horrified. Mom had told the truth.

Yet everyone laughed, including my mom, who had spent several days crying, drinking vodka, and trying to cover the blackened and purple skin with pancake makeup.

Lessons at the Dinner Table

Who started everything? How do we know there's a God we can't see? How far away is the sun? Why is there starvation in the world? Why does the church teach no birth control when there's a population problem?

These were the serious philosophical questions that Dad asked us at the dinner table. He believed he was educating us, presenting critical questions for our minds to explore. But I feared a possible wrong answer. If I remained silent, he hollered, "What good are you if you don't think? Think! Use that damn brain!"

By the age of eight or nine I had memorized a few facts: The sun was ninety-two million miles from the earth. The earth's circumference was 24,000 miles. The church should not encourage its parishioners to keep on having babies. This was not a fact, but an opinion that became fact because it was Dad's. It pleased him to hear us repeat his ideas. It pleased him to believe he was raising thinkers who explored important questions.

If pleasing him meant avoiding yells and shouts, a punch or a shove, I would please him. It never dawned on me that it didn't matter what I or anyone else did. It never dawned on me that it wasn't Mom's fault or my fault that he grew angry. In my young mind, we were to blame for his violence. Because of some lack or some irresponsibility, we caused Dad to get upset and lose control of his temper. And so I prepared myself. I memorized what I thought he wanted to hear.

Each weekday night I stood watch at the bay window for Dad's car to pull into the driveway. I greeted him with a smile. I asked, "How was your day?" I behaved as best as I could. Night after night, Dad washed up and changed out of his work clothes. Then he entered the kitchen or dining room where Mom and we kids sat at the dinner table, ready to eat with him the meal Mom had prepared. After a philosophical discussion, a report of his day, or a list of his grievances concerning Mom and us, he returned to his twin bed in Mom and Dad's bedroom. I had heard Mom explain to a relative that he could not sleep with anyone else in the bed. He returned there and read the newspaper, then opened a book he had saved from college days: Rachel Carson, Paul Tillich, Loren Eiseley, or Thoreau. Sometimes tears slid down his cheeks over some phrase that moved him. Sometimes he marked a page and read passages to us at a later meal. Sometimes he napped for a while. Then he headed to the family room in the basement and spent the rest of the night watching TV until after the ten o'clock news when he turned in for the night. Every weekday night he went to bed by 10:30.

This weekday schedule varied little. We kept the house as quiet as we could to avoid disturbing him. Sometimes we joined him for a TV show. We were always in bed by 10:30 until we entered high school. In high school I remained up later if homework required extra time. I loved homework, especially reading literature. I loved poems, short stories, and novels. I loved entering other worlds, other conflicts, other peoples' lives, other songs. Sometimes I made up extra homework for myself to remain awake in a very quiet house. The clock ticked. Distant train whistles shrilled all the possibilities of distant terrains. The refrigerator motor hummed. As Dad got older, he snored softly, a great snore, a snore that meant peace, finally some peace. And in that peace I whispered the words of great books. Such glorious words stitched together in miraculous, musical, and mysterious ways.

Sunday Afternoon Drives

Some Sunday afternoons we behaved like a family. We loafed after a leisurely breakfast. We separated. Mom looked through a cookbook, selecting recipes to try out. Dad lounged on the sofa, a book open, his eyes scanning the pages. Mike built a Lincoln Log house, and his cowboys and Indians fought against one another. I took care of Chatty Cathy, bathing her, changing her, and holding her close.

"Why not take a ride?" Dad asked after lunch on occasion. "Good day for a ride." We all agreed and readied ourselves. Sometimes we drove to Gilson Park in Wilmette and watched the boats dotting the horizon. Sometimes we drove along Sheridan Road through all the wealthy North Shore suburbs. One Sunday Dad pointed out Senator Charles Percy's mansion, and for years I looked at that mansion in Kenilworth with indifference. However, after one of Senator Percy's twin daughters was murdered in 1966, I stared at the mansion as we drove past, pondering her death. Who killed her? Was it the mob, a family member, or possibly her own dad? Could Senator Percy have a side that the public didn't see but his family members did? Were they covering up the awful crime? Were they pretending to feel the kind of devastation a perfect family would show under such circumstances?

My mind spun, imagining and worrying about Senator Percy's daughter Valerie. I didn't worry about myself. We were a family like any other. We took Sunday drives. We relaxed together. In silence, we relaxed and drove.

Three Months in Third Grade

Doctor Shaw could not figure out what was causing the fever and why medication was not working. Blood tests revealed a blood infection that perhaps stemmed from an abscessed tooth that had swelled my mouth and cheek earlier that year. Perhaps the bacteria from that abscess had found its way into my bloodstream. Whatever the source of the infection, the doctor ordered bed rest until the blood tests showed normal counts. For the next three months I remained confined to bed.

During that time I slept and watched TV. When I could concentrate, I tried to read the books Dad's sister, my Aunt Lorel, brought over— *Across Five Aprils, Five Little Peppers and How They Grew, Little Women.* Consumed with thoughts of my illness, Aunt Lorel pampered me with all kinds of gifts—new books, magazines, stuffed animals. She liked to share her memories of all the illnesses she had suffered through. Dad called her a mental case and a hypochondriac. He said that she would claim any ailment or disease anyone else ever had and talk for hours about medical conditions. Even though he badmouthed Aunt Lorel, I loved her because I sensed her deep love for me. Not only that, she introduced me to various arts and crafts such as decoupage, rock painting, and collage making. Though she was sick a lot and became obsessed with anyone who was ill, I treasured her attention as a child.

During this three-month period, Mom hired a tutor to come over a few afternoons a week so that I wouldn't fall too far behind in school. I liked the tutor. She helped me understand the difficult math problems in a workbook, read from the books Aunt Lorel gave me, and had me read aloud to her. One afternoon she brought over her family's guinea pig and let me feed it a carrot.

Mom also set up a tiny TV near my bed. I watched *Bewitched, I Love Lucy, Gilligan's Island,* and steamy soap operas—*As the World Turns, Another World, The Guiding Light.* TV, TV, and more TV. TV on the screen and TV in my imagination—I could live whole other lives by imagining myself as one of the nicer characters from one of the soaps, someone wealthy, beautiful, and loved by another character who was handsome, caring, and perfect.

Late one afternoon, perhaps two months into this confining illness, Dad returned from work and entered my room. I greeted him, stiffening. "Did you have a good day?" I asked.

He didn't answer. He stormed toward me, hollering, "I'm sick of this! It's all in your damn head. You're not sick! You just think you are. You're just like your aunt, just like her!" He threw his fist at me, pinned me to the bed, slapped my face, continuing to holler. Then he left the room and continued to rant and rave at Mom.

After changing my nightgown and sheets, wet with urine, I lay back down and slipped away. I roamed a beach and speculated aqua waters, surfers balancing on the waves roaring in. Beneath palm trees, I crossed the sand with a handsome man who would never beat me, who held my hand and expressed his love to me there on that beach in Hawaii. Our love existed without fists, curses, shouts, or tears. Our love was painless. We lived happily in one unreal tale after another.

Separation

In fourth grade I heard about divorce on TV. Couples ended their marriages and began a new life separated from one another. I thought this was the answer for our family. We could get a divorce, couldn't we? We could exist without all the screaming, belt lashes, and flying dishes. We could live without the embarrassment of neighbors overhearing our family feuds. I told my mom about this and begged her to divorce my dad.

One morning about a year later, after Dad left for work, Mom explained to Mike and me that we were not going to school, that we were going to Grandma's instead. A tear curved down her cheek, and she wiped it away with the back of her hand. "I'm leaving your dad. We'll stay with Grandma and Nonnie until I work something out."

Though I had begged Mom to leave Dad, I now trembled and felt nauseous at the idea. Mom was dialing a number on the phone, stating our address, and asking for a taxi. She climbed the attic steps and lugged down suitcases she had packed without anyone knowing. We buttoned our coats and left the house on Colfax Street, Mom perching a note against the salt and pepper shakers on the kitchen table on the way out.

The ride down familiar streets seemed unreal. We passed two-story stucco and brick homes. The leafless elms and maples, bare, almost skeletons in winter, blurred into one another. The gray sky hung heavy over the suburb we left and remained gloomy as we entered the North Side of Chicago. Apartments replaced homes. And soon we were walking up the cement steps of Grandma's building. She had returned with her mother, our Nonnie, to Chicago after Grandpa died. The two-bedroom apartment was fine for them. Grandma worked at Old Orchard Shopping Center for Kroch's & Brentano's, a bookstore. Since money was tight, she did not remain home that day to greet us. Instead, Nonnie stood at the door, trembling. Though she tried to hide her worry by greeting Mike and me with a hug, we could see it in her eyes.

We settled in, and until early evening the day was rather uneventful. But by five, Mom had posted herself at the window. Her eyes narrowed and her mouth was one sealed line. She leaned against the wall smoking.

She kept one hand on the edge of the drape, lifting it away from the window now and then to peer out onto Tripp Avenue.

Every few minutes, Nonnie checked in on us from the kitchen archway leading into the dining and living rooms. She wiped her hands on the full-bibbed apron and peered at us from behind her wire-rimmed bifocals. She took a deep breath and then turned around and disappeared into the kitchen to finish dipping chicken pieces into egg whites and cornflake crumbs.

Mike and I sat on the sofa. Mike was penciling in all the *o*'s in one of Grandma's *Good Housekeeping* magazines. Grandma had promised him a dime for every page he completed. He was on his seventh page, hundreds of *o*'s darkened. Earlier I had completed a few pages but after a while felt bored, so instead I sat with a book in my lap. I turned the pages to *Lotta on Troublemaker Street*. I scanned the lines, moved my eyes across the words, but read nothing. I glanced at the TV screen. Ricky Ricardo stood three inches in front of Lucy, his eyes bulging. He hollered at her in Spanish. She stood frozen, her eyes widening, her lips trembling. And then she bawled her famous cry. Ricky stopped yelling, like he always did. He apologized. They hugged and kissed and the audience laughed.

"It's him!" Mom shouted out. "It's him. Nonnie, hurry! Get the kids. Mike, Kim, Go. Go with Nonnie."

Nonnie ran in from the kitchen. We jumped up and sprinted toward her. We headed for the bathroom in the hallway. Once inside, Nonnie closed the door, turned the lock, and tore the shower curtain open. Mike and I climbed into the bathtub. Nonnie held the wall for support and lifted one leg and then the other into the tub. She pulled the shower curtain shut, mumbling something in Norwegian. I understood *Gott*. I understood "Jesus." I looked up at Nonnie's eyes. They looked out from those glasses at the white tile. She trembled. Seeing her trembling caused me to shake even more. I tried to stop the shaking by folding my hands together tighter, tighter, even tighter. I heard Mom across the hall in Grandma Esther's bedroom, unzipping her suitcase. I imagined her digging through her underwear, pajamas, and shirts for Dad's gun. I had overheard her explaining to Grandma that she brought the gun with her because she was afraid Dad would return home from work to an empty house, find the note, fly into a rage, and come after us.

"It's OK. Not him," Mom finally called in to us.

We all let out an audible sigh. Nonnie lifted Mike's chin. "It's OK, little man." And then she caught my gaze. Tears spilled from her eyes. "It's OK."

While Mom remained stationed by the window, Nonnie set Mike and me up at the card table in the kitchen. She brought over two small plastic juice cups and a pad of paper for each of us. "Let me show you how to make moons," she offered. She set the rim of the cup against the paper and traced a sharpened pencil around the circumference. She repeated the gesture until she had made a few moons. "How many moons do you think you can make?"

"Hundreds," Mike said, smiling. "I can make hundreds. How much do I get for that?"

"I have some quarters tucked away," Nonnie said.

"I like quarters."

Mike started right in. I followed along. I enjoyed the smooth sweep of my hand around the cup. I loved the sharpened point of the pencil. I picked up the cup and looked for a moment at each moon I had created. I imagined myself on that moon. Just like an astronaut, I could leap and jump and not be bound by gravity. I could float and bounce. I made more moons, hundreds of them. I filled the pad of paper. My moons were different than the moon in the sky to which I couldn't escape. My moons were earths where I could live safe and whole, free, finally free.

A few weeks later, however, we returned home.

Dad controlled the finances, and because of his unrealistic views of what it cost to feed and clothe a family, he had given Mom far less than was needed. Mom, who handled her mother's bank account, had taken money she thought she would repay—ten dollars here, fifteen dollars there. The amount, over the years, totaled up to about a few thousand dollars. How would she ever pay it back?

Dad promised to help her. He promised to give her more money each week for living expenses. He promised to change. He could be a good man. He never meant to hurt her or us. He couldn't explain his past actions. But he could change and he loved her, loved us all.

Though I don't know their exact conversations, I was told life would be different. I shared with Dr. Emerson that I believed my father did love us, did want to change, and actually believed that he could. His intentions were sincere but his skills were deplorable. He was too proud to seek out help to learn how to handle his anger, how to communicate effectively, and how to allow room for the typical unpredictable nature of family life. Emotionally untrained, culturally shaped, his promises lasted only a short time.

Initial trips to museums, parks, and the zoo occurred. One Sunday we went to Brookfield Zoo. Giraffes stood with their long necks, their open mouths reaching toward the leaves of high branches. Gorillas scratched their bellies, sucked their thumbs, stared out at us mortals. Dad leaned down and said to Mike and me, "Do you like those gorillas—those big hairy, amazing gorillas?" Oh, yes, we did, we liked them. Mike thought the gila monsters, iguanas, and rattlesnakes in the reptile exhibit were cool. Dad pointed out that the elephants' gargantuan legs were larger in diameter than the trunks of some oaks and maples.

We held hands that day and smiled at each other. We were a family to be admired, a family coming back together after a separation that would remain a secret. Even those who knew—our grandparents, particular relatives—would not mention the separation, would not ask if things were better.

That day and in the days that followed, I felt as if I were playing a part in a drama that would soon end. We would resume the old parts. I could still sense those old parts—the father who stormed and raged when something was out of place; the mother who cleaned and cleaned and attempted to put everything in order to prevent the outbreak; and the children, planets, separate from one another, far away, existing in the vast darkness, just existing.

Overheard

My friends' eyes widened and the conversation halted. Mrs. Winona, my fifth-grade teacher, stood behind me. "What is going on here? What kind of talk is this? To your desks," she ordered.

Though I didn't know much about boys, I had watched enough TV to share a dirty joke in the coat room at school with Liz, Melinda, and Jan. Their laughter caused me to believe I had earned their friendship. For those few moments, I fit in and I felt cool. The more they laughed, the more I shared details about lovers and French kissing, that is until Mrs. Winona entered.

I sat down at my desk, feet firm on the floor, hands folded. I looked at my hands, little fists right there on the desk, and I unfolded my fingers. I shifted and felt something come up in me, from the belly to my ribs, ribs to chest, chest to throat. I opened my mouth and a deep belly laugh escaped. I couldn't stop. I pressed my fingers to my cheeks and bowed my head onto the surface of the desk, still exploding with uncontrollable laughter.

"That's it!" Mrs. Winona shouted. She marched over to my desk with a roll of adhesive packing tape. She ripped off a piece big enough to cover my mouth and sealed my lips.

Instead of showing humiliation, I continued to laugh, my persistent giggles leaking through the tape. Everyone laughed, but Mrs. Winona held up the wide roll of tape used to seal boxes and asked, "Anyone else want this? Anyone else?"

There was silence.

"Let's have order, then. Order now." And there was order in my fifth-grade classroom. Even I calmed down and sat there until recess with pencil in hand, scrawling the answers to math problems.

Several weeks later on a Sunday morning, I was charged with the task of walking Rudolph, our dachshund. I shuffled over stones, broken glass, and litter all the way down the alley, an aisle between two sets of houses—a dozen or so on Colfax and a corresponding dozen on Lincoln. I named the neighbors on our side as I passed their homes—Sanders, Wolfes, Armstrongs, Wells. An elevated train clacked, speeding by. I hated the sound, so unlike the smooth Amtrak trains. None of the Wells kids were in the yard. They went to church on Sundays. The Armstrongs were probably still sleeping because they, like us, didn't go to church.

Halfway home, I yanked the chain to stop the dog because I heard something. What was that sound? Where was it coming from? Maybe that house between the Wells and Armstrongs, the people I didn't know.

The muffled sound receded. "OK, Rudy, let's go," I said to the dog and started walking. I walked several more yards and then pulled on the chain and stood still again. Not our house. Please, not our house.

I stopped and turned around. I didn't want to go home, didn't want to walk up those gray wooden steps to the back door. I headed back to the end of the alley and loitered. Even the stupid clack, clack, and squeak of the el was less stressful than going home. The dog, happy with the longer walk, didn't stop me from worrying. Would I get in trouble for taking so long? Would I be grounded for the rest of the school year? Would Dad hit me?

Eventually I forced myself to return. At the end of the alley, just as I was about to turn onto the smooth cement of the sidewalk, I glimpsed Liz, Melinda, and Jan. They stood on the sidewalk outside our front yard—mulberry bushes and a stretch of lawn between them and the house. I spun around and ran full-speed back down the alley. My heart raced. Tears fell. Not my friends, not my friends, not my friends. Stupid, stupid, stupid! No one was supposed to know, no one!

Back at the end of the alley, I wiped my face and kicked a few sticks and rocks. I told the dog that I hated this, hated this, hated this. I told the dog I didn't want to go back home, ever. And I didn't want to see any of my friends. I couldn't go back to school. I'd rather just die, I told the dog. The dog looked at me and then sniffed around some more.

The fear of punishment pulled me back home. I expected a beating for taking so long. But when I returned Dad hadn't even noticed I was gone. The yelling had stopped. I swallowed and held in my anxieties. I didn't know what I'd say to my friends. Maybe they would pretend they hadn't heard anything.

The next day, however, riding home on the school bus, Liz asked in front of everyone on the bus, "What happened at your house yesterday? There was yelling and cursing. It sounded awful."

"My brother," I said. "He was home from college for the weekend and he's nothing but trouble. He was carrying on and on, and no one could control him. I think he has drug problems, really. My parents are so upset. It's embarrassing." How this lie gushed from my lips, I don't know. How I could so easily conceive something to somehow excuse what happened surprised me. But I had to do something. No one was supposed to hear Dad.

"You have an older brother? Hmm, I didn't know that," Liz responded.

I nodded but wondered if she believed me. "Yeah, I do, he's just a lot of trouble." I tried to sound as convincing as possible.

I don't remember the rest of the conversation. I don't remember if I searched the faces of my friends for some sign that they believed me or didn't believe me. But I remember that lie, the first of many more to come that would begin to weave excuses and a story that I could bear. I think of the tape on my mouth, intended to silence me for a few uncontrollable moments, and that tape didn't matter at all. I was already taped like a mummy, paralyzed, wrapped and wrapped with all kinds of tape, tape that silenced me, tape that programmed me, tape that I would one day wonder how I would ever undo.

Crank Calls

We were three young girls, fifth graders, with nothing much to do during those long lazy summer days. We lived in a time when parents didn't worry about child abduction and molestation. We had freedom to roam our neighborhoods. We had hours to invent and reinvent ourselves from preteen girls into movie stars. We still swung in swings at the park, twirled into dizziness and oblivion on the merry-go-round, and hid from one another for hide-and-seek. Sometimes we put on Sarah's mom's makeup—the soft pink lipsticks and blush, deep blue eye shadow—and pretended we would find ourselves rich and handsome men, get married, and have babies. Our lives would be filled with joy, not the despair of our warring parents, our controlled mothers whose husbands ordered them around, yelled at them, handed out ten- or twenty-dollar bills as if that alone could feed a family.

My best friend, Siegie, and I didn't talk much about our parents. But we knew, we sensed, how similar our lives were. Our friend Sarah lived with her mom, who tired of the controlling man she had married and obtained a divorce. She worked every day, so we hung out at Sarah's, where no adult could stop us from dialing number after number.

"Hello, is John there?" I asked in a pretend sexy voice.

"No, he's at work."

"O darn! He's at work?" I responded.

"Who's calling?"

"No one. No one," I said, imagining myself the disappointed lover. "Who's this?"

"I'm his wife."

"His wife?" I asked, feigning astonishment. "He has a wife. You are his wife?" I pretended to stumble over my words. Both Siegie and Sarah held in their cheeks, trying not to laugh. But we couldn't control ourselves. We burst, the giggles hopefully overheard by the woman on the other end.

Our own lives hurt enough that we chose to distract ourselves. We were ten. Our parents drank, fought, and ordered us around as if we were robots or soldiers, not children, not souls. We had to find ways, as all children do, to fill our time, to dump elsewhere the chaos we felt inside.

We opened the phone book, read each other phone numbers, and laughed, delighted that we could sound like other people, that we could develop our own soap operas in an empty apartment to fill those empty summer days.

Tabasco

No didn't work. *Stop that, quit it, go stand in the corner, I'm going to tell your father* . . . none of Mom's attempts to stop the swearing worked. Charles, my brother, a four-year-old with gorgeous brown curly hair and bright blue eyes, repeated the atrocities that so often spewed out of Dad's basic-training drill sergeant's mouth. He said the *f*-word, the *s-h*-word and God's name prefacing damn. Mom tried to control him. She tried everything. One day she stormed to the refrigerator, grabbed the small bottle of Tabasco sauce, and stomped toward Chuck. She smeared his lips and dotted his tongue with the red pepper sauce. His lips and the surrounding skin turned red. He didn't swear the rest of that day, too distracted by the burn.

Within days it was the same battle all over again—Chuck still repeating what he had heard Dad say. Mom threatened and scolded, beside herself with trying to figure out how to stop such embarrassing behavior.

Nothing worked. Chuck survived Dad's madness by trying every way possible to identify with him. At four he swore. By ten he sat in front of the TV, cheered and hollered at the Chicago Bears, acting like the man Mike, his older brother, wasn't. Mike, who liked music, was beaten for wanting to play the flute, which Dad considered an instrument for *fags*. Chuck showed no interest in music. He acted far more macho than any other male in the family. He cursed. He watched football with Dad. He joined the Air Force, following in Dad's footsteps. His basic training was held at the base where Dad had spent most of his Air Force career. He hung up Playboy centerfolds in his locker. No one would consider him a *fag*.

Unable to Cross

A whole tree lay on its side, serving as a bridge from one side of the river to the bank on the other side. Children, agile as monkeys, walked that balance beam of a trunk and hoorayed and hurrahed upon reaching the other side. No one fell into the deep rushing river. "Come on," they shouted to me. The trunk appeared as narrow as a needle. How could a needle serve as the pathway for me to get from where I stood to where the other children laughed and played? How did they get their bodies to maneuver across that treacherous bridge? How could my body, trembling as it was, inch across the log without falling in?

I never ventured onto the trunk that particular day, never shared with the rest of the teenagers the adrenaline of risk-taking, the exuberance of accomplishment. Though I considered hugging the trunk and sliding across the bark, I knew the kids on the other side would laugh at my babyish attempt. My body froze as I pictured the worst: falling into the deep river and—since I could not swim—being consumed by the dark water.

I wandered back toward the adults and the younger children at the park site. Though I wanted to join in and have fun with kids my own age, I was too afraid and unskilled. I played with the children of my father's work associates. And, of course, the adults praised me. Such a responsible young woman, not wandering off like the rest, doing God knows what.

A Prince Dies

I often wonder how I learned anything. I spent hours in fantasy—at school, at home—to get myself to sleep. I stole themes and storylines from the soap operas my mother watched during the day and at night. *As the World Turns, Peyton Place,* and movies such as "Love Story" provided me with the grist I needed for some excitement. Lovers arrived and died, and more lovers relieved me of my grief with their adoration, care, and money.

Fantasy worked to relieve me of some of the pain of home life. But the tool that served me in childhood had different effects as I got older. The first time I considered fantasy as a dangerous thing occurred during my sophomore year in high school. My family had moved from Evanston to Glenview, Illinois, and I left one high school to start at another. I felt the typical awkwardness many new students experience when entering a school where cliques are already in place. Some people tried to include me, asking questions about what I liked to do, whether I had seen a certain movie, or what music I liked. Others invited me to sit with them at lunch. I boasted to some of the girls who had boyfriends that I, too, had a boyfriend. His name was Ben, and I hated being forced to move away and leave him, I explained.

Ben was an actual person, very good-looking I thought, with his long brown hair and dark penetrating eyes. He was known to smoke a little reefer and hang with the cool crowd. He and I were not close in reality. In fact, if someone had asked him if he knew me, I think he probably would have said no. But having a boyfriend seemed to make a girl acceptable, and so I told several girls about Ben. They sympathized with my situation and began to include me, which I believed wouldn't happen if they knew I didn't have a boyfriend.

One day I arrived at school with tears in my eyes. Jennifer, Laura, and Liz asked me what was wrong.

"It's Ben," I said, sobbing. "He was killed in a car accident."

"Oh no!" Jennifer responded, hugging me. They all offered their sympathy and warmth. For days and weeks they inquired, "Are you missing him?" "How are you doing today?" "Let me know if there's anything I can do." "If you need to talk, I'm here." Their attention felt great; I had friends, friends I didn't believe I would have without pretending my life was other than what it was.

Several months later I heard from a friend in Evanston that Ben had been killed in a car accident. After the initial shock, I felt guilty. Because I had fantasized Ben's death, I reasoned, perhaps I had caused it. Was I a murderer? Was I an accomplice? To avoid my feelings and the perplexity of the situation, I spent even more time in fantasy. Not about Ben. Not about anyone who was real. I wouldn't risk that. But I continued utilizing characters from soaps and movies, believing that I couldn't destroy what was invented.

Fiddler and Dinner in the Round

For my sixteenth birthday Dad drove us into Chicago. I can't remember which theater we attended, but I can still see our dinner table, one of many circling the stage. Mom and Dad had asked me what I wanted for my birthday. I always received something special. The year before it was furniture from Pier One—a headboard for my bed and a dresser that Mom had painted Wedgwood blue and added an antique glaze to. Since I loved theater, I told Mom and Dad that I'd like to go to a play. Mom checked out various possibilities, and we settled on "Fiddler on the Roof."

Sitting in the theater in the dim light among several dozen families and couples all dressed up as we were, candles glowing on all the tables, thrilled me. But the play affected me more than I expected. I was amazed how words on a page, the script, could be infused with actual life and spirit. The music moved me in profound ways, more profound than what I had experienced in church or anywhere else. The stage, through the artistry of the crew, became a real setting, a place for this drama to be acted out. The actors and actresses surrendered to the script and to some innermost part of themselves that claimed the words and the plot and the interactions with other characters. They moved across the stage as if they were in the world of the characters they performed, and I sat there seeing who I considered to be the real Tevye, Golde, Yente, Lazar . . . all in their Russian town, all struggling with traditions. I laughed. I wept. My parents did, too. I felt connected with Mom and Dad that night. I felt connected as we watched another family's struggle, another family's loving, and the pain of that loving.

Ironing

One school morning downstairs in the basement of our home, I opened the squeaky ironing board, turned on the iron, positioned one of my blouses that I wanted to wear to school that day, and waited a few moments for the iron to heat up. That's when I heard the words: *You little slut. No good son-of-a-bitch. Fat slob.* Though my Dad had called me these names before, he was in the shower at that moment. These words were coming from inside me. Somehow Dad's threats, insults, and emotional battering had become lodged in my head. I stood there in the basement. I held the iron upright. I looked at the wrinkled blouse and paused. I didn't know what to do with this awareness of my own internal barrage. It would be years before books and therapists introduced me to the concept of erasing old messages. I swallowed. I placed the steaming iron on my blouse, maneuvered it forward and back, and pressed out every wrinkle, every single wrinkle.

Headaches

Every day as I walked the halls of Glenbrook South High School from one class to the next, my head pounded. After I had endured a few months of dealing with headache pain that was unrelieved by aspirin, Mom made an appointment with Dr. Salk. When I sat in his office a few days later, Dr. Salk listened with a stethoscope to my heart and lungs. Then he checked my throat, nose, and eyes. "Under any stress?" he inquired as he checked my ears.

I shook my head.

"School's going OK?"

I nodded.

"Busy with after school activities?"

"I'm not really into anything right now."

Dr. Salk kept his focus on me. "Have you just finished participating in activities?"

"No."

"How about homework? Do your teachers assign a lot?"

"Not really."

"So, if school is not a source of stress, what about things at home?"

I looked at my feet.

"Kim, I know a little bit about your family situation. Your headaches might be related to what's going on with your dad. I'm going to prescribe something that will help relieve the pain. But I want to make another suggestion. Would that be OK?"

I nodded, wondering what his suggestion was, wondering how he knew about Dad.

"You're getting close to the time when you will be leaving, possibly going off to college. That would be a good thing. Are you considering college?"

I nodded, though I had given college little thought.

"When you are at college, Kim, please seek out some professional counseling. You will need some help to come to terms with what has occurred in your home. I hope that you will come to realize not all men are like your father. They're not." He shook his head emphasizing that point. "It may be hard for you to learn how to trust a man after growing up with your dad." Then he repeated, "Get some help. Not all men are like your dad."

When I shared this memory with Dr. Emerson, she asked me what it was like to have my family doctor express his concern. I remembered wishing I were someone else at the time—someone who had such a great home life that they could report to their doctor all the fun they were having. But reflecting on the incident in her office, I felt grateful that he cared enough to offer me that advice. In the years ahead I would need that advice. I would need it when I struggled in therapy, when I had a hard time trusting men, and when in my own marriage the tangled web of my past made it difficult for me to relate to my husband.

First Act

Sandy Dayton stood up in front of the classroom. She had curled her hair for the occasion and wore blue eye shadow, mascara, blush, and even a little lipstick. I envied her perfection—the skintight Gap jeans and Limited aqua T-shirt that showed off her slim figure and accented her blue eyes. She nodded to Mr. Kornwell, our theater teacher, and he dropped the phonograph needle onto the album. The music to "Riders on the Storm" began, and Sandy, in the most confident and lyrical voice, recited by memory the words to Genesis. She was beautiful to watch. The music worked well with the Biblical creation story, and everyone in class was enraptured. How would I ever follow such an act? She was popular, talented, beautiful, and I hadn't even thought about including a musical background to my monologue.

The applause following her performance made me even more nervous. Would anyone clap for me? Should I continue with my plans—to act out my secret life, the life of a young woman whose father abused her? Would anyone guess that my act was no act? What would they think of me if they knew what I was pretending was reality?

Before I had time to ponder these questions, Mr. Kornwell asked the class to identify the strengths of Sandy's performance.

"The music was cool," Dan called out.

"Yeah, it really went with the Bible, which sort of surprised me," added Janice, the girl who prayed before she ate her lunch.

"She seemed unaware of the audience and totally into the performance," Josh said.

"She read really clearly, too, and we could hear even with the musical background," Melinda piped in.

Mike interrupted the lull that followed Melinda's remark. "I haven't memorized the Bible, but from what I can recall I think Sandy memorized the passages."

"OK, these are great comments on the strengths of Sandy's performance," Mr. Kornwell said. "Any suggestions for improvement?"

Silence hung over us. Several students shook their heads. Someone muttered, "Not really."

"If we wanted to aid Sandy to make her next performance stronger than this excellent performance, what would we suggest?"

"Maybe she could move around some. She stayed in one spot the whole time."

"Not a bad idea," Mr. Kornwell said, looking out to the class for further feedback. "What about varying the sound of her voice? Remember how we talked about that?"

Several students nodded.

"Those might be two things to work on, Sandy," Mr. Kornwell said. "Outstanding performance."

Sandy sat down, and then Mr. Kornwell invited me up to the front of the room and asked if I needed him to do anything. I shook my head no and said that all I needed was a chair, which was already there. I sat down and everyone quieted down, their eyes on me. I could feel my heartbeat in my throat.

"I need to get out," I started. "Out. I can't take it anymore. No, my parents are not getting a divorce. They're not." I paused. "That's the problem. They stay together. They fight. My dad . . ." I looked down at the floor. I couldn't look out at the counselor I was imagining myself talking to. "I came here for advice, for help. I know you're a trained counselor. I hope you can help, but I don't think anything will ever change." I paused as if I were listening to the counselor I imagined asking me some questions. "You want to know what I was going to say about my dad? You know, he'd probably kill me if he knew I was about to share what I'm about to share. He beats us. Not just a slap. Not just a single belt whipping. He takes his fist and gives us black eyes, broken bones. I don't know what's wrong with him. I don't. Something has to be." Again I paused and glanced up to the face of the woman I saw in my mind's eyes. "What do you mean how do I feel about this? How do you think I feel? You can't even imagine how he terrifies me, my mom, my sisters." I said sisters instead of brothers so that no one in the audience would make any associations with my family, but then I spotted Karen and Ellen looking down at their feet. Their facial expressions were so serious, so grim. I sighed a heavy and audible sigh. Because I feared the class would interpret that sigh as the real me sighing, not the person I was portraying, I fumbled for words. "I have to get out. That's how I feel," I almost shouted. "Don't you understand. This is a hell. A home is not supposed to be a hell, but my home . . . it's hell. He'll never change. They've separated and he promises and promises he'll stop. But he never does." I noticed that most of the students, and even Mr. Kornwell, could not look at me. I had to stop. They knew this was my life and not an invented one. "I'll make it though. I promise you that I'll make it because I will leave someday. You just wait and see. I'll leave and I'll go somewhere else where it's not hell, where it's maybe just normal, where I can go shopping at the mall with friends, where I can eat a meal without fearing anyone, where I can spend a day without hearing one darn shout. It will happen. You wait. You wait and see. It will happen."

A long silence hung. I forced myself to stand up. The class stared at me, and Jennifer, thank God, started to clap. Then others followed suit. Mr. Kornwell stood up and he, too, was clapping. "A very powerful performance, very powerful," he said, nodding to me, looking at me with what appeared to be concern in his eyes. Or was it knowing or recognition that I had just performed my life, the secret life that my family made every effort to keep from everyone else?

Class was over. The bell rang. No time for comments on my performance. Just as well. I wasn't sure I could take in the comments. I just wanted to leave the classroom, head to my locker, catch the bus home, even though that home was the very hell I had just mentioned in the performance of my life.

Babysitting and Freedom

Dad did not want me going out with any of my high-school friends who might smoke pot, drink, and get into trouble. Home was where I belonged. That was that. I was so accustomed to not being allowed the kind of freedoms and liberties that most of my friends experienced, I didn't bother to argue. Since I was allowed to babysit and earn money to help buy the clothes, makeup, and accessories that most teens desire, I discovered a way out of the house. I could pretend that I was babysitting. I could tell Mom and Dad that, hey, the Hayaks want me this weekend. Since I did a lot of babysitting for that family, Mom and Dad wouldn't suspect anything.

I usually walked over to the Hayaks' house when I was going to sit for them because they lived only half a mile away. I said my good-byes, began my walk, and instead of going to the Hayaks', met up with some friends at a church parking lot just a few blocks from the house. Everything Dad feared I would do, I did. I smoked cigarettes, I drank, I interacted with high-school friends who came from families with problems or from families who were far too lenient and permissive. Sometimes we drank right in their homes in front of their parents, who also drank and smoked marijuana.

The inebriation unloosed me from my worries, problems, and the hell of home life. I loved the total lack of self-consciousness I felt when I danced and spun to Bruce Springsteen or Paul Revere and the Raiders.

I took pleasure in falling because I never hurt myself. Flat on my back, I marveled at the trees changing colors, ablaze with autumn. In winter, the skeletal trunks and branches and twigs, the bare essence of trees, bowled me over. The buds filling those same bare branches, I considered an absolute phenomenon.

One night I returned home seeing triple. Mom and Dad were entertaining another couple. They sat in the living room, each of them holding a glass of wine. "How are you?" I asked. "Nice to see you." They were a haze of smiles and words. "Have fun. I'm off to bed . . . so tired. Even though the kids were great, it was a long night." My tongue felt heavy. I worried that my words were slurred. I went into the bathroom right across from the living room. I locked the door and looked in the mirror. I couldn't even see my own image. I leaned against the blur of myself reflected in the glass. I asked God for help. I couldn't move. I couldn't leave the bathroom. What if they could tell I was drunk? Perhaps they knew. Perhaps Mom and Dad sensed my state of inebriation. But I had to get out of there. If I stayed in the bathroom, they would suspect something. I convinced myself to open the door, walk down the hallway to my room, say good-night, nice to see you, before entering my room and closing the door and falling into bed. Sleep would not relieve me of the effects of too much beer and wine. I woke the next morning with a splitting headache, a sour stomach, and a prayer that Mom and Dad would not suspect anything. They didn't. They said nothing about the night before.

Venting

I traipsed through the backyard, my backpack weighted with geometry and Shakespeare books. I opened the door to the jalousie porch and went on into the kitchen.

"Kim, after you set your things down, I need a hand." Mom stood over the sink, her brow dotted with sweat, her hand pulling out the inside of a chicken.

"I've got homework," I retorted.

"Your dad will be home early and I'm behind."

"Behind in what—serving him? He's thankless." The sassiness gushed like an open wound. "I have other things to do. You're always nagging me to help. Why should I help?"

"Kim, please put your backpack away. Just set the table for me, OK?" Mom's pleading was accompanied with a sigh—that helpless sigh. I hated her helplessness. I hated that she put up with Dad, a tyrant, a maniac, a monster. I hated that I already was feeling guilty about all this hating. I knew I would set the table. I would shut my big mouth when he walked in the door. I would sit there at the table and answer stupid questions about politics or listen to Dad drone on about his day.

I stomped into my room, tossed the backpack across my bed, and went to the bathroom. In the bathroom I stared at myself in the mirror. I brushed my hair back into a ponytail and clipped it up in a bun, but strands hung out and it looked awful. I stuck my tongue out at myself, then smiled, tried to look good, beautiful. If only the reflection looking back weren't me, but Karen. She had a great life. Her parents got along. She was allowed to use their charge card and buy jeans and shirts and get her hair cut at the hair salon at Plaza Del Lago.

"Kim, hurry up. It's getting late," Mom called, sounding nervous. Yes, the clock was ticking, ticking. Soon it would be five and Dad would be home. Then we could all die for the night. He had threatened to put Mike's head in a vise the other night. But I already felt as if I were in a vise. We were all in a vise, his vise.

"Kim . . ."

"What do you want?" I screamed. I opened the door and stormed out of the bathroom. "What do you want? You want me to sweep? You want me to vacuum? You want me to dust? You want me to become some kind of maid just like you. You just want me to do what pleases him. But don't you get it? Nothing pleases him!"

"Kim, that's not true. Calm down."

"That's not true? That's not true? Listen to you! You don't even know what's real anymore. Why do you stay with him? What's wrong with you that you stay with him?"

"I know it's been hard the past week. Your father is under a lot of stress with his new job . . ."

"I'm tired of his stress!" I screamed. "I'm tired of his yelling. Every single day he screams and yells, and you just take it." I couldn't stop the yelling. Years of pent-up emotion were pouring out of my emerging adolescent self.

And then Dad appeared. He looked at me, then walked to the closet to hang up his coat. He turned around and took one step, then another, and another . . . toward me. I stood there, frozen, unable to breathe or move.

Even before he raised his arm, his fingers curling into a fist, even before he hit me, I lost bladder control. He punched me and then shoved me into the wall. "Get the hell out of here! Don't you ever talk to your mother like that. Get out! Get to your room," he ordered.

But I couldn't get up. I was shaking. I couldn't seem to think, stand up, walk to my room.

"Did you hear me? Did you hear me?" he screamed.

I crawled, managed to get to my knees, then onto my feet.

I closed my bedroom door. I changed my clothes, climbed in under my sheets, and somehow managed to stop the trembling, the weeping.

First Jobs

Conveyor belts of lipstick, pancake makeup, eye shadow, perfumes rolled by day after day. I was part of the human race responding to bells. A bell shrilled when work began, shrilled at the beginning and ending of the morning break, shrilled to launch the lunch break, and half an hour later shrilled to mark lunch's all-too-soon end. The days seemed endless. How boring could life get? I tried making up stories to pass the time, but then I made errors. I was a sophomore in high school, not a factory worker. After a week, I quit.

Laundering sheets at a nursing home didn't impress me either. My supervisor should have provided a gas mask so I wouldn't have to smell the stench of those sheets. I was almost sixteen, not sixty. I had a whole life before me. A paycheck motivated me to spend a couple of hours after school, three days a week in that forsaken laundry room. I stuffed sheets into the washing machine, measured soap, pulled cleaned and dried sheets from the dryer, and folded them. I managed to last a month at this job.

The following month I was hired as a secretary at a tucked away golf association, though I only typed twenty words a minute with close to ten mistakes. I enjoyed working in a business environment with many other secretaries, administrative assistants, executive directors, and mailroom clerks. The golf association sponsored a major golf tournament, and during the summer months I joined several other staff members and stayed in a hotel to help prepare for, manage, and conduct post-tournament operations. I made a few thousand dollars during that time because I worked overtime. The glamour of meeting professional golfers, journalists, and even celebrities excited me.

Once, while I was riding down to the lobby from my hotel room, a gentleman poked me and said, "Do you know who this is?"

I apologized and said I didn't know and explained that I was new to the whole golf tournament business, assuming the man was a golfer.

"It's Bing Crosby," he said.

"Sure," I chuckled.

"Really, it's Bing Crosby."

I looked at the man, who smiled but didn't nod his head or say a word. I repeated, "Sure," convinced this was not Bing Crosby and these two men were trying to pull my leg. When we entered the lobby, dozens of people thronged around, who else, but Bing Crosby. Bing winked at me as he began signing autographs.

During the few years I worked at the golf association, my immediate supervisor, Peg, became aware that I was suffering from a difficult home life. A couple of times I showed up to work bruised, and when she asked about the marks, I didn't let on. But one time Peg asked if there was trouble at home, and I broke down. She became very motherly toward me and encouraged me to consider going to college. That would never happen, I told her. My dad didn't believe that girls should go to college, and I didn't have enough money. Peg arranged for Mr. Cook, the executive director of the association, to meet with me. He was an alumnus of the University of Missouri in Columbia, and he encouraged me to consider his alma mater. He had friends there and could arrange for me to work part-time while I went to school. The University of Missouri—a great school for journalism. I loved writing. Journalism seemed like a possible career. But I didn't know if my dad would allow this, and I couldn't imagine proceeding without his consent. Mr. Cook encouraged me to talk with my parents anyway. He said that he would be willing to talk with them as well.

A few weeks later I initiated that conversation. My dad, confined by his traditional perceptions of women, couldn't fathom that a career was something I desired. "Most girls want to find a husband. Most girls want to become a mother. Don't you have any interest in doing what's normal?"

"Dad, of course I want to get married, but not yet. I want to get an education. I want to have a career."

"A career?"

"Yes. I really like journalism. I like writing, and maybe I would even like broadcasting."

"I don't get it. You don't even date. You don't dress in an appealing, sexy manner. You do nothing to try and attract someone, and you're at the age where you need to find someone to settle down with. This college stuff is crazy. Women get married, maybe become nurses."

"I can't handle the sight of blood, and Mr. Cook made these arrangements."

"That was very considerate of him, I think," Mom piped in.

"Carole! Considerate? What are you talking about? He's interfering. An out-of-state school! It's a waste. If Kim's going to go to college, the best thing would be down the street at the community college. They've got good nursing programs. She could live at home and go there."

"Dad, Mr. Cook found a part-time job for me at the University of Missouri. I've been accepted there. This could work out. It's a great school."

Dad went round and round with the marriage talk, with the becoming a mother talk, with the acceptable profession of nursing talk.

I broke down and wept. "What's wrong with Missouri? Mr. Cook said he would talk to you. Please, just talk to him."

"Bullshit! Why in the hell should I talk to someone who is meddling with our life?" Dad stomped out of the room.

Mom looked at me and mouthed, "Don't worry. He'll come around." But I didn't think he would. Dad never came around. He wanted full control of everything, including my life, and I just didn't know how to escape that emotional vise.

Though Dad refused to fill out any college financial aid forms because he feared the communists would get his private information, and though he refused to help with any of the costs, several months later, just as Mom predicted, he drove the eight hours to Columbia, Missouri, and moved me into Johnston Hall. It was late August of 1975.

Part 3: Released Inmate

Caught

When the secretary I was hired to assist took her breaks, I sat at her desk, answered her phone, and snooped in her top desk drawer where she kept a lipstick, a brush, and several quarters among the pencils, pens, and staples. I pocketed a couple of quarters, not enough to be noticed. Each time I sat there I took one, maybe two, one time five quarters because I figured that Joan wouldn't notice the missing five among the more than dozen quarters piled in the bin next to the paperclips. For weeks and weeks, on through the holidays, I pocketed the quarters.

In February my boss, Dr. Leonard, wanted to speak to me. I sat in the chair in his office. Every secretary had gone home for the day. I was the only worker who remained, except for him. He sat there for several moments without saying a word. The long silence was unbearable.

"I have a serious matter to share," he started.

"Oh."

"Yes. For several months Joan has had money taken out of her desk drawer. Never anything big . . . some change, never all of it, but it's adding up."

"Oh, my," I responded, feigning disbelief.

Dr. Leonard continued sharing that he had already talked to other employees and a few of the custodians who told him that they didn't know anything about the missing money. "How about you? Do you know anything?"

"No," I responded.

"Are you sure you don't know anything?"

"No, not a thing," I said, shaking my head, sensing that he didn't believe me.

"Would you be willing to take a lie detector test?"

I didn't respond.

"Would you?" he repeated.

I broke down.

Dr. Leonard wanted to understand what might have caused me to do such a thing. "Is everything OK with your family, with your classes? Are you having any problems with your friends or boyfriends?" he asked.

His questions could have helped me explore the reasons why I had taken the money, but they didn't even penetrate because the shame was so dense. I wanted to run, but where to? And would Mr. Cook find out? He had made the effort to help me find work in Columbia, and now I had betrayed him. He had wanted me to go to college. He believed I was bright and capable and needed an environment, he said, that was safe, where I could flourish. He had made it possible for me to escape from hell, not to create it.

"What about your family situation? Can you tell me?" Dr. Leonard asked.

I couldn't even look at him, let alone tell him. There was the window. There was the steel gray sky outside, the leafless trees.

"You might feel better talking about it."

"I don't know," I managed. "Besides, there's no excuse for what I've done."

"Maybe, but sometimes exploring the reasons can be helpful in making changes. I have some information for you. There are several good counselors on campus." He handed me a sheet of paper with names and phone numbers written on it. "We'd like you to stay. Everyone likes you very much. No one needs to know, except Joan."

"I can't stay," I said.

"Think about it," he said and then pointed to the sheet of paper that he had handed to me. "Please call someone," he encouraged. "Please."

I nodded and managed to rise from the chair and shake Dr. Leonard's hand and leave his office. I walked down the long hall, down the stairs, and out of the administration building, knowing I could not return.

A few weeks later Dr. Richard Stevenson wanted to know what had brought me to see him. As if he didn't know. Surely Dr. Leonard had called him. Stevenson was the name at the top of the list with a star next to it. Dr. Leonard had handwritten the names on that list, made a point to star that particular name, and mentioned Stevenson not once but twice. What choice did I have but to tell the precise truth? Yet the truth seemed lodged in my throat. I opened my mouth, but the words wouldn't come. Instead, I felt tears welling up, but no, I would not lose control of myself. I pushed back my emotions and managed to say in a matter-of-fact voice, "I stole some money." And I looked Stevenson in the eyes so that just maybe I wouldn't appear as disturbed as I was feeling. Though he was a handsome man with dark hair, a groomed moustache and beard, and brown gentle eyes, I couldn't hold my gaze. I stared out the window at the brick building across the way, the leafless trees, and the gray sky above us all.

"You stole some money?"

I nodded, continuing to look out the window.

"Do you want to tell me what happened?" he asked.

I shot a glance at him. He sat there, all patience, looking at me, waiting for me to respond. He didn't show any sign of the disgust I felt toward myself.

"Not really," I responded, looking out the window.

Silence hung between us. *I should speak. I should say something,* I thought to myself.

After a few moments I managed to offer a summary of events. "I worked in the financial aid office, just a few afternoons a week. I answered phones. I typed a few memos. I helped the secretary. And, well, I took some money that belonged to her—change that she kept in her desk drawer—fifty cents here, fifty cents there. Sometimes those quarters added up to a couple of dollars. Over time it added up to a lot, and then I got caught."

"Hmmm, I see," Dr. Stevenson said.

I was trying to avoid feeling anything, but my heart started pounding. I broke out in a sweat. And then . . . the tears. I tried to stop them but I couldn't. I just sputtered and cried and felt ashamed.

Before the hour was over, Dr. Stevenson asked if I wanted to return to try and figure out what had caused me to steal. He said he wasn't so worried about the actual stealing as what the stealing might represent. Though I wanted to run far from that office and never return—never have to look at myself through someone's eyes mirroring me back to myself the way his did, with gentleness, a desire to understand, and genuine curiosity—I nodded. We set up another appointment. I thanked him. I went through the cordial motions I had been taught to perform. But I felt worse than I had before entering the office.

Right after that session, I headed to the dorm cafeteria for dinner. I ate and ate. I had seconds, thirds, desserts, more desserts, and then headed off to a bathroom stall, where I relieved myself not only of all the food I had just eaten, but also of all that shame, years and years of shame, of which I was not even conscious.

This was not the first time I had used food the way an addict might use drugs or alcohol. In high school I had received positive attention during my junior year when I began losing weight. I pursued the diet and received praise from teachers, other students, and relatives. Thin was good. Thin made me acceptable. I continued to decrease my calories: I ate eight hundred calories a day, then seven hundred, then six hundred. When a couple of friends shared that they had found a way to eat whatever they wanted and still lose weight by making themselves throw up, I tried out their formula, a formula I didn't realize would lead to disaster.

I returned to Dr. Stevenson, but we didn't make much progress. I always insisted that I was fine. The tears must have been good for me to get out. I knew I wouldn't steal again. I needed to control myself and act like the adult I was becoming. School was going better. I hadn't missed a class. I had a new job. I was fine. There was no need to return. Though I'm sure he asked some questions to try to help me ponder my decision, I don't recall them. I recall my determination to exercise my willpower and not steal. I would not steal. I would not.

But that failed.

Once Sunday afternoon in the laundry room of the dorm, while tossing a load of wash into the dryer, I spotted Victoria's Secret underwear hanging on the line. Later when I returned to fold my clothes, the underwear was still hanging there. I snatched a few pairs and tucked them into my laundry basket. At the time, though I knew what I was doing was wrong, a more powerful craving existed in me. I wanted to be other than who I was. Rather than transform myself through the hard work required of honest-to-goodness therapy or a spiritual practice, I sought to escape myself.

Just as the quarters I pocketed were used for such things as a haircut, shampoo, and the kind of items that would transform my outer self, just as the binging and purging would take off extra pounds to make me thin, beautiful, and desirable; the Victoria's Secret underwear—the kind of underwear that models in magazines wore, that my friends wore, that promised popularity, sexiness, and beauty—would do the same. I had internalized the cultural messages geared toward adolescents and young adults. I would be acceptable if my hair was just so, my body adorned with particular underwear and clothes, my body thin, thinner, the thinnest. I had not received messages about my internal world that penetrated and inspired the kind of transformation that would build my self-esteem. I feared examining my inner self, which I sensed on a deep level was flawed.

That unmanageable self was the source of nightmares. It held my past and more shame than I knew how to handle. It was uncontrollable, but my hair was not. I could have a beautician provide a perm. I could clip it just so. I could lose weight—one pound, three pounds, five pounds. I could eat six hundred calories a day, measured just so. But ridding myself of shame? Extinguishing nightmares from which I couldn't wake up? I couldn't begin to touch that part of me. I couldn't even articulate such complexities.

On the heels of the Victoria's Secret theft, I was in the dorm room of a new friend whose father was an executive for McDonalds. I figured someone like her wouldn't notice missing money. When she went to the bathroom I pocketed twenty of the fifty dollars on her dresser. Her parents sent money to help her pay for sundry expenses. I envied her. I wanted parents who helped fill out university applications and those lengthy and cumbersome financial aid forms. I wanted parents who sent checks. I wanted to feel supported the way my friend and others in the dorm were supported by their families.

A few weeks later a high-school buddy, Donald, who lived only two doors away from my family's home, asked me if I wanted to go for dinner. He was someone with whom I drove home from school for the holidays and then back. When we returned to my dorm room, Donald said that he had something on the serious side to share. "First, I want to say how much I like you, and this will not change any of my feelings of friendship toward you. Laura and Tracy approached me recently. They shared that a lot of things have been missing on your floor of the dorm. Laura's underwear was taken out of the laundry room. Mary had money taken off her dresser. They've gone round and round trying to figure out who could be doing this, and, well . . ." Donald paused. "I guess they're thinking it could possibly be you."

"Me?" I repeated in a questioning and stunned tone.

"Yes. They've pinpointed you, and they're worried about you. Everyone really likes you, and they're fearing something is going on inside of you."

I couldn't speak. Once again I was in the position of being confronted. I felt nauseous. Tears filled my eyes.

"Kim, we all care about you. This has nothing to do with not wanting you in our lives. We want you. And we want you to get some help for yourself so you can be happy."

I didn't come out and admit to the stealing. I didn't deny it either. I just cried and felt ashamed. What I had done was despicable. I couldn't understand why Donald was being so kind.

Years later I learned from my younger brother, Chuck, that he was riding his bike home from an activity one day and could hear Mom and Dad screaming from more than a block away. Donald's parents were walking their dog and stopped in front of our house. They shook their heads. They walked on, then stopped. Were they wondering what to do? Should they intervene? No, they must have decided. They walked on. Chuck shared that whenever they saw him, they treated him with pity.

I considered that Donald, aware of the situation at our house, had shared that information with my resident advisor and friends. The tenderness with which he approached me revealed no judgment, just deep concern.

Visitor

One night a prominent man, a visitor to the university who read poems and discussed poems and wrote poems and loved all of us who aspired to the same lofty goals, was scheduled to read his poetry. The venue was a coffeehouse. He stood on the small stage holding a silver microphone. In the dimmed light, he read his original work. His voice rose and fell to the rhythms of the words he had arranged. His eyes latched on to me and didn't scan the audience. I smiled. I stared back. I felt giddy.

Then the table where I sat with Diane, a friend from poetry class, became the setting. He pulled up a chair from another table, sat down, and asked if he could join us. I giggled because he already had. His eyes remained latched on me.

"I like your poems," I said.

"Thanks. I like your poems, too."

I felt pleased that he liked the poems I had shared in the class he had visited earlier that day. I couldn't help but smile. He kept on looking at me. I was attractive, attractive to someone.

My friend decided to leave. Knowing what was going on, she made up some excuse about meeting someone else.

Left alone, he told me about the newer poems he was writing, how he wished he could show them to me. But wait, he could! He had them back in his hotel room. Why not? Why not go pick them up?

"That sounds great," I said.

Minutes later he inserted the key, opened the door, and invited me into his hotel room. He closed the door behind us, turned, grabbed my arm, and pushed me across the room.

"Hey," I said. "What's going on?"

"I know what you want. I know exactly what you want," he said, lifting me from the floor, pushing me onto the bed and tearing open his shirt, unzipping his pants.

My heart raced. I couldn't breathe but said to myself, *Breathe, relax, pretend.* How else could I get out?

He flopped down next to me, pulled me into him, took my hand and asked me to stroke his chest. I didn't want to, but I did. I felt sick but pretended I was fine.

"Like this, goddamn it!" he ordered, showing me how to stroke his chest.

I did the best I could. I touched him to avoid being pushed again, to avoid getting hit or raped. I played along. When he moaned, I felt sick playing along. I kept stroking his chest, hoping, *Only there, please, only there.*

But he took my hand, slid it down to his underwear, the hard bulge there.

I obeyed but whispered, "You know, we could have the whole night to ourselves. I just need to catch up with my roommate. She's expecting me to meet her to study. She'll worry if I don't show up. I need to let her know I've met someone and that I'm going to be with you tonight."

"So call her, then."

"She's in our dorm study hall. There's no phone there."

"No phone?"

"Why don't we just drive on over there? I'll run up and tell her."

"What dorm did you say you were in?"

"Mason Hall," I lied.

I held his sickening hand as we walked to the car, and I directed him to Mason Hall, which was not my dorm. He pulled me to him, kissed me before letting me go, and I tried to kiss as if I didn't despise him. I said I would be right back. He squeezed my hand. I opened the door, stepped out into the cool air, and tried to run as if I weren't running for my life. I reached the door to the dorm, entered, and ran through the hallway toward a back exit and then ran a few blocks to my own dorm. I entered a back door and stormed up the stairs, muttering that I hated men. I hated them. I hated them. I made my way to my room. My roommate was gone for the weekend. I didn't call anyone. I couldn't let anyone know that I had been so stupid as to go to a hotel room with a man I didn't know.

Opening the Door

Diane, John, and I entered a pub just off campus at 3:30 in the afternoon and started in. We ordered a pitcher of beer, put quarter after quarter into the jukebox, talked about the meaning of life, the poetry we would write, and the poetry we were reading. We ordered some dinner and more beer and then headed off to a party, where we danced and drank and watched a couple in a corner make love. A young woman stripped naked and ran outside. Reefer was passed around. Music blared. I swayed and entered a universe where the one person I saw became two, three. I passed out on a sofa and woke at noon the next day. My head throbbed, my stomach felt sour, and my esophagus burned.

Alone, back in my dorm room, my roommate gone, I stood at the mirror. My image brought up the snake, uncoiling more shame. I saw triple because I couldn't see me. I saw the universe without a sun, starless, empty, void of any possibility. Vials of several different kinds of drugs sat on top of my roommate's dresser. I lifted one of the bottles and stared. I opened the cap and spilled several capsules into my palm. I put the capsules on my tongue, sipped some water, and swallowed. I opened another bottle and repeated the process . . . then another bottle, and another one. Then I lay down on my bed. As I prepared to pull up the blanket, cover myself, drift off to sleep and then to starlessness, I decided I should open the door. Did I really want out of my life? Maybe not. Maybe someone would walk by, say hello, see me, and wonder. Maybe not. I opened the door and left it to fate. Then I lay down again and pulled up the blanket.

I spun as if in Auntie Em's house, but I was not anything like Dorothy, whose mantra "there's no place like home" brought her back to Kansas. I spun with a tree yanked from its roots, a book of poems, the witch with her pointed nose and wrath cycling through air. My brother throwing a rock shattered a glass window, missing me. A rainbow disintegrated into the gut of a crocodile. A simple daisy floated. The bed in the hotel, his hand grabbing my hand . . . pizza, more pizza. The empty desk in Levis's classroom, an ice-covered canal holding somewhere in its immense self, two classmates—a brother and sister who ventured across the surface on their way to school.

The ambulance floated too. Red flashed in leaflessness. My body rose from the stretcher and fell back, a paramedic's demand or hand. Then the race through a hallway, swinging doors, a tube burning, a tube going down my nose and into my stomach and out, over and out.

I woke to a window and more spinning. All night I felt that same kind of groundlessness, but I did not soar to the beyond. My body remained in a bed, and when I woke there was a nurse. Ten minutes later, a therapist appeared. By the end of the day, I had promised to commit to outpatient therapy.

During the remainder of that semester I returned for therapy twice a week. Sometimes I arrived ahead of time and sat in the hospital cafeteria, writing poems that took me to the wounded space inside where the awful truth existed.

Ray's Cafe

I dropped all of my classes at the university except for one—creative writing: poetry. I moved out of the dorm and into the Wabash Arms apartment with my friend Deborah. I worked from 5:30 in the morning until 1:30 in the afternoon, five or six days a week as a waitress at Ray's Café. This diner attracted truckers, farmers, a group of retired men, and some local business people. A large group of regulars came in for early morning biscuits and gravy, eggs and steak, and strong black coffee each and every day. These were the retired farmers, all widowers, who had nicknames like Happy and Clown and Shadow. These men, grandfather figures, became my friends. Even though I knew very little about them, they treated me with courtesy and respect. They smiled and always asked how I was doing. They left generous tips and encouraged me to save up so I could return to school full-time.

I sensed, however, a particular loneliness about them. Even though they smiled and interacted with me and with each other in warm ways, sometimes they sat against the back wall in the longest booth of the café and stared out the window onto the streets and the sky beyond the buildings. No one said a word. Theirs was a silence as complete as death. The jingle of the cash register, Ray hollering about one of his daughter's mishaps, the ding of the door opening and a customer entering were welcome interruptions to that silence.

Ray, my boss, hollered at his three daughters; his wife, Charlotte; and me. He was not like my father, though. My dad hollered and carried on in private, but Ray didn't care who heard him. His public scenes indicated to me that he believed he had nothing to hide, that his yelling was the normal response to any kind of mishap. One time I spilled cottage cheese on a businessman's suit and Ray swung through the doors from the kitchen to the dining area, roaring, "Holy To-le-do. You've gotta be the damn klutziest waitress I ever hired."

"Sorry," I muttered, trying to scoop up the cottage cheese I had spilled on a customer's pants legs.

"Sorry?" Ray bellowed. "Sorry? You'll have to do more than say you're sorry. This week's wages can pay the cleaning bill."

"Oh, that's not necessary," the man said. "We're getting it cleaned up."

It was just after lunch rush hour and all eyes in the filled dining room were on me. I felt mortified.

"You do it again, you're out of here," Ray hollered, "understand?" He didn't wait for my answer, and in a quieter more reasonable voice, apologized to the man, who took pity on me and left me a five-dollar tip.

One morning after a late night party, the alarm sounded at 5:00 a.m. and I slammed the snooze button. Five minutes later the beep, beep, beep startled me. I sat up and pressed the off-button and collapsed back onto the pillow. There was no way I could work. I would miss one day, just one. I fell back asleep. About twenty minutes later, the phone rang. It rang and rang, and I sat up and stared at the phone, picturing Ray cursing at the black box, at me.

Finally, silence. I stood up, pulled all the shades, and took the phone off the hook. Though I felt some remorse and enough shame to picture myself slipping on my waitressing outfit, racing into work, apologizing for being late, the symptoms of my hangover possessed more gravity and pulled me back into bed, back to sleep.

At about two o'clock in the afternoon Ray and my landlord stood in my bedroom.

"Thought you might be dead," Ray said in his typical loud manner. "Can see you're almost there. Didn't even hear us knock."

I sat up holding the covers around me. "I'm just sick. I'm sorry I didn't call in. I must have slept through the alarm."

"Sure did," Ray said. "Good thing Char managed the breakfast and lunch rush like she did. We sure can't have you doing this again, or you're out. Got it?"

"Yes," I responded, embarrassed, not just at being caught but at having Ray see the mess, the entire inside of my apartment—empty wine bottles, filled ashtrays, our tiny kitchen right at the entrance with a week's worth of dirty dishes on the counter.

Praise

One evening a week I walked over to campus for the single creative writing class I was taking. Most of my poetry was incomprehensible to an audience. It was atrocious in terms of form. In Larry Levis's class I received ample criticism. Thank God, though, I wasn't told to quit, something he had suggested to some of the more cocky and smug students.

One time I submitted a poem about a friend from high school who had suffered from inflammation of the brain during our junior year. The disease had disabled her, resulting in a loss almost as great as a death. Initially, I had to explain to Levis and my classmates what the poem was about because they hadn't a clue by the various images and words I had thrown together. The poem, comprehensible only to me, needed major attention. After spending several weeks revising the poem, I resubmitted an almost entirely different one to the class. When up for discussion, the poem received some praise. Readers could now grasp it. Evocative images and attention to language earned me encouragement even from my well-known professor. He said to me and to the entire class that I exemplified the qualities of a true writer, for it takes stubbornness and drive to return to a work and stay there and labor and labor until it is right. I had been given so little praise and encouragement that I almost couldn't believe it when I did receive it.

Back Home

I woke to my father's screams and pulled the pillow around my ears. His voice, his cursing, belted into me anyway. My mother had not made his eggs the way he liked. Damning her wasn't enough. She was worthless, she was ugly, he said. She hadn't even combed her hair, for

Christ's sake, hadn't even put on some lipstick for him, her husband, whom she obviously didn't appreciate. On and on and on he went, and nothing, not even a combination of my hands pressing over the pillow and the three inches of foam, worked to shut out his boot-camp insanity.

Several months before, I had phoned from my apartment in Columbia, Missouri, where I was exhausted, I assumed, from what I considered the financial struggle to make ends meet. I had nowhere else to go, but I told my mom that I didn't want to return if *things* with Dad were the same. Mom claimed that he wasn't yelling as much and that there had been no major outbursts. "Come on home," she encouraged.

I returned home to Glenview and soon found work at Hackney's, a local and very popular restaurant. Within the first week, I developed a friendship with Catherine—an outdoorsy, energetic, curious woman infused with vitality. She inspired me. She had two jobs and worked almost around the clock, as she was saving for a trip out West. Her destination was Washington state, where she planned to join her boyfriend. Along the way, she planned to hike in the Colorado Rockies, tour Bryce and other canyons, and visit with friends scattered in Arizona and California. When she asked me to join her and I responded, "No, I really can't," she didn't turn away.

"Kim, why don't you think on this some more? Your parents aren't very healthy, if you ask me. What you've described, well, personally, I'd never make it in an environment like that."

"I'll think about it," I responded, almost wishing I hadn't confided to her how hard it was returning home. She was horrified by what I was used to and encouraged me either to move out or to travel with her. Anyone who hasn't endured violence and abuse can recognize such behaviors as deplorable. But I couldn't see my way out. How would I make it? With what money would I travel? What would Mom and Dad do? Could I make it somewhere else? I had made a mess of almost everything in Missouri. What if I were to move somewhere out West where I didn't know anyone and created another hell? Was I destined to move from one hell to the next and then back to the same hell?

Crossing

Frightened and cautious, I inched along the slippery road. Other cars passed me, honking, frustrated by my slowness. When I approached a bridge I pulled over. The snow drifted from the riverbanks and rose all the way to the bottom of the bridge. How would I ever make it across in whiteout conditions? I sat in the car, fidgeting with my coat buttons, trying to come up with a solution. Then a flash of red caught my eye, followed by a flash of green. I looked up. One car after another, without mishap, crossed the bridge. When I woke, the words "Go, you must go," echoed inside me.

I realized then that fear and despair had caused me to say no to my friend Catherine's invitation to drive out West with her. I had attempted college life and had failed at everything but creative writing and partying. I had received my first bit of freedom and had not known how to handle it. If PhDs could be earned for socializing, I would have received one. After falling short at starting my adult life, I had left the nightmare I created and returned to the nightmare I came from. I didn't want to fail again. But this dream, so powerful, urged me onward.

Blueprint

Before Catherine and I departed for the West, I explained to my parents that I was joining her for a ride to Columbia, Missouri, to visit some of my friends at the university. I would take a Greyhound Bus home the following week. I knew that if I told them I was planning to explore the West with my friend, they'd insist that I not go. Even though I was almost twenty and legally free, I doubted my capacity to resist their disapproval, so I avoided telling them the truth, avoided confrontation.

The morning I left home for this so-called week away, I had one large suitcase packed, a full backpack, and a letter that I had received the day before. The letter, postmarked Australia from the poet Philip Levine, was a blueprint of my future. I had enjoyed the privilege of studying under Levine in Bloomington, Indiana, at a writer's conference in 1977. I had written to him several months earlier sharing that I had returned home unsure about what to do with my future. I asked his advice on where I might go. He knew from the content of my poetry some of the history regarding my upbringing and seemed sympathetic to my situation, but when I didn't hear back from him, I figured that this famous poet didn't have the time for a fledgling like me.

In fact, he wasn't too busy to remember me. He was just busy teaching across the world in Australia, where he had received my forwarded letter. He encouraged me to leave the unhealthy conditions of my home and to try to do so without guilt. He recommended that I go to Tucson, Arizona. Provided with a list of poets both at the University of Arizona and in the community at large, I felt disappointed that he hadn't recommended a mountainous and oceanic environment like Oregon. I nonetheless tucked the letter into my backpack, grateful at least to have a sense of some destination.

I left the yellow brick ranch home on Robincrest Lane with both parents standing on the front stoop, just a small rectangular slab of cement, a single step onto the short jog of a walkway, which led to the driveway. They stood together as any parents might when seeing off their young adult child. They stood with some reluctance, some of what every parent feels when they know they must let go but still carry some concerns about safety. I said *good-bye* and *see ya* as if I were returning in a week. I offered a quick hug, making no eye contact. I was in a hurry to leave. As Catherine pulled out of the driveway, I managed a longer look. They remained standing close together as if such closeness commonly occurred. Dad's wave seemed to contain a sense of relief and good riddance, but my mom's posture seemed to say, "You better come back," as if she sensed that I would not.

The letter I sent home was loving and kind. I was unable to stand up to my parents and say, "I can't take the insanity anymore." I wasn't ready for such honesty, and I felt uncertain. Maybe things weren't so bad. Maybe I imagined or exaggerated the beatings and yelling that terrified and hurt me when they occurred but perplexed me later. No one talked about the violence in our house. My mother's motto was *Tomorrow is a new day*. Even today she will say, "You just have to move forward, get on with life, and forgive because it's all too short." So if I was entering a new day, and life was short and these were the only parents that I had, why dwell on the bruises, the broken bones, the words such as *slut* and *fuckface* that were so ingrained in me that I sometimes responded to my own mistakes with the same language.

I explained to my parents that my decision not to return home had nothing to do with them. I needed to find myself, figure out my future, and explore. I provided them with a list of states that Catherine and I were planning to visit. I promised to call. I apologized for the hurt that I knew my decision would cause them. I took full responsibility for leaving.

When reflecting on my decision to leave, Dr. Emerson and I concluded that if I had stayed, I would not have survived. I was drinking every day, binging and vomiting sometimes several times a day. I didn't know how to handle the complex and intense emotions that the violence evoked. Everyone was in denial. I had to inebriate myself. I had to eat and eat and eat and stuff down every ounce of anger, every pound of fear. Then my obsession with gaining weight and, in my mind, becoming even more unacceptable, caused me to make myself vomit everything I ate. Dr. Emerson explained that bulimia is not only a dangerous and destructive cycle but also an addiction because the vomiting releases endorphins and the resulting euphoria is sought after by the binger and purger.

Runaway

I didn't know how to drive a stick shift, so in a city of hills—Kansas City, Missouri—Catherine handed me the keys one morning and said, "Best place to learn." I was terrified because I knew there was no way to learn on these hills without making a mistake. But Catherine rejected my, "No, not here."

"So what if you stall? It's no big deal," she said with a smile.

"But it's rush hour," I stammered.

She laughed. "It's OK. Don't worry."

A people pleaser, I inserted the key, started up the car, and began an hour of stalling and starting and inching forward. Catherine cheered me on the whole time, much as her parents had encouraged her, no doubt.

We took turns and drove the long Interstate 70 stretch through flat Kansas, admiring the cornfields and the thunderclouds, miles off. Catherine played the harmonica when I drove, shared trail mix and organic juices, discussed her trips to Europe and her love of nature. I felt a new life stirring in me.

After a week of visiting friends and hiking the Rockies in Colorado, we headed for Bryce Canyon in Utah. Placing the straps to our water canteens over our heads and filling our fanny packs with trail mix and granola bars, we geared up for a hike. Catherine pointed out a few different trails on the map, and we decided on a challenging three-mile hike. We set out on flat land but soon ascended rocks and boulders. The views were so intoxicating that, half a mile into our trek, we ventured away from one another. I settled into a cranny and maneuvered myself against the rust-colored rocks and shale. I took in the hoodoos, distant mesas, and grottoes. The unpolluted blue sky extended to distant peaks and beyond. The only sounds were my own breath and heartbeat. I dared not move, dared not interrupt the absolute stillness. A spectator to the moment, all I wanted was to be present and breathe. I felt emptied of the past. I felt emptied of every fear and worry. The occasional rush of a mourning dove's wings startled me, but I didn't mind. Out here in this wilderness, I doubted any creature could be as terrifying as what I had endured. Out here I sensed divine mystery. I sensed the presence of that God I had sometimes doubted. The beauty here was unhampered by what we humans can do to our physical reality. I felt my whole being relax and surrender, and I uttered two words: *guide me.* And I uttered them without breaking the silence. I uttered them in my mind for the very God I found myself so completely sensing for the first time in years, there in Bryce Canyon.

Our next destination was Arizona. While Catherine visited a good friend in Mesa, just outside of Phoenix, I planned to take a Greyhound to check out Tucson. Catherine was in no hurry, so I could take several days and then catch up with her, and we would resume our travels through California and Oregon to Washington. Even if I decided that I wanted to settle in Tucson, I wanted to complete the journey to see all the beauty of the West Coast.

We stayed with Catherine's friend Cindy in Mesa. Cindy's parents, Fran and Dick, a couple from the Chicago area who were about the same age as my parents, happened to be visiting when we arrived. I liked Fran and Dick. They radiated warmth and possessed a genuine interest in their young-adult children and their friends. Dick, a social worker in private practice, raised his eyebrows when I confided in him that I had left Chicago and didn't know where I was going. When I shared a few details of my childhood, he encouraged me to continue building an adult life away from my family. Fran also thought that the letter from Phil Levine offered some great guidance.

Both shared details of the challenges they had experienced in their own family life. Dick, a recovering alcoholic, admitted his drinking had just about ruined their marriage and prevented him from being the kind of father he was trying to be now. Missing work, getting fired, driving while intoxicated, and even ending up in jail were all part of his history. Fran managed to put into practice what she had learned from Al-Anon and refused to bail him out. In jail he went through withdrawal and hallucinated that he was digging his own grave. This was the turning point for him, the bottom that was truly the bottom. He agreed to commit himself to an inpatient program and begin the long journey to abstain from alcohol and achieve a full sobriety where he would learn to express his emotions and deal with day-to-day challenges without resorting to liquor.

I fell in love with Fran and Dick. I was starved for the kind of human relating that occurred with them. It was honest and down-to-earth. They did not hide behind the typical social conventions of showing only one's perfect self and hiding the complexities typical of all humans.

During this time, however, I drank—and not just a glass of wine or a can of beer, but a bottle of wine, a six-pack or two. One night while attempting to retrieve a book from Catherine's car, I staggered around parked cars and weaved through the rows, aiming for the Volkswagen I couldn't find. Where had we parked? Where was that darn car? Did it even matter? I didn't even know what I was going to do with my life. I didn't know where I was going. Dizzy, I leaned into a car that didn't belong to Catherine. The breeze tousled mesquite and palo verde leaves. I turned and spun, wanting to become the invisible breeze beneath the full moon, whisking between the silhouettes of saguaro and prickly pear toward the mysterious dark mountains in the distance, darker than the night itself, mountains leading into other mountains, ranges impossible to traverse without paths.

Later that week, before catching the Greyhound to Tucson, I asked Fran and Dick, "What makes you so different from most adults I've met?"

Dick shrugged.

Fran thought for a moment. "Maybe it's our faith," she said. "We're Bahá'ís."

"Bahá'ís?"

"It's a worldwide religion."

"Hmmm. I don't really like organized religion," I said.

Fran nodded and changed the subject. Neither of them mentioned "Bahá'í" again. This surprised and impressed me.

Fran and Dick took me to the station and stayed with me until the bus departed. They would be returning to Chicago before I returned to Mesa.

"You are truly a brave woman," Dick said. "I have total faith that you'll be able to build a great future for yourself. Your parents might never understand or give you the support you deserve, but don't let that stop you."

He hugged me, and then Fran took my hand and repeated similar sentiments. Their faith in me made the remainder of my journey seem less like running away and more like building a new life.

Entering the Desert

I watched the mountains, dozed, and woke to exchange a nod with the woman sitting in front of me on the Greyhound from Phoenix to Tucson. Even though I had more complications than I cared to admit, I was traveling with a single embroidered handbag in my lap. In it were a toothbrush, a book of poems by Louise Gluck, and a bottle of rose oil, which I used as perfume. No toys, no diapers, no baby bottles, no fussing. The woman in front of me kept one eye on her daughter, who drove a Matchbox car along the upper edge of the seat in front of them.

"Brrrrooom," she screeched. Her brother crashed his Matchbox truck into the car. The girl scowled at him. He pinched her. The mother scolded them, and the baby she was holding began to fuss. My life, at least for that particular moment, seemed relatively uncomplicated.

The bus continued heading toward Tucson. A few mothers shushed their little ones, a few people snored, and several of us gazed out the window. The full moon lit up the desert valley and the distant and ominous mountain ranges. The open space provided me with a sense of hope and possibility. Never had I known land like this, and I felt mesmerized. The people, too, in all their variety, attracted me. The bus carried us all— mothers, fathers, grandparents, Americans of every descent, especially Mexican and Native. I felt the border on this bus. I felt fascination for the land, the plants, the people, and the languages I could not comprehend.

The Tucson Greyhound bus station was a hub of people arriving and departing, of children riding the plastic stallions for a quarter to mariachi tunes. Both English and Spanish were spoken over the loudspeakers. Everyone understood the names of cities—Los Angeles, Phoenix, Albuquerque, Houston . . . I found a pay phone and dialed Tim, the son of a woman I had worked with at the golf association. I had arranged to stay with him for a few days.

Tim picked me up and we headed over to his cool adobe apartment. Bars covered the front door and windows. "Lots of robberies in this area," he said as he unbolted all the locks. He limped inside, still recovering from a rock climbing fall that had taken the life of a friend. He shared a number of details of the horrific accident—a thirty-foot fall that had left him unconscious with various fractures. Still, he hoped to resume rock climbing. "In due time," he said, though I wondered. Grief etched his eyes. Sadness seemed to wrap his being. As I struggled to get to sleep that night, I thought about his accident. The physical survival, even with all the injuries he had sustained, seemed manageable compared to the more challenging impact of losing a friend. I had heard about survivor's guilt. I wondered if he felt guilty or grateful or guilty for feeling grateful.

The next afternoon I wandered the paths of the Desert Museum with Greg Pape, a poet and friend of Philip Levine. The sun penetrated me in astonishing ways. I felt as if I had been given a pitcher of sunlight, had guzzled the entire quart, and then proceeded to hold out the empty flask, fill it, and then devour the next quart . . . and the next.

I leaned against a railing overlooking a huge rock pit. One of the staff members was preparing to feed the coyotes housed there. He dropped slabs of meat. One of the coyotes emerged from a cave, grabbed the meat, and carried it to another location, claiming his share. The feeding behaviors of these sleek and alert mammals intrigued me. I identified with their relentless hunger. While demolishing their portions they glanced back as if fearing attack. They circled their food, claiming it. If given immense quantities of food, they would keep on, never stopping even when hunger no longer motivated them to eat.

Greg loved the bird sanctuary, and we spent more than an hour listening to the warbles, tweets, and clicks—the amazing symphony of the various desert birds. I enjoyed watching Greg as much as the birds—the gaze of a poet taking in every detail, the ear hearing what a typical tourist might not. He possessed a knowledge of the desert birds and shared freely, pointing to, and naming, particular birds flitting through leaves or perched on branches.

The next morning I visited the University of Arizona Poetry Center, a small and cozy white house that shelved thousands of books. Lois Shelton, the director of the center and another of Phil Levine's friends, explained the creative writing program at the university and showed me around. She set me up in a room that contained hundreds of tape recordings of writers who had visited the university. I relaxed in a big and comfortable chair, placed earphones over my head, and listened to W. S. Merwin and Lisel Mueller.

During the three days I spent in Tucson, buses transported me from the east to the west ends of the city. I walked miles. Mountain ranges cradled the sprawling city—a city of cloudless skies and cacti. I had thought the desert was an empty, barren landscape, nothing but a dusty basin filled with rattlesnakes, scorpions, and tarantulas—a bunch of sand, the symbol of death, blistering hot, a place where you learn to flee the sun. But I was attracted to the landscape and how the light fueled me the way Prozac might; it penetrated my core with the healing properties of the dry heat, nature's sauna.

Catherine and I left Phoenix a few days later. We drove west from Phoenix through the desert and crossed the border and decided to spend the night in Indio, California. The motel featured a musty-smelling room, cockroaches racing the floors, and smelly linens. We opened the windows, and the curtains fell to the floor. Not a smoker, Catherine suggested we both smoke some of my cigarettes to clear the room. We lit up. We sang a few songs out the window. We decided to sleep in our clothes and shower somewhere else the next day, as the mildew and mold in the bathroom disgusted us.

While spending a few days with Catherine's aunt and uncle in Palo Alto, I called home to let Mom and Dad know I was safe. I managed to dial the number and say hello. Mom answered. I was silent a moment. "Mom it's me," I said. There was a pause.

"Hello, Kimberly," she said, grief coursing through her voice.

My dad grabbed the phone. "What do you want from us? You've hurt your mother. You've hurt us all. What you need is a shrink and a priest." And then he hung up.

Placing the phone back in its cradle, I wondered if I had done the right thing leaving home like I had. I didn't want to hurt anyone, especially Mom. I sat there for a while, staring out the window. Catherine and her family chatted in the Jacuzzi. Across the room, dozens of bottles of wine stood lined up on the bar. I walked over, grabbed one, and brought it into the guest bedroom. I gulped down several mouthfuls. That afternoon, every time I came in from the pool to use the restroom, I soothed myself with another gulp.

Catherine's aunt, a refugee from Hungary, was a potter and a soulful woman. Her story of escaping from Hungary but losing her children in the process grieved her. Everyday something reminded her of the loss of her children, and she wept. Her husband held her and wiped her tears. She tucked her head into his chest. I admired them—her tears, his tenderness. I wondered if I would ever be able to express my emotions as easily as she did, or if I would ever find someone as loving as her husband. My musing lasted a few moments, and then I preoccupied myself with her story. I asked questions. I thought about her grief, her pain, her anger, and in so doing, escaped my own story, my own pain.

Catherine and I said good-bye to each other at the Greyhound Bus Station in Santa Cruz, California. Though I had wanted to travel all the way to Washington with Catherine, I was anxious to return to and settle in Tucson. During the long ride, the bus driver picked up a hitchhiker south of Los Angeles near the Arizona border. The man plopped down next to me, said "hey," and opened up his guitar case. "You like music?" he asked. Before I answered he started singing and proceeded to entertain the whole bus. Between songs he shared some of the colorful details of his life. He had escaped from the watchful eyes of his probation officer. He was falling in love with me, sensed I was his soul mate, wanted me not to go to Tucson but to Phoenix, where he was heading. He had some friends there. I could stay with them. He could tell by my beautiful eyes—mirrors of the soul, he said—that I was for him.

I smiled and nodded and listened to his ballads, clapping like everyone else but trying to figure out how to escape. The more he talked, the more he touched me, going so far as to stroke my thigh. I was terrified that if I did anything to express my fear or disinterest, he might hurt me. The fear was so great that all rational thought slipped away. I didn't consider that the bus was crowded and if I were to complain someone would assist me. It didn't occur to me to shout stop, to rise and march up to the front of the bus to insist he be removed. I had no idea how to protect or defend myself. I had never known there was any alternative but to absorb and accept questionable and violent behavior. But, just as I meandered away from my parents, I often found a way out of other potentially dangerous situations. In the Greyhound Bus Station in Phoenix I excused myself, headed for a restroom, and then left the bus station.

An hour later I returned and took a bus to Tucson. Rather than start off at the YWCA, which I had assumed would be the cheapest place to stay, I paid for a week's stay at the Deseret Motel, which was thirty dollars less that the Y. In the weeks ahead, I masked all the fears and anxieties that a move across country without a steady job and income would evoke in most. I drank daily, consuming at least a bottle of wine. Like many heavy drinkers, though, I managed and settled into a new community. My intent was to find both a job and a place to live that first week. I succeeded in achieving the first of those goals. I took a job as a waitress at the Plaza International Hotel. Transportation to and from work was not a problem since Tucson's public transportation system enabled one to get just about anywhere in the city and its outskirts. For the first few days of work, however, I missed the bus and resorted to hitchhiking. I didn't want to risk losing my job because I was late.

On the third day, during the lunch-hour rush, several gentlemen who were eating together snickered each time I returned to their table. One man finally said, "We know what you do."

"Excuse me?" I questioned.

"I said, we know what you do," he repeated in a taunting way.

"I don't know what you're talking about," I responded.

"I saw you hitchhiking on Miracle Mile. We know what the women who hitchhike on Miracle Mile do," he said, winking.

"You'll have to excuse me. I have other tables." I spun around and headed for the kitchen, where Susan, another waitress, was waiting on an order. When I shared with her what had just transpired, she shook her head and said, "Kim, they think you're a prostitute. It may not be common knowledge to you, but anyone who knows Tucson well knows that Miracle Mile is the prostitute strip." Had I known prostitutes hung out on Miracle Mile, the motel and hotel strip of Tucson, I would have stayed at the more expensive Y. It took everything in me to finish up the lunch rush that day. Susan offered to finish serving that particular table. Even so, I couldn't wait until those gentlemen left the restaurant. I could feel their eyes trailing me. I felt embarrassed about being accused of something I had never done and never intended to do. I wished I had had the same convictions about hitchhiking. That encounter ended my short-lived experiences with thumbing a ride.

Waitressing, too, was a short-lived occupation. I applied for and received a secretarial position at the University of Arizona. I would make more money and receive benefits. The security of the position enabled me to settle down. I moved in with a middle-aged woman, Doris, renting one of the bedrooms of her two-bedroom home. My rent included sharing all other living space—the kitchen, living and dining rooms, bathrooms, laundry room, and backyard. Doris worked as an executive secretary downtown and had an active social life, so while we shared the home, we both enjoyed some privacy.

Though I faced many new challenges settling into a new community, my attraction to the desert continued to grow. While some days mercury levels rose to 105, 107, 110, 115 . . . and I fled the scorching sun for the inside of a library, the work place, or my own bedroom where I lay on the floor with a wet washcloth on my forehead and swamp cooler vents directed at me, I sensed I had found a new home, my first home, a home where I could begin to thrive.

The new language I studied, the language of the Sonoran Desert, brought to my poems a new and intoxicating vocabulary: ocotillo, cholla, prickly pear, saguaro, Joshua, creosote, birds of paradise, cottonwoods, ironwoods, palo verde. I studied field books to learn the names of all the unusual plants, cacti, trees, and the mountain ranges, too. I memorized the names of the Tucson, Catalina, Santa Rita, and the Rincon Mountains, the ranges that cradled the desert city. The mountains entered my poems and so did the sky. I loved being able to view the entire sky from horizon to horizon. Its incredible brilliance astonished me. I had never known such a deep blue in the Midwest, a blue resulting from the intensity and quality of light that brought the likes of Georgia O'Keeffe to New Mexico, invigorating her artistic sensibilities.

Love-struck, I hiked the canyons where the lush vegetation thrived and dotted the mauve landscape green and yellow. I made many new friends and discovered through them numerous hiking areas—Sabino Canyon, Mount Lemmon, and trails in the Rincon and Santa Rita Mountains. I loved finding something physical that I could do to challenge myself. I had never been very athletic or very comfortable with my body, but I was about to embark on a process of learning to use my body in physical ways. Hiking, biking, jogging, swimming, and taking yoga classes would help me begin to discover that I was not an object to be hurt and beaten. My body would become *my* body, and I would learn to treat it with respect.

Every day sunrise and sunset were sacred events that often drew shopkeepers and business owners and employees out into the parking lots to view the flaming red and orange artistry. I, too, admired the vastness uninterrupted by skyscrapers and elm trees. In those moments, I experienced eternity not as some abstraction. Eternity was magenta and lavender crisscrossing into yellow flames. Eternity was my breath. Eternity was the gift of being in the moment, being present.

Work at the Medical Center

A bald man with an eagle tattoo sat on one of several cement, backless benches. His grayish stained T-shirt bore holes and a jagged tear. He grinned a toothless grin, his open mouth a dark cave. I carried that darkness, too, that silence, but I hurried past the recognition of our resemblance and connection. I joined, instead, people who appeared to have somewhere definite to go—the doctors, residents, nurses, administrators, even moms pushing strollers, who walked against and with me toward the set of three glass institutional doors of the University of Arizona Health Sciences Center. I loved the long walkway from the street to those doors. I loved having a few extra moments to appreciate the blue sky, deep and brilliant, almost primary, sweeping over me. The Catalina Mountains caught the sunlight, curved and swooped into shadow. The view of the range in its entirety humbled and centered me. Once inside, I joined dozens of anonymous others, shuffled down the green-tiled hall, past radiology, human resources, and turned left to the office of the director of nursing.

Joann Crouch nodded brief hellos to the receptionist, Roxie, who was already on the phone at the first desk; then me, the newest secretary, at the second desk; and finally Mary, her own secretary. Her taupe orthotic shoes reminded me of Nonnie. Her glasses, her gray permed hair—signs of Grandma and Nonnie. But she was the director of the entire Department of Nursing. She sat at a paper-filled desk, rushed off to meetings with top hospital administrators, and attended national conferences. Mary screened her calls, scrawled names, numbers, the urgent and brief messages that kept Miss Crouch in her office for hours after we left each day. If she minded the sixty- to seventy-hour work weeks, she didn't let on. Her mysteries, complexities, emotions, I didn't witness. Tasks tunneled us away from the private interiors of who we were.

I slipped a rectangular mint-flavored piece of gum in my mouth and crushed the wrapper, tossing it into the trash filled with all of my mistakes—at least a dozen pieces of paper filled with a zillion typos. I couldn't pronounce half the words I typed for Amy Sara Housman, RN, PhD, a professor of nursing and one of the country's leading researchers.

I wondered why I had applied for this job as I blew a bubble with the three pieces of Doublemint gum filling my mouth. I leaned toward the manuscript. Arrows pointed to scrawled handwritten words squeezed in the margins followed by another arrow pointing off the page with the word *over* scrunched beneath the arrow. I turned over the paper. The entire backside was filled with more of the unintelligible writing I was hired to read, type, proofread, and then submit to Dr. Housman.

Housman wore knee-length cotton skirts and blazers, nylons, and black or navy pump shoes. Her brown, distracted, and hurried eyes blinked from the bifocals she slipped on to look at my efforts. Her sighs fell across the page. Her finger pointed to the penciled sentence I had missed. "This will need to be retyped by 5:00. We're behind in sending this out," she said without emotion.

After several more attempts, I completed the letter, studied the lines, picked the gum from my mouth, and crushed a Kleenex around it. It looked good to me.

Every Wednesday I pressed the little round button with the number 7 printed on it and rode up in the hospital elevator during my lunch hour. I exited, hurried across the scuffed checkered tiles and through the doors to the Department of Psychiatry and then on through another set of doors and down a hallway to the group therapy room. Four of us slunk back into the cushions of separate chairs or love seats. Eyes darted. Feet tapped—up, down, up, down. Not mine. I held my feet together and forced them to be still through the power of my own thought. I looked the two therapists in the eyes and said, "Hello, how are you?" as I arrived. I didn't belong here as a patient. I could fit in as a brilliant leader.

Short, perfect, natural curls capped Anne-Marie's drawn and solemn almond-shaped face. She described the rituals, the imprisonment, as if she had nothing to do with her own torture. Why couldn't she see that she was her own judge, a judge who had sentenced her to a lifetime. And for what? For gaining what she thought was two extra pounds, but, the counselor reminded her, she had actually lost two pounds. No, she insisted. She had weighed herself. She knew the numbers. She was her own judge, police officer, and victim. She was the security guard who handcuffed and pulled her through the windowless hallways, the dank interior of the prison she had built herself. She pushed herself into the cell—a racetrack. There, she ordered herself to run. Soldiers guarded the sidelines. They pointed revolvers. They fingered the triggers. Anne-Marie ran, eyes wide. She was not allowed to stop until she ran eight miles. *Idiot,* I wanted to tell her. *All you had to do was say, "walk." All you had to do was grab one of the guns and say, "I have more power than you. Stop the torture."* I hated her stupidity, those perfect curls, the pathetic silence, the up, down, up, down, up, down of the black laced tennis shoes beneath the size zero white Levis accenting the black rib-tight tank top. I hated her guilty face, her eight-mile-a-day body that subsisted on ten counted-out Cheerios and lettuce leaves dotted with fat-free salsa.

I managed to tone down my reaction and suggested that she exercise a little willpower. "Maybe you need to create a new inner judge that's a little less demanding," I suggested. "Consider yoga. It's easier on the joints. And how about adding a few grains to the dinner plate?"

Both counselors interceded. They asked Ann-Marie how she felt.

. . . Silence.

They asked her to describe a run.

. . . Silence.

Then they asked me how I felt.

"She's so stupid," I responded.

"But how are you feeling right now? Let's get to the feelings, not just the thoughts."

What had I said wrong? Why this focus on feelings? Why couldn't the counselors see how stupid Ann-Marie was? Why weren't they asking Ann-Marie, the obviously sick one who couldn't stop tap, tap, tapping her pathetic feet for even a second? My hatred of Ann-Marie, I didn't realize at the time, had more to do with my hatred of my own disordered eating and my own rituals, which I denied having.

After that session, I returned to the steel desk with three drawers, bins filled with articles in draft stage, the phone, and the fluorescent lights. No one asked me how lunch was. No one had a clue where I went.

Several months later I received my first performance review from Miss Crouch. I felt confident about my growth, so the word *probation* startled me. "Numerous errors, inadequate proofreading, missing deadlines. These problems are serious to Dr. Housman and Dr. Brown. They've even noticed a decline lately and wonder if something has happened to cause that," Miss Crouch said after starting with a few sprinkles of praise about my personality.

I took a deep breath. Why had they not let on sooner? They interacted with me kindly, never sharing anger over my work. I couldn't lose this job. I needed to pay rent, my car payment, and my insurance. I thought everyone liked me.

"Are you OK?" Miss Crouch asked, sensing I was overwhelmed.

I wiped my cheek, but that did little good.

"Has something been distracting you?"

I tried to look at her, but my eyes remained on her desk. "I'm in counseling," I said. "I'm dealing with a rape that occurred." My shoulders shook, and I saw the poet who had shoved me and the cigarette burn on the carpet I fell against.

"Oh, my. I'm sorry. I'm so sorry." She placed her folded hands over the review form.

"I can work harder. I have forgotten to proofread, but I'll do better," I said.

We talked another twenty minutes and devised a plan for my improvement. I felt guilty as I returned to my desk. Though I was dealing with the near rape in individual and group therapy, was I using that to explain my inadequacies as a secretary?

Over the next few months I started to type slower. There were fewer errors that way. I still pressed the key on the Selectric marked with an X that whited out the errors. I read each line, checking it against the draft. I double-checked, sometimes triple-checked, and then submitted my work. I succeeded. Rather than retyping, I received new articles, graphs, or queries.

In early June, Joann Crouch was mugged in her backyard. Her secretary explained the details of the robbery—how she had been shoved to the ground, gagged, her purse snatched. Yet Miss Crouch returned to work and appeared unchanged. The same pearls hung around her neck. Her acrylic dress gathered at her waistline and fell to her knees. The laces of her shoes were tied and bowed. She continued with her busy schedule of meetings, continued with phone calls, continued interacting with everyone. "I didn't even go through what you did," she confided in me one day. "I can't image how difficult it has been for you. This is hard,

hard for me . . . but you . . . my, it's too much," she said, her worry grave, intense, fresh from the assault to her own body in her own yard.

We were united through tragedy. Though thirty years apart, though Miss Crouch lived each hour with mission, focus, purpose, though she possessed a title that had earned her the respect of many, we both held memories of assault and violation.

The hum of fluorescent lights pressed against me. I surveyed Miss Crouch's desk. Stacks of files clipped with notes lay next to hard-covered nursing books. Sticky notes covered her phone. Lines and curves, Miss Crouch's handwriting filled pages of legal pads. Would I ever discover my purpose the way she had her own?

"Marked improvement," she said, looking up from my latest review. "I have to say that I'm impressed." She smiled, then grew more sober.

Was there something I was failing to do?

"I have whole chunks of time when I can't concentrate. Did that happen to you?" she asked.

My brain raced. I didn't see the poet. I saw the clothesline, the palo verde trees, the trash cans, Miss Crouch pulling her purse toward herself, letting go at the first glint of steel. I nodded and managed to say, "It's been very hard."

"Nothing like this has ever happened to me."

Lucky, I thought to myself.

"I guess a good thing is that I have more empathy for those who have experienced this."

"It's too bad that so many of us have to go through something to develop more compassion," I responded, not sharing my relief that I was the lucky recipient of her newly born empathy. A part of me had feared this review, feared all the mistakes that would be brought to my attention, feared that I could lose the job that paid my bills.

I continued learning to pay more attention to details, to proofread, and to develop the skills that earned me a raise. I also continued with group therapy each week. I continued to dislike the other women and didn't want to be identified with them. In my mind, I was nothing like the pea-counting, frizzy-headed ninety pounds of skin and bones, nothing like the track-pounding wife whose husband begged her to stop, nothing like the binger and purger who wasted dollars at the 7-11. I wanted to argue with these women each time they spoke. I wanted to tell them to stop their insanity. I wanted to run out of the room when we met each week as I struggled to disavow myself from the truth.

Finding Faith

One night I discovered several pamphlets in a zippered compartment of my suitcase. The pamphlets were about the Bahá'í Faith. I smiled, realizing Fran and Dick must have put them there. I skimmed through the first one and considered the others because I was so impressed. Here was a religion that espoused one God, one progressively unfolding religion, and one humanity (varied as it may be ethnically or racially). Bahá'ís were forbidden by the teachings of their faith to proselytize, and they encouraged the independent investigation of truth. The elimination of prejudice of all kinds—racial, ethnic, religious, class, and gender—was asserted. The harmony of science and religion was another incredible teaching, as well as the need for the elimination of extremes of wealth and poverty.

I searched the yellow pages and found a phone number for the Bahá'í Faith. I dialed the number, and someone by the name of Gail Powers answered the call. I explained to her that I had met a Bahá'í couple while traveling and had read a little on the Bahá'í Faith and was interested in learning more. She asked if I would like a visit or to attend a meeting. I invited her to visit with me a few days later.

The doorbell rang and I opened the door to an attractive woman with short light brown-reddish hair. "Hi, I'm Gail," she said, her voice soft-spoken and her manner on the shy side. I invited her in and since Doris was home, showed Gail to my room, where we both took a seat on my bed.

"So you mentioned that you met a Bahá'í couple in Phoenix and you've read a few pamphlets?" Gail began after we shared a few introductory details about ourselves.

"I've read a few pamphlets and like that the Bahá'í Faith accepts all the world religions. I never liked it when the priest closed the church doors and yelled that we were sinners and going to hell and that people who didn't believe in Christ—followers of other religions—were going to hell, too. I had a hard time with that because I had some friends at school who were Jewish and Buddhist and I couldn't believe such nice people were going to hell."

Gail nodded her head and lamented that some religious leaders, but not all, use fear as a tactic. She affirmed that Bahá'ís believe the major world religions were created by God. "God is not in competition with God. There is one God, and that God is the source of all the world religions. In some parts of the world God is referred to as *Alláh*, other parts *Dios,* other parts *Gott*. We speak different languages and have different words for God, but there is only one God."

"That makes sense to me. I also like the teachings on equality—the equality of men and women, the equality of all people no matter what their race or ethnicity is. I've always believed that. The independent investigation of truth is neat, too. The teachings just make sense. I just wonder why I've never heard of Bahá'u'lláh before."

"A lot of people wonder that when they first hear of the Faith. I grew up in a Bahá'í home so I didn't have that experience, but I've heard other Bahá'ís explain that when they pondered that question, they realized it was kind of like Christianity and other religions. The Bahá'í Faith is just over a hundred years old. Many of the early Christians, for example, did not hear about Jesus until hundreds of years after His Revelation. It takes some time for the Word to spread, for the earliest believers to share their newfound Faith."

I asked how I could learn more, and Gail opened a bag and pulled out some books. "I'd be glad to leave you with some of these books, and there are meetings you can attend. We have meetings called firesides for people who want to learn more about the Faith. There's one this coming Saturday. Would you be interested in coming?"

"Sure," I said, feeling ready to attend a meeting. I was ready to meet more Bahá'ís and see what they were like.

For the next several days I devoured the books that Gail had left. I read during my lunch hour, after work, and before bed. I read about equality, social and economic development, and the history of the Faith—more challenging to read about because of the Arabic and Persian names.

Reading the actual scripture was like reading the Bible, not easy. The elevated and lofty language made it hard for me to grasp the meaning. I had to read and reread. The prayers were a little easier to comprehend, but words such as "Thou" and "willest" and "conferreth" were new to me. If I had been more biblically literate, I would have had an easier time. Nonetheless, I opened the books and took in as much as I could, wondering why I had not heard of the Bahá'í Faith before. Having grown up so close to the Bahá'í House of Worship in Illinois, how had I remained oblivious to the fact that a sensible, beautiful worldwide religion existed?

The first Bahá'í meetings I attended surprised me because of the diversity of the people. One meeting, held in south Tucson at the two-room home of Paule and Moro Baruk, was memorable. Paule, a stunning woman with long black hair and radiant eyes, welcomed me. I loved her French accent and assumed she was from France but later learned she was from Algiers. Her Egyptian husband, Moro, an exuberant person, opened his arms and hugged me. "Welcome, welcome. We've heard so much about you." He proceeded to introduce me to Bahá'ís from Sells, the home to the Tohono O'odham Native Americans. Bahá'ís from the Navajo reservation were visiting as well. I met Bahá'ís from Iran, Mexico, Canada, and even Africa. I met people who came from diverse professions and religious backgrounds, young and old, and even people my age. The meeting began with prayers—prayers spoken, prayers chanted, prayers sung. French, Persian, Arabic, Navajo, and Spanish were some of the many languages I heard that night. Though I was taught at church to love all Christians regardless of their race, I had never been to a church service with this kind of ethnic diversity. As a little girl I sang, "Jesus loves the little children, all the children of the world, red, yellow, black, and white. Jesus loves the children of the world." I sang that over and over in a predominately white congregation.

That night the diversity and the quality of the discussion impressed me. The Bahá'ís grappled with the teachings on equality. They deliberated about how to transform their lives to eliminate the prejudices they had inherited from their culture, their families of origin, the educational system, and so on. They realized they had to work on achieving equality. They also did not act as if they were the "saved" group and then go on to regard everyone else as inferior or destined for hell. I was impressed with how some of the Bahá'ís proposed the idea of preferring members of other religions above oneself and how that kind of attitude might help to weed out the root cause of many of the world's wars.

Though I left Paule and Moro's home feeling transformed by the experience and very drawn to the teachings of Bahá'u'lláh, I still did not want to join an organized religion. I could take the Bahá'í teachings I liked and incorporate them into my belief system. I preferred the notion of collecting the good from various philosophies and religions rather than becoming a follower of one particular path. And in Tucson, a spiritual Mecca of sorts, I had been meeting people of all faiths—Christians, Jews, Sufis, Buddhists, and people treating the New Age movement like religion. I loved receiving what my new friends and acquaintances had to share and deciding which gems to make a part of my own philosophy and worldview. I felt that if I selected one of these paths it might look as if I were discounting other paths and, therefore, other people.

Yet another part of me yearned to be a part of a community and wondered, if I were to join a faith, which one would be the best to join? One night I prayed to my dead Grandpa Max and asked him to give me a clear and definite sign through a dream.

That night I dreamed of numerous people standing and sitting around a campfire in the desert. The yellow and orange flames flickered and rose, illuminating the desert floor, the nearby arroyo, the saguaro, and the prickly pear. Entranced, I moved closer to warm myself. I stood among a variety of people wearing the native dress of their countries. I swayed to music that I recognized. A woman strumming a guitar sang, "The answer, my friend, is blowing in the wind. The answer is blowing in the wind."

Waking, I felt disheartened. "The answer is blowing in the wind" was not the answer I was after. I wanted something concrete like "Buddhist community," "Baptist Church," "Bahá'í Faith." Unable to return to sleep, I switched on the light and opened the book *Prescription for Living,* which Gail Powers had given me. The very first line of the book read, "The answer will come to you like straws on the wind and only you can determine the direction in which it is blowing." Startled, I reread that sentence, connecting it with my dream. I couldn't stop there. I read chapter after chapter, staying up into the wee hours of the morning, learning more about the history of the Bahá'í Faith.

In my free time I studied more with Carl and Suzie, a young couple who I enjoyed spending time with. We read prayers together and then analyzed them, discussing what the various verses meant to us. I loved doing this and was beginning to memorize prayers and make prayer a part of my daily routine. I now woke earlier in the morning and took ten or fifteen minutes to focus on and say aloud various prayers before going to work. I loved one of the verses from a morning prayer: "Illumine my inner being, O my Lord, with the splendors of the Dayspring of Thy Revelation, even as Thou didst illumine my outer being with the morning light of Thy favor."[3] I imagined myself bathed in pure light. To consider that I was worthy of such illumination felt good. During the day at work, I found myself beginning to rely on phrases from the prayers. When I felt disheartened, I would remember the verse "I will no longer be sorrowful and grieved; I will be a happy and joyful being." When I regarded myself in a negative light, which was all too often, I repeated, "O God, Thou art more friend to me than I am to myself. I dedicate myself to Thee, O Lord."[4] I connected with the idea that God was more of a friend to me than I was to myself. I had mistreated myself. I had made so many decisions that didn't reflect strong self-esteem or a sense of worth. But maybe now, with this spiritual input, I could revise the way I thought of myself. I could change.

I continued to attend Bahá'í meetings and met more of the Bahá'ís in Tucson and Pima County. As I did so, I learned about the laws of the Faith. Some of them, like praying every day, made sense to me, especially since I had begun praying and found it beneficial. Fasting once a year, however, for nineteen full days from sunrise to sunset, scared me. How would I be able to fast? No food, no water, nothing in the mouth from sunrise to sunset. If I had my period or I was sick, the Bahá'ís told me, I would be exempt from the Fast. The thought of a nineteen-day menstrual cycle suddenly appealed to me. I shared this with a Bahá'í who laughed and counseled, "It's a process, Kim. Don't worry so much about the laws.

---

3. Bahá'u'lláh, in *Bahá'í Prayers*, (Wilmette, IL: Bahá'í Publishing Trust, 2002), pp. 123–24.

4. From a popular prayer attributed to 'Abdu'l-Bahá.

Little by little, you'll get the hang of it, and you might even come to appreciate the experience of fasting." Abstaining from drugs and alcohol was another law that bothered me. What was wrong with a glass of wine here and there? And how would I give up drinking?

Because I didn't believe I would be able to follow the laws, I continued attending Bahá'í activities, praying, learning more, but convincing myself that not officially joining would allow me to have the best of both worlds—fellowship with great people and following whatever laws I found suitable. Of course, at the time, I didn't dare examine my addictions. I didn't consider the two to three glasses of wine, sometimes more, I drank daily as problematic.

One night I dreamed I was asleep in bed. The nightmare started slowly. An invisible yet tangible weight spread over me. This heaviness, this mass, draped my entire body and pressed against me. I tried to move, to wrestle myself free, but whatever this force was, it was paralyzing me. I felt terrorized, even though I knew this was a dream. "Wake up! Wake up!" I ordered myself, but the words remained trapped in my head. I tried to scream for help, but my tongue wrangled around itself, and only frantic, silent gasps and moans escaped. There was nothing I could do. I believed this paralyzing weight was going to suffocate me, and no one would know the truth. Whoever found me would just believe I had died a simple death in my sleep. But then the words of a short prayer I had learned circulated in my mind: *"Is there any Remover of difficulties save God! Say: Praised be God! He is God! All are His servants, and all abide by His bidding!"*[5] Exhausted, I gave up the physical struggle and surrendered. I repeated the prayer over and over in my head, and I woke, my hands heavy on my chest. I wondered if I was the weight, if the dream was trying to convey that I was suffocating myself.

I continued to attend meetings, getting to know more Bahá'ís, reading and reading. My initial concern that I would have to deny my belief in Christ waned. Bahá'u'lláh's writings on Christ were among the most eloquent I had ever encountered. I couldn't become a Bahá'í without accepting everything I had already learned about Christ. Bahá'u'lláh upheld the divinity of Christ.

---

5. The Báb, in *Bahá'í Prayers*, (Wilmette, IL: Bahá'í Publishing Trust, 2002), p. 56.

After several months I decided to enroll, giving myself private permission to defect if I ever detected anything I didn't like. A week later I met with the Spiritual Assembly of the Bahá'ís of Tucson, a democratically elected governing body of nine believers representing the community. The Assembly had invited me to attend part of its meeting to welcome me more officially to the community. The meeting was held at the home of one of the Assembly members, Mary Ray. Mary, a tall and thin woman, suffered from a number of physical ailments, but she radiated enthusiasm and optimism. Her love for the Bahá'í Faith was evident in the way she selflessly served the community. She hugged me and led me into the living room where all the other members were waiting and smiling. We began our time together with many wonderful prayers—prayers said in Spanish, chanted in Persian, and sung in English. Afterward Mary asked me to share what attracted me to the Faith and what made me decide to declare my belief in Bahá'u'lláh.

"I have to say that I didn't think I'd join at first. I thought I'd just hang out with all of you," I started. A few of the members chuckled. "But I absolutely love the teachings and the diversity of the community. I've also learned so much at the meetings, and I've even had some powerful dreams that have pointed me in this direction. The books I've read all make sense, and I just don't want to hold myself back."

"Well, Kim, we want to welcome you and tell you how thrilled we are to have you as part of our community," Mary said, speaking on behalf of everyone present.

"There is one thing I should mention," I added, wanting to be up front. "It's about the laws. I'm not really a person who's into laws, so I don't plan on following them. But I love reading Bahá'u'lláh's writings and learning about His life."

No one said anything negative in response to my statement about the laws; I think the members of that institution had enough wisdom to understand that I was engaged in a process of learning and transformation. They trusted the process and other community members to continue to offer their patient and loving guidance.

After becoming a Bahá'í, I moved in with Carl and Suzie and their two-year-old daughter. One weekend when they were away, I went to bed praying for relief from depression. Though I had joined the Bahá'í community and felt a sense of belonging that had been missing in my life, I was still caught up in addictive behaviors. I was trying to drink less since I thought I should try to follow some of the laws of the Faith. As I cut down on drinking, I turned to food. I couldn't see a way out of the eating disorder. My morning affirmation, "I will not binge and vomit today," did not work. By day's end, every day, I was either at the cupboards or driving to a 7-11 to get something, something sweet and filling, something to take away the pain I didn't want to look at, didn't want to feel. So I prayed, begging God to heal me, to provide some relief.

During the night the jangling of the doorknob startled me. Someone was outside, right outside my window, which was close to the back door. Terrified, I froze. If I barely breathed, maybe I would just disappear and the intruder would not harm me. I imagined him breaking in, as he was endeavoring to do. I imagined him stalking through the rooms, finding what? Carl and Suzie were struggling to make ends meet. I didn't have much either. There was nothing of significance to steal—a small TV, a stereo, nothing more.

The sound of metal against metal, maybe a knife picking at the lock, continued. I somehow decided to gather all my courage and face the intruder. I flung open the door and faced Jesus Christ. Jesus stood there looking at me with love, understanding, and concern. I uttered no words; I couldn't. The thief in the night was the Lord.

"You have opened your mind to My teachings, but now you need to open your heart and allow me in. Then the healing will begin," he said.

I woke with a start and lay there holding on to the images of the dream. The thief in the night awakening me was my Lord, my Savior, "the Healer of all thine ills."[6] The Lord said that I needed to open my heart. What did that mean . . . to allow the Lord in to heal me? I didn't know. I was always trying to take charge and heal myself, to exercise my own willpower. Let the Lord in? Some friends in twelve-step programs often referred to God doing what they couldn't do for themselves, and that notion seemed to work for them.

---

6. Bahá'u'lláh, *The Hidden Words,* (Wilmette, IL: Bahá'í Publishing, 2002), Persian, no. 32.

That night the dream was so powerful all I could do was pray. I asked God to help me understand what it meant to fully open my heart to Him. Then I reread one of my favorite parts of "Letters to a Young Poet" by Rainer Maria Rilke. Rilke explains that we need to love our questions, even the most difficult ones, and not force answers, for we will live into the answers. Though a part of me was impatient, yearning for instant healing, instant rebirth, instant perfection, I sensed the truth of Rilke's words. I understood that the dream was another link in the long chain of healing, a process, not a one-time event.

Back Home Again

During the summer of 1980 I returned to Chicago to visit my family and ended up staying for a few years. When I first arrived home, my expectations and hopes were high. Mom had shared that Dad was changing, not losing his temper as much, and handling stress better. Mom's perceptions, perhaps born out of desperation or hope or a combination of both, fueled my own sense of hope. Even though I had heard Mom express the same sentiments before and ended up disappointed when I realized little had changed, I wanted to believe her. I hungered for my family to be just that—my family, and one that handled stress and typical life challenges the way other families seemed to.

At the same time, Mom's optimistic views made me feel guilty for the times I didn't feel hopeful and for being the one in the family who acknowledged the violence. Perhaps I had exaggerated the past. Perhaps something was wrong with me for reacting to the violence as I had. Maybe what I labeled violent wasn't really violent. Maybe my take on the disunity in our family relationship increased the problems. If so, I prayed to God to be healed, to serve as an instrument of love and unity. Perhaps then my relationship with Mom and Dad would improve. Perhaps they would forgive me for running off. Perhaps any desire they still had to disown me would vanish. Perhaps we would have another chance to mend our relationship.

A week after moving back home, I woke one morning to the sounds of Dad putting Mom down. I could hear him even though the bedroom door was closed. "You look like a pig. What's this crap you call breakfast?" I knew all too well this tone, these words, his voice. Why had I left Tucson? Why had I returned to Glenview? Nothing had changed. How Mom could interpret this as an improvement, I didn't understand, but then I followed suit. Dad left for work. I showered, dressed, and ate breakfast without mentioning a word to Mom about what I had overheard. I went off to work and enjoyed my day as if nothing had happened that morning.

I obtained a summer job working at the Bahá'í Publishing Trust in Wilmette in the Department of Special Materials. For eight hours a day, five days a week, I focused on editing pamphlets, postcards, and cassette recordings. I had lunch with coworkers. I developed friendships and made plans in off-hours to attend movies and parties. Because I was living with my family, I was able to save most of my earnings. I had no electric bills, no phone bills, no rent to pay, and I had set up an actual savings account. The lack of financial pressure and the ability to save inspired me to remain in Chicago for a while. Perhaps I could save several thousands of dollars and return to school. Even though living with Dad was a challenge, I could just tune him out, I decided. I could do my best to avoid conflict.

It was wishful thinking. Conflict with my parents became a more fre-quent occurrence. Some of it was the same old painful raging, and some of it was the very normal kind of conflict related to my comings and goings and my sometimes forgetting to call if I was out with friends later than usual. Since I had grown accustomed to living on my own and not checking in, and I was still immature, it didn't occur to me to consider that my parents would worry about my whereabouts. Mom and Dad decided at one point to charge me rent so that I would become more responsible. That's when I decided that I might as well move out and pay rent to someone else.

For a year after moving out, I moved a few times and worked a few different jobs after my summer position at the Bahá'í Publishing Trust ended. I endured the young adult challenges of trying to figure out how to handle money and roommate problems. I experienced an unethical work situation in which a boss was embezzling money. When I caught on, he tried to have me fired before I reported him. During this time my dad criticized me for moving so much and for repeatedly switching jobs. He didn't ask why I moved or why I left a job. He just criticized me, and I internalized his opinion that I was irresponsible for flitting from one job to the next, that I would never grow up, and that I was obviously disturbed.

One day shortly after moving into a basement apartment in Wilmette, my brother Chuck telephoned me. "Thanks, Kim. Thanks a whole hell of a lot."

"What's wrong, Chuck?"

"What's wrong? Do you really care? You and Mike just pick up and leave. Mike's way the hell in Alaska. You're out of here again. And I'm stuck living in this hellhole."

I asked Chuck what had happened. He reported that Dad had beat up Mom and him the night before. "He almost strangled Mom," Chuck said.

When I hung up, I obtained the hotline phone number for Child Protective Services, dialed the number, and reported my dad to the state of Illinois. In therapy I had come to realize that I was not the cause of my dad's violence, and this realization enabled me to make that call. I was surprised to learn from the social worker assigned to the case that the state already had a file on my dad. Years before, neighbors had reported him when they overheard fights and spotted bruises. The laws were so weak back then that not much could be done unless someone witnessed the abuse. But teachers were informed that there was a strong likelihood that abuse was going on in the home and were told that if my brothers and I acted out in school, they should try to handle the problems there, without bringing in my parents. I was surprised to learn this. My dad had an actual record. What all of us had tried so hard to keep secret was not a secret.

I asked the caseworker what would happen next. He said that a social worker, probably himself, would make a visit to the house to begin an investigation. My dad, mom, and brother would be requested to meet with an assigned therapist. If my dad refused to comply with these orders, Chuck would be removed from the home.

Two days later my mom telephoned and shared with me what had happened. I listened and, toward the end of the conversation, confided in her that I had received the call from Chuck and had decided to report Dad to the state. I begged her not to tell him.

But after being pressured, Mom told Dad. Of course he fumed and made it clear that he considered me a betrayer, disloyal to the cause of family. I was so anxious during this time that I sought out help from the Spiritual Assembly of the Bahá'ís of Wilmette. When I first met with them, they obtained as much factual information about the situation as they could. I shared details of the past as well as the present. The Assembly praised me for reporting my dad to the state and remarked that what I had done was very courageous. I didn't feel too courageous at the time, but nonetheless I appreciated the compliment. They set up another meeting at which they would give me more specific counsel, and they advised me not to have contact with my family in the meantime for my own protection.

Within a few days we met again. The Assembly's advice was for me to have no contact with my family. I could talk to my brother and mother over the phone, but I was advised to remain away from the family home, to allow the state to do what it deemed appropriate, and to update the Assembly with any new developments. They encouraged me to continue with counseling and assured me of their love and prayers, letting me know they were there for me.

During this time Chuck telephoned to express his outrage about what I had done. He concluded that I had betrayed the family and that I had only made matters worse. He had never asked me to intervene, nor had he wanted me to report Dad to the state.

While Chuck's reaction startled and hurt me, I couldn't undo what I had done, and I didn't regret calling the state. I did feel anxious about the major upheaval the report had caused in the home and wondered what was going to happen. Years later, after Chuck had forgiven me, he shared that Dad had hired a lawyer to clear his name and that when they drove to the required appointment with a psychiatrist, Dad told Mom and Chuck what to say in the session, which included bad-mouthing me, labeling me the mental case with an eating disorder whose perceptions were skewed because of my problems.

One afternoon during this difficult time, Janet Marks—a member of the Wilmette Assembly and an angel of a woman—stopped by to check in on me. She handed me a beautiful yellow rose and a card in which she had handwritten a passage from the writings of Bahá'u'lláh. This was one of many home visits she made, and she always left assuring me that the Wilmette Assembly was praying for me. Those visits were a lifeline.

Though I had been praised for my courage in reporting Dad, though I was back in therapy, I didn't feel the courage of either act. Instead I swung from grief to depression. The more I lifted the veils of denial about my situation, and the more I looked at my life, the more the pain increased.

One afternoon I visited the Wilmette Public Library, which was a few blocks from my apartment. I checked out a copy of Picasso's famous "Old Guitarist" painting from his blue period. In this piece an elderly artist is depicted in fetal position, curled around his guitar. There was something about this painting that I believed in, something that gave me hope. I hung the painting in my apartment and studied it. The guitarist curled around the instrument seemed to depend on the instrument as a fetus depends on the womb and the umbilical chord and the life of the mother. The guitar, the artist's salvation, would birth music not yet known.

As the next several days passed, depression devoured me. I prayed but could not visualize anything beyond the painful present. Reporting my dad, severing contact again with my family, and examining my own problems in therapy overwhelmed me. I couldn't imagine freedom from the wounds.

One night I fell into a deep sleep, and a powerful nightmare followed: Curled up like a fetus, I was sleeping on the exact same twin bed I was in with the sheets wrapped around me like a mummy. The torture began. I dreamed I was a machine—metal, screws, washers, buttons, play, stop, record, rewind, fast forward, speakers—all in a box just like the 1960 Wollensak tape recorder Dad brought home from work. I was that machine. My tongue was the metal strip of tape crossing the rollers that produced sound. Everything about me had conformed. I was not flesh and blood and heartbeats and my own thoughts and dreams. I was a machine. I was man-made. I felt the metal of myself. I felt the anguish of expressing what someone else had impressed on me. I tried to break free, but I was confined. I was in a prison cell, the jail, the metal box, and the buttons were being pressed by an outsider. I had no control, no power, nothing that was my own, and I could not wake up from this nightmare. I tried. I couldn't even scream for help because my tongue was not a tongue. It was the three-quarters of an inch tape crossing the rollers. Stop. How to press stop? How to get out of this predicament, this war?

When I did awaken, I sat up. The dark room enclosed me and felt safer than the setting of the nightmare. This darkness in this tiny basement, this womb, was real. I was not a machine. I no longer lived with my parents. I was a young adult. I didn't know where I was going, but it was not backwards, not rewind. There was no rewind button. There was the guitar man on my wall, sad man, a sad Picasso, but still, some kind of hope existed in that painting—the possibility of music. I sat there in the dark wanting to believe that suffering could be a pregnancy of sorts, could shape possibilities, virtues, growth. I wanted to believe that my survival could occur through the arts, through the support and love of friends and community.

For the next ten months until right before the next Christmas, I had no contact with my dad. Traditionally, my extended family came together for Christmas. I doubted that any of our relatives knew I had reported my dad to the state. My absence would arouse some suspicions. Most knew that I had disappeared and moved to Tucson. That couldn't be kept secret. But everyone had come to believe we had reunited and that our relations had improved. Sure enough, my mom called and invited me for the holidays. I explained that I was not yet comfortable seeing Dad, which displeased her because she took the brunt of such decisions.

My dad called a few days before Christmas and pressured me. "It's one thing to hurt me, your father. I can take it. But do you really want to hurt Dinn and Gramps, your aunt and uncle, all your cousins? It's a few hours out of your life. Can't you, for the sake of the family, get out of your own anger and selfishness and come?" Though I wanted to say "no," though I felt apprehensive, I complied with his wishes and agreed to spend a couple of hours on Christmas Day with the family.

On Christmas morning I woke early, sipped some coffee, and tried out some new relaxation exercises from a cassette recording. The wonderful breathing exercises relaxed me so much that I fell asleep. I didn't even hear the window break, didn't even hear Dad enter the room. I woke. He towered over me. "Dad, what is it?" He fell to his knees and put his hands to my throat and squeezed. I wrestled to break free, but he was stronger. His grip tightened. I couldn't breathe. I was going to die.

I woke up and sat bolt upright. My face was wet with tears, my forehead sweaty. I stood up and raced into the kitchen, picked up the phone, and dialed the number for Janet Marks. Within ten minutes she and her daughter-in-law Amy Marks, another Assembly member aware of the situation, drove over and stood right there in front of me so that I could look at them as I made the phone call to my dad. I dialed. My mom answered, and I explained that I had reconsidered my decision to come. She didn't understand why I couldn't come for just an hour. Dad grabbed the phone and said, "You know, Kim, you are really screwed up, an absolute mental case. You need to be institutionalized."

"Dad, I'm sorry to do this," I interrupted, keeping my gaze on Janet and Amy, "but I can't listen to you talk like this. I'm hanging up."

Both Janet and Amy embraced me. I allowed them to hold me and comfort me, but a part of me exited from the scene. I could barely fathom that I had stood up to my dad and refused to continue the conversation when he became abusive. I never would have been able to do that without Janet's and Amy's presence.

Part 4: Breaking the Cycle

New Intentions

I turned on George Winston's "Winter into Spring" to provide background music. My friend Laurie poured alcohol-free wine into three plastic juice cups. My roommate, Shawn, lit a few candles we had set on the trunk that served as our coffee table. Then we plopped down on the floor and sat cross-legged around the flickering flames, the jar of pens, and the stationery Laurie had brought for our "evening of intention."

The three of us had lamented our sorry state of affairs when it came to men. We wanted to find that special person to spend the rest of our lives with, but we had not had much luck. Ideas from the book *Creative Visualization* by Shakti Gawain had intrigued us. She believed that our imagination and our thoughts could create the kind of life we desired. Why not give it a try! We could come together, read prayers and poetry, listen to music, and meditate on what we wanted in a relationship. Then we would write letters to God listing the qualities we desired in our future partners. We marked the calendar for Friday, October 19, 1984, after sunset, and that night had arrived.

After reading several prayers and passages from our respective faith backgrounds—Laurie from the Old Testament, Shawn and I from the Bahá'í writings—we took turns reading excerpts on marriage from Khalil Gibran's *The Prophet.*

"You know, I like Gibran," I said, "but all this on having a lot of space in your loving doesn't grab me at the moment. I'm tired of empty space and wouldn't mind some closeness."

Laurie laughed. "You're missing the point."

"I know," I said. "It's all that sentimental and emotionally healthy stuff about being in the same house and being separated. I don't want to think about the separate part just yet."

We all giggled and then somehow managed to quiet ourselves and turn to the empty page. Each of us began writing. My letter read,

O God, My God, Thou art my Haven and my Refuge. The following qualities I would like in my marriage partner:
1) That he is an active Bahá'í (active as defined by God)
2) That he is a giving person of himself
3) That he is truthful
4) That he knows himself
5) That he is steady and provides a sense of steadiness
6) That he exercises the principle of the oneness of humanity
7) That he is committed to maintaining and developing the marital and family relationship
8) That he is intelligent and career-oriented
9) That he is sensitive and compassionate
10) That he is health-minded
11) That he is active outdoors
12) That he is optimistic and has a sense of humor
13) That he will inspire me to progress spiritually
These are the qualifications that I kindly request to be found within the next year if God so wills. Praise be to God, the Lord of all the worlds.

We then dated and signed our own and each other's letters. We placed our letters near the candles and then continued to ritualize our evening of intention with creative movement. We held each other's hands and whirled and swayed to the music.

Within a year Shawn was married, but this was not a surprise. She had shared with me that she started saying the Bahá'í marriage prayer while in middle school. Back then I engaged in flawless fantasies, but not Shawn. She studied hard to prepare for college. She asked God to prepare her and whoever her future husband might be for marriage. She figured it was never too soon to start praying even for her unborn children back then.

Laurie continued her adventuresome life of teaching at a school for deaf children and traveling to attend weddings and birthdays of friends all around the country. She had not indicated any timeline in her letter, like I had. She dated and had to ward off the men. She would even try to look unappealing so men would stop paying attention to her. I remember one time at the laundromat, she was wearing an oversized T-shirt with a hole in it, cut-off shorts, her glasses, and no make-up and still someone was eying her and even asked her out.

After a few months I slipped my letter between the pages of the *Creative Visualization* workbook, a little disheartened that no one had showed up looking like the man of my dreams. I forgot about the letter until three years later during my first year of graduate school. One Saturday afternoon I sat in a blue Ford Escort thinking, "Why, dear God, did I say yes? Why did I agree to this?" We were rounding the next curve coming down the highway from Mount Lemmon back to Tucson, and if I had had the nerve to lean over and read the speedometer, I believe the marker would have pointed to at least fifty miles per hour. This was a thirty-mile-per-hour road. We spun on some gravel and I gasped. My date chuckled. "Could you please slow down?" I said between gritted teeth.

"Don't worry. I know what I'm doing," he responded.

"I don't think so," I said. "This is a mountain road. I think you're supposed to slow down before curves, not speed up."

"You worry too much. I've driven this road a thousand times and I'm still alive."

If I could have stopped the car, jumped out, and jogged down the mountain road rather than drive with this maniac, I would have. But we still had miles to go and dozens of curves and overlooks offering views of a nine-thousand-mile descent into rock and scrub. Why had I said yes to this guy? He seemed nice enough when I met him at Elena's party the week before. Was I that poor a judge of character or just unlucky? I closed my eyes and prayed.

Back in Tucson, he stopped at the Good Earth Restaurant. I wanted to say, "See ya! I'll catch a cab from here. And don't bother to call again." But I had not yet developed the virtue of assertiveness. Instead, after the hostess seated us, I excused myself to the restroom. I didn't say good-bye. I exited the restaurant, walked three blocks, and then called a cab to take me home.

Back in my apartment, I phoned Jean-Marie. "Never again. Never. This is it. I'm not dating anymore unless it's with someone who has absolutely every quality I placed on that list I told you about." I explained what had happened, and Jean-Marie laughed.

"Kim, you'll have another date by next weekend. Just wait and see."

That week I met with my therapist and repeated the saga along with my decision to quit dating.

"What do you like about your decision?" she asked.

"Well, I'm sick of going out with guys who I know I would never want to spend my life with. I'm sick of wasting time. I could be writing. I could be doing yoga. I could be hiking. I want to do what I want to do instead of flying down the mountain with some jerk."

I tend toward the theatrical, and my therapist knew me well enough to try and steer me in a productive rather than dramatic direction.

"So you want to use your time in more constructive ways?"

"Yes."

"Since you've shared that you're tired of dating before and even suggested you might not date again, but then continued to date, maybe you need to consider what you're going to replace dating with."

"What I'm going to replace dating with?"

"Yes. What else might you do? You spend a lot of hours teaching, taking classes, studying, going to Bahá'í activities, and dreaming about finding someone."

"Well, that has been a topic this past year, hasn't it?" I asked, referring to the latter point. I was tired of dreaming about marriage. I just wanted it to happen. It wasn't as if I hadn't been praying.

That week, while reading some unliterary self-help book about learning how to fill your own holes and not expecting someone else to, I had what I considered a brilliant idea. I would date myself. I would not just date myself, I would buy myself a ring and propose to myself and act as if I were preparing to marry me.

I dialed Jean-Marie right away and shared the idea. "I love it, Kim. That's great. I might do that, too. Let's just give up on men. We don't need the headaches they bring. But I'll have to start after Saturday night because I have a blind date."

"You might be sorry," I said, giggling.

"One last try, then I'll join you in the experiment."

That week I bought a silver band and placed it on my left finger. I knocked on the door of Deb, the graduate student who lived next door in the duplex we rented. "Guess what?" I said, as she opened the door.

"What?" Deb asked, her eyes widening.

I held my left hand out in front of my face and wriggled my fingers.

"You're engaged!" she said in total shock. "Who's the guy? I didn't know you were going out with anyone."

"I'm not," I said and burst out laughing.

"You're engaged and you're not going out with anyone? OK, Kim, come on in and explain this."

Inside, I shared what I had been realizing: that the whole American dating thing didn't work, that I finally understood I needed to treat myself the way I hoped someone else would someday treat me, and that I was tired of being pulled along doing what someone else wanted to do.

"Deb, I want to decide where I want to go. Should I go to a foreign movie or a poetry reading? Should I get up early and hike Sabino Canyon or spend a quiet night at home? Imagine a date where I sit on the front porch, sip sun tea, and read a novel."

"What if you get lonely?" Deb asked, turning inward as if she were pondering this whole phenomenon for herself.

"Well, I probably will. And maybe that's OK. Maybe everybody has moments like that. I'm not sure dating someone is the best medicine for loneliness. I'm not sure marriage is either. I think that's just something I'm going to have to accept—that there will be times when I feel lonely. And I'll have to figure out what I'm going to do when that happens."

For the next several months I did my best to take care of myself. Loneliness was the least of my problems. My life was very full, as my therapist had pointed out. My challenge was to carve out the time to date myself. It took some practice, but I learned to take a little time every day to do something I wanted to do rather than something I had to do or felt pressured by someone else to do. I began to sense that this practice was helping me to become more whole and complete within myself. I was discovering my likes and dislikes. For the next year I continued this practice, learning what I wanted to say yes to and what I wanted to say no to.

Sometimes a *no* turned into a *yes*. That occurred one January morning during Christmas break while thumbing through the pages of *The American Bahá'í* newspaper. I skimmed a few stories about international and national activities and then spotted a brief story about an upcoming singles conference. The conference was going to be held at Bosch Bahá'í School in Santa Cruz, California. What would a Bahá'í singles conference be like? I wondered. I didn't want to go and look like some desperate female, even though I sometimes felt desperate. I couldn't imagine that the kind of pick-up scene that could occur in a bar or at a party would happen at a Bahá'í conference. But still, it could be weird. I didn't want to put myself in a situation where people were on the hunt.

I turned the page and spotted an article about a poetry fellowship. I read that the Louhelen Bahá'í School was taking applications for the 1988 Robert Hayden Poetry Fellowship. I had read Robert Hayden's poems both as an undergrad and as a grad student. The article stated that his accomplishments included winning the first World Festival of Negro Arts and that he was the 1975 Fellow of the Academy of American Poets. He was also a member of the American Academy of the Institute of Arts and Letters, and he had served two terms as Poetry Consultant to the Library of Congress. He had still been working as a professor of English at the University of Michigan when he died in 1980. The fellowship would provide room and board and give poets time and space to work on their poetry for four to six weeks during the summer.

The thought of having concentrated time to work on writing appealed to me. I could work on the manuscript for my master's thesis. But then Robert Hayden was amazing. I was not an amazing poet. I was struggling. I believed my chances of winning were next to nothing. What poems were good enough to submit as part of the application? The deadline was two days away. I couldn't pull together an application in that frame of time.

The next day I sipped coffee on my front porch while watching the sunrise. I opened my prayer book and read the morning prayer and a few prayers for guidance. Then I sat in silent meditation. I heard two directives: "Go to Bosch, and apply for the fellowship. Don't let your fears run your life. Take some chances."

My dreams had always served as a source of direction and guidance. After studying yoga and meditation and becoming a Bahá'í, I had developed ways to listen to what was deep inside. I loved Bahá'u'lláh's exhortation to "listen with heart and soul to the songs of the spirit."[7] For too much of my life I had no idea how to access my inner world, but I

---

7. Bahá'u'lláh, *The Seven Valleys*, (Wilmette, IL: Bahá'í Publishing Trust, 1991), p. 37.

was starting to enjoy the process of quieting myself and listening. I was also learning to respond to what I heard and act on it. Because I had some extra money from the accident settlement, I could and did make airline reservations to fly to California to attend the singles conference. A few months later, I made another reservation to fly to Detroit, Michigan, after applying for and receiving the Robert Hayden Poetry Fellowship.

The singles conference held at Bosch Conference and Retreat Center, located in the Redwood Mountains outside of Santa Cruz, California, was held on a weekend close to Valentine's Day. The scenery captivated me. Redwoods towered into the sky. Wild flowers and ivy carpeted the ground, except where trails had been cleared. Though I didn't spend much time outdoors that weekend, I managed to squeeze in a few short hikes with new friends during meal breaks and enjoyed the views from the windows.

The first session started at seven o'clock on Friday evening. Almost a hundred individuals crowded into the conference room. How wrong I was to expect that everyone would look just like me—young. My vision of those who were single expanded. Singles were young and old, divorced and widowed. Maybe there were two dozen like me who were in their twenties and not yet married.

The administrator of the school introduced the speakers, a married couple—Dr. Hoda Mahmoudi and Dr. Richard DaBell. She then turned the lectern over to Hoda, a tall and attractive woman with short black hair. Hoda looked out at all of us. "Don't fool yourself," she said, "getting married and raising a family is the hardest work you will ever do." She paused and there was a long silence, allowing us to ponder her statement that began the conference, a statement I would never forget. I was still in la-la land about marriage, which is surprising considering my background. But Hollywood and advertising had indoctrinated me well. An idealistic part of me was hoping for some kind of modern version of Prince Charming to come along and help me create a life of joy. So, hearing that marriage would be the hardest work I'd ever do startled me.

Both Hoda and Richard went on to elaborate about the fact that bringing together two lives shaped by different life-experiences would inevitably bring some trials and opportunities for growth. Married couples face a number of challenges, such as figuring out the demands of child-rearing, handling money, sexual intimacy, sharing home maintenance, and more. Hoda shared some of her own experiences, explaining that even with education and skills, she considered marriage and child-rearing the most demanding work that she had ever engaged in.

The next morning we studied some of the Bahá'í writings on pre-paring for marriage, the purpose of marriage, and raising children. I felt affirmed in my decision to quit dating. The writings talked about the value of investigating one another's character and working together, since marriage involves the tasks of managing money, maintaining a home, and raising a family. Recreation and having fun can be a part of getting to know someone, but making a decision to marry must include opportunities for a couple to see various sides of each other, to see how they handle stress and fulfill the obligations of living a responsible life, and to determine how well they work together.

"You know," Hoda said, "in America dating is like turning the stove on high, and within minutes the water in the tea kettle is boiling and you can hear the whistle. But in India dating is like turning the stove on low—it takes much longer before the water boils and then there's steam. We might learn from our neighbors abroad."

I had the opportunity to eat lunch with Hoda. I shared with her that I was almost thirty and ready to get married. I mentioned that I had spent a lot of years in therapy and still continued to work on overcoming the effects of a violent past. "What about the writings?" I asked. "It says that abused children will be scarred, their characters even perverted. That scares me. Does that mean I can never marry?"

"The effects of abuse are damaging, and it's great you are in therapy and that you have done so much work. It also says in the writings, 'The healer of all thine ills is remembrance of Me.'"[8]

"I've prayed a lot for healing and I've worked hard. But it still hurts to hear the negativity of well-intentioned individuals who spew out the warning, 'Don't every marry someone who's been abused or comes from an unhealthy family situation. You're just asking for trouble.' When I hear that, it makes me feel like I'm damaged goods, beyond repair."

---

8. Bahá'u'lláh, *The Hidden Words*, (Wilmette, IL: Bahá'í Publishing, 2002), Persian, no. 32.

Hoda put her fork down and placed her hand over mine. "Do you still feel like you are damaged goods?"

I took a deep breath and thought for a moment. "Maybe a little," I said.

"Kim, a lot of people will have a variety of views on abuse and violence. I've known people who never get well because they don't seek out sustained help or they give up when therapy gets rough. I've known others who steadily face the challenges of marriage. Marriage is hard for everyone. It's doubly hard for those who come from violent backgrounds. You seem like a mature young woman who knows the value of therapy. If you really want to get married, continue to prepare and believe in yourself. Don't let a few statements prevent you from fulfilling your dreams."

I returned to Tucson feeling even more determined not to look for a partner through the old practice of dating. Dating, a cultural activity, didn't interest me. I still joked around about dating myself. But I realized I wasn't really dating myself; I was developing myself by continuing to live my life and pursue my goals, trusting that I would meet someone along the way.

Five months later I journeyed to Louhelen Conference and Retreat Center (a Bahá'í school in Davison, Michigan) for the six-week Robert Hayden Poetry Fellowship. I arrived in late June to a tan earth and blistering hot dry days. I was worried that the humidity of the Midwest would challenge me, but the dry heat of the drought almost matched that of the Sonoran Desert.

Bluey Diehl, the administrator of the school, welcomed me and showed me the layout of the school and property, where I would sleep, and where I could set up my office. The outdoor trails and acreage provided great scenery. I couldn't wait to sit on the patio with the sunken garden and write. I could share meals with participants attending the various conferences held throughout the summer. I was welcome to sit in on any sessions, but not obligated to do so. Bluey invited me to share my poetry at the art and talent night that concluded each session.

For the first few weeks, I followed a productive working routine. I woke for dawn prayers. I ate breakfast with session participants and then excused myself to go to the office set up for me in the archives, a long and narrow room inside an old white farmhouse. Before writing, I said a few more prayers. I had heard many visiting writers at the University of Arizona share that to write well they had to learn to let the ego lie down at the door. Others shared that their best writing occurred when they got themselves out of the way. Praying helped me to strive for that kind of humble posture before taking the pen to the page. Following prayers, I would write for a couple of hours and then, tired of sitting, go for a three- to four-mile walk. I returned for lunch and then took a short nap. Then I put in another three hours of writing. Before dinner I either practiced yoga or visited with new friends, mostly teachers and volunteers working at Louhelen for the summer. After dinner I returned to my makeshift office and wrote until I couldn't write anymore.

I never tired of this routine and the break from everyday life. I didn't miss phone calls, running errands, attending meetings, or cleaning my apartment. The intense pleasure of reading and writing filled me up.

My primary focus in accepting the fellowship was to work on my writing and advance my master's thesis, but during the third week of my six-week stay, I decided to participate in one of the sessions offered by the school on the Word of God. The session was described as an opportunity for participants to immerse themselves in the ocean of God's words and to explore the depths of their meaning. Participants would also have an opportunity to reflect on their own use of language and the power of human utterance. As a seeker of truth and a writer, I was excited about the focus on both the Word of God and language.

During lunch on the Friday the session was to begin, I looked up from my conversation with Carol Handy, an old friend. A tall, dark, and incredibly handsome man stood in the lobby. He wore a light blue suit and even a tie. He had black curly hair, and wire-rimmed glasses framed his dark brown eyes, which glowed as he smiled and greeted a few others standing in line to check in at the front desk.

"Carol, who's that?" I asked.

"Who's who?"

"That guy standing over there."

Carol looked over toward the door. "Oh, that's David, David Douglas."

"Do you know him well?"

"Yes. He lives near my community."

"Is he married?"

"Nope."

"Well, you've got to introduce me."

Carol chuckled and promised she would.

Several hours later, I entered the classroom where the session would be held for the next five days. David Douglas was the instructor of the course. Within a day I realized he possessed many of the qualities I had listed in my letter to God. Through his sharing in class and over meals, I discovered that David had been a Bahá'í for about fifteen years. The Bahá'í Faith was the focus of his life. By profession he was a counselor at an elementary school. His teaching skills revealed his intelligence and his giving and humble nature. In his interactions with the students in the class, he revealed compassion, sensitivity, and optimism. His sense of humor and sweet laugh touched me. In his role as a teacher, he was inspiring me to progress spiritually. He seemed to know himself well and exuded steadiness and reliability. In our class, he shared that the teaching of the oneness of humanity was what had initially attracted him to the Faith, as he came from a biracial family. In terms of his commitment to health, he was a jogger. I couldn't tell about his commitment to maintaining marriage and family life, but I was very hopeful that I might mentally check off that item on my list after getting to know him better.

But how was I going to do that? He was leaving in a couple of days, and I was leaving in a few weeks. He lived in Michigan. I lived in Arizona. Though we had had some nice interactions, he mingled with everyone else in the same kind way.

On the fourth day of the five-day session, I didn't waste any time and asked David if he would like to go for a walk during the break before dinner. He agreed. We met up on the patio at about five o'clock and walked across the big open field toward the trails that led into the woods. We chit-chatted about the beauty of the surroundings and offered a few more details about our lives. I learned that he lived in Benton Harbor, Michigan, had an eleven-year-old daughter, and was raising two of his nephews. He had been divorced for a couple of years.

I could barely resist David's dark brown eyes and soft-spoken voice. He exuded sincerity and kindness. Spotting the sunlight at the end of the trail and a glimpse of the open field, I knew I had to tell him. Then the dinner bell rang.

"Are you hungry?" David asked.

"Yes," I said still thinking, *Tell him, Kim. Tell him.*

"You know, David, there was something I wanted to share with you." We were at the end of the trail, and I stopped walking before entering the field.

"What's that?" he asked, following suit and standing still, gazing at me with those deep eyes. I wanted to look away because I didn't want him to sense how attracted I was, but I resisted.

"I feel a little nervous saying this," I said, thinking that if I acknowledged my anxiety it might diminish. "I just . . . well, I, um . . ."

"What is it?"

"Over the past few days I've found myself admiring you. You have a lot of qualities that I find . . . well, attractive. I'd like to get to know you better." There. I had said it without breaking my gaze. But I sensed something was wrong.

"I'm flattered, Kim. You have a lot of qualities I admire, too, but I'm engaged."

I managed to stumble over a few words and proceed into the open field and the paler light of dusk. We headed back to the conference center for dinner. I felt disappointed and struggled against my feelings of attraction that intensified during the last day of the session.

A week later, hard at work on new poems, I heard a rap on the door of my office. I opened it expecting to see a staff member or resident of the school. But there was David—tall, handsome, taking me in with those eyes.

"What a surprise!" I said.

"Are you busy?"

"I'm writing, but I don't mind a break. Come on in." I offered David a chair and we both sat down. "So what brings you back?"

"Well, I wanted to share with you that I broke off my engagement."

"You what?" I said, shocked.

"I figured I had no business getting married if I could find myself attracted to someone else."

"Someone else?" I asked, dumb for the moment.

"Yes, I also found myself attracted to you. I realized that I'm just not ready to rush into marriage with that happening. I can't and won't do that again. But I did want to let you know. And I would like to get to know you better—slowly, though."

"Wow," I said, still surprised and almost speechless.

We continued our visit for a while, had dinner together, and then David left to return home. Before my return to Tucson, I visited David for a day at his home in Benton Harbor. We enjoyed a meal he had prepared and then went for a long walk in a park along the St. Joseph River. We found a picnic table and began the first of many talks to deepen our friendship. David offered a few details of his first marriage and divorce, taking responsibility for his part in the dissolution of that marriage. I shared some of the details of my upbringing, eating disorder, and recovery work. Though we said good-bye that day, we continued learning more about one another through phone calls and correspondence.

Back in Arizona I thought about David a lot. His dark brown eyes, tall and muscular physique, and receding hairline attracted me. His community efforts to promote racial and ethnic harmony complemented my own commitments to improve human relationships. I admired his sense of responsibility and his skills as a parent, as an educator, and as a community member. I found myself thinking about him and possessing feelings I had never experienced to that degree before. Was this love or infatuation or just chemistry? Was it meant to be? I didn't know, but I wanted to explore this profound connection.

I knew attraction wasn't enough. Chemistry was nice, but it wasn't going to make for a wholesome and healthy marriage. Infatuation was not an ingredient to keep one out of divorce court. Love was important, but I had observed that love could dissipate; couples, so in love and married one year, were divorced the next. Even though we were getting to know each other through letters and phone calls, I didn't like the long distance because it provided no opportunity for us to examine each other's character in the context of day-to-day life.

During my prayers and meditations, the idea came to me to take a leave of absence from my teaching position the following semester, arrange for an independent study course, and spend a semester in Michigan. This would enable me to get to know David without the veil of long distance. I felt even more excited about these plans when I asked for and was granted a leave of absence from my graduate teaching position. I arranged with my graduate advisors to complete a project through independent study. I made arrangements to stay with Carol Handy, my friend who lived near David. I advertised and subleased my apartment. All this fell into place with such ease that I believed it was God's will for me to go. However, David was not as enthusiastic. He thought this would put pressure on him to rush into developing our relationship. I felt heartbroken by his reaction until my therapist asked, "Who's your higher power—God or David?"

"God, of course," I answered.

"Well, then? What are you waiting for?" she responded.

I informed David that I would be coming to Michigan. Whether we were meant to be together or not, we would find out more quickly if we were working together and getting to know various aspects of each other without the veil of long distance, I explained. I didn't want to rush things, but I also didn't want to wait a year or two before spending sustained time together only to discover then that we were not compatible. Though still worried about feeling pressured to rush into something, David accepted the plan.

Whiteouts

That winter, while David worked, I wrote, keeping up with my independent study projects. During the late afternoons, evenings, and on the weekends we worked together on race unity and related activities for the community.

One Saturday in March I tagged along with David, who was scheduled to facilitate a youth retreat. I wanted a change of scenery and figured I could fit in a walk and find a coffeehouse to work on my studies. We left Benton Harbor and drove toward South Bend, Indiana, about an hour and a half away. Though the snowfall was light when we left, about twenty minutes into the drive we found ourselves inching along the highway in whiteout blizzard conditions. David had years of experience driving in such weather, and I trusted his judgment. He slowed way down and concentrated. I focused, too. I found the phenomenon of the whiteout disturbing. I wanted to see something beyond where we were. I wanted to see the field or the dark asphalt that slithered into the distance and revealed the horizon. We five-miled-an-hour through the blinding snow, and here and there a view emerged: the car bumper ahead of us, a snatch of field, a telephone pole, and then back into it—those blinding moments of wind and snow entangled with each other.

So far our winter together resembled the drive. We were both excited by the possibilities of a future together, yet we were both afraid. At certain moments, even though we couldn't see the future, just as we couldn't see the horizon, we relaxed and trusted that each step would evolve into the next. We talked about marriage and family life as a strong possibility. We believed we had the skills to create a healthy home life. At times I worried that I was not healed enough from the past, that I would make a mess of things, that I needed to stop this car we were in and race through the blinding and chilling snow until I couldn't run anymore. David, too, was concerned. He had had an excruciating first marriage and an even more heartbreaking divorce. He proceeded with caution.

We crossed the border into Indiana and drove into the sun. Patches of snow etched the earth, but signs of spring were more evident. Sarah, the woman hosting the event to which we were headed, had provided directions to a park on the river. After an hour in the car, I was ready for a walk. I said good-bye and left David behind with a few other adults and several teenagers who would pray together, study scripture, and create dances to demonstrate the Bahá'í teachings on the equality of men and women, the elimination of prejudice, and living a holy life. When I arrived at the park and began walking, I wondered what it might have been like if as a teen I had had such a circle of adults and friends. What challenges might I have circumvented? What different decisions might I have made?

I picked up my pace for the aerobic effect. The park was beautiful, though winter hung on this March day. A few spots of snow dotted the tan earth, mist filled the air, and the gray sky hung low. Ducks extended their wings and lifted themselves up to the surface of the river and then dipped down and submerged themselves, their scratchy quacking piercing the cold air. Some scrambled up on the grass for pieces of bread tossed by an elderly gentleman, then returned to the water, dipped themselves in, extended their wings, and repeated the cycle all the while squawking at each other.

The cold and heavy river wound through the golf course. I walked the nearby greens, not yet green. The trees were like bones—no flesh, no luster, just bones. Branches hit branches hit branches. Twigs on the ground caught in a leftover piece of ice reminded me of my own worries and insecurities. I was tired of my fears of men, marriage, and having children. Why did I sometimes feel anxious and want to run when David looked at me so tenderly? Some days I felt ready. Other days I didn't. I just didn't know. The river, thawed and moving, hooked around the course like a question mark. I walked the curve.

I remembered how in fifth grade, two other students at Haven Junior High, a brother and sister, risked the winter ice covering the canal on their way to school. They slipped under. After several days of searching, their bodies were dragged out. *Never cross the frozen river or your body will be dragged out,* I told myself. *The flesh will not be flesh anymore, there will be no breath, you will die, you will go through the ice and die if you cross the frozen river.* I dreamed back then that my body slipped through an ice crack, I paddled my arms, struggled to catch my breath, hyperventilated, and struggled to scream against the breath I couldn't catch. My own anxiety caused me to go under.

But David had shared with me a story from his childhood about how his Dad filled a plastic swimming pool with fish one autumn. When the water froze, his dad warned him not to walk on the ice. "Any disturbance of the ice could kill the fish. If this was a pond and skaters took advantage of the ice, they could kill the fish frozen near the surface. Those way down deep, away from the surface, even though still frozen might survive, but it's best not to risk killing the fish." Just before spring, David's dad informed him that soon the fish would be swimming again. For weeks David checked the pool after school, waiting for the water to thaw. In late March the fish began swimming, picking up from where they had left off, as if nothing had happened, as if they had never been frozen.

Perhaps I could allow God to thaw my frozen fears. Perhaps I could return to those moments when I recognized in David the qualities I had asked God to provide in a lifelong partner. Perhaps I could marry David, raise a healthy family with the help of my faith and guidance from others, taking one day at a time and not projecting so many fears into the unknown future. I didn't know what the future held. The future was like this question mark of a river. I continued to walk around the curve, chanting the names of God—Splendor, Beauty, Power, Will. Could I just try to *be* and let go of the questions, the fears? Could I give my dreams to God and surrender like the river to the forces of winter and spring, of freezing and thawing, of being swum in by the ducks, being ridden through by boats, and experiencing even death, the death of the child crossing what appeared to be but was not a frozen river?

I did not want my own frozen fears to destroy my dream to marry. Maybe I could live into my hopes rather than my fears. If I ran into one of those fears, didn't I have enough proof that I was good at seeking out help, that I had learned the power of consultation with friends and professionals, and that I was never stuck? With the help of others I could discover the array of choices available to deal with any given challenge. Even now, I could decide to keep walking with the river that stretched beyond my vision or turn back and return to my love, in a house in South Bend where he was teaching teenagers about self-respect, about expressing one's needs, about communication.

Though I turned back, I was really walking forward, with a river that stretched beyond my vision. I reached the house on Fourth Street, climbed up the front steps, opened the door, and entered a room of teenagers eating pizza. David looked at me and smiled, his eyes embracing me.

Shrine

I planned my pilgrimage with the same determination and type-A mentality with which I embraced just about everything. Before leaving for Israel in early January 1990, I filled several pages in my journal with a list of all the prayers I believed I needed to say. Even though I felt more confident about my healing process, I worried about how the past prevented me from achieving my potential and reflecting the light of God. I wanted the mirror of my heart to shine. I wanted my soul to be transformed. I wanted to be fully healed, not just partially healed, because maybe then I could forgive myself for all the past misdeeds and feel more confident about the future. I would pray about marriage, pray for all my unborn children, and pray for direction in terms of career and writing.

My first night in Jerusalem, exhausted and needing sleep to prepare for the next few days of tours, I showered and had just tied my robe when a knock at the door surprised me. "Yes?" I called through the door.

"Waiter, here. You forgot credit card in restaurant," the voice behind the door said.

I opened the door and the waiter who had just taken care of me handed me the card with one hand. In the other he held a metal pitcher. "Massage. Israeli hospitality. Massage." He entered the room and pointed to the bed.

"No. I don't need a massage."

"Israeli hospitality," he said.

"Israeli hospitality? No, I'm tired. Sleep," I said in chopped English, unsure of his English skills. I held the door open and pointed to the hallway. "Thank you, but no."

He didn't move. He didn't budge. I didn't know what to do. He walked over, closed the door and said, "Relax. Help you sleep." I wanted to tell him to leave, to get out, but I didn't. He had me lie down, and after a few minutes of his massaging my back, I jumped up and said, "Enough. Come back tomorrow morning. Better time."

"What time do you leave in the morning for tour?"

"Eight thirty. Come at 6:30."

"I will come. Israeli hospitality."

When he left the room, I double-locked the door. The next morning I ignored the knocks. After breakfast I spoke to the manager at the front desk and shared what had happened. I told him that I didn't want Israeli hospitality of that kind again. Though initially challenged and unable to respond in self-preserving ways, I was making at least a few inches of progress. In this situation, like so many others, I managed to distract the individual and find my way free of possible harm. This time I also reported the situation to an authority figure, who did indeed apologize and no doubt reprimanded the waiter involved, for I did not see any sign of him again.

On the first day in Jerusalem, my tour included a trip to the Old City. Following our guide, about a dozen of us from all parts of the world entered Lion's Gate with the intent of retracing the steps of Christ. We followed the Via Dolorosa, or the Way of Suffering, stopping at each of the fourteen Stations of the Cross. I had expected a sanctified and holy atmosphere filled with reverence and stillness. But tourists fled into shops as cars honked and sped by, prayers from the mosques filtered onto the cobblestone streets, and shopkeepers competed for our attention. Our guide reminded us that Jesus taught among this same kind of noise and commotion. In this clamor, I tried to picture Christ carrying the cross along this path to the place of His crucifixion and burial. I imagined the crowds back then, some cheering, some silent, all witnesses. I tried to sense the enormity of the Lord's walk to His death and our salvation. I felt humbled by my efforts to grasp the significance of the Way of Suffering, the significance of the Lord. I photographed the stations where Christ fell under the weight of the cross. I understood falling. My own personal suffering included numerous falls. I knew I couldn't or shouldn't compare my life to the Lord's, but I wanted to feel a deeper connection to God and this was how I achieved some semblance of closeness.

The next day, I stood with hundreds of women on the left side of the Western Wall that I also learned was called the "Wailing Wall." I learned that this most holy spot was the remaining outer wall of the Second Temple destroyed by Rome. I took my place and inched forward. The chanting, cries, and sometimes sobs engulfed me. I felt as if I were a miniscule ripple in an ocean of endless waves reaching the shore and receding and then reaching for the shore again. When I placed my hands against the stone, the wall seemed to vibrate. I knew so little about the particular history of this wall made up of rocks and boulders, some weighing as much as two million pounds, yet I cried as I regarded it. The wall constructed to protect the Temple was what endured. Even though the Temple was destroyed, the spirit of the people was not obliterated. I, too, had constructed walls to protect my soul, walls that I had at times considered faulty because they isolated me and kept out even those who cared. I needed to protect myself even though my childhood war was over, even though the Temple of my soul—my body—had not been destroyed, only harmed. I didn't know whether these interior walls served or harmed me, but I prayed to become more conscious. I inserted a slip of paper into a crevice of the wall that held thousands of similar slips with prayers written to Almighty God. My prayer read, "Keep on healing me."

After arriving in Haifa by bus, I checked into the Dvir Hotel and then joined about ninety other pilgrims to tour some of the gardens that had transformed Mount Carmel into an oasis of beauty and calm. I walked the paths, pausing to photograph a stone peacock and then a row of manicured cypress trees. As I ascended the mountain to the next garden, the perfect geometry of the garden below caught my attention. I positioned myself to capture pictures of the lush green lawns in the shape of rectangles. Gardeners had hedged bushes into the shape of nine-pointed stars. Clear pools of water reflected the overcast sky and the green of the cypress trees. Water trickled from ornamental fountains. Inspired by the beauty, I slipped the camera in my purse to say a few prayers.

One night I sat with dozens of other pilgrims to listen to a member of the Universal House of Justice, the international governing body of the Bahá'í Faith. The representative discussed the process of developing our communities throughout the world, many still in the stages of infancy. He said, "When a child falls down, a loving parent will comfort her and encourage her to get back up and try again. We must not be critical of ourselves, dear friends. In our efforts to develop our communities we are like infants. If we reprimand ourselves, criticize by saying 'Just look at you. You're so clumsy. You fell again. Can't you do anything right,' then we will thwart our efforts. We must be infinitely patient, filled with encouragement, and focus on what we are accomplishing rather than what we are not."

I sat there spellbound. Those words were meant for me. I needed to take them into the deepest part of me. I needed to parent myself with love and encouragement. I needed to stop focusing on all that was undone and consider what I had accomplished.

The next day I visited the most sacred spot on earth for Bahá'ís, the Shrine of Bahá'u'lláh. Two white brick planters stood at the front of the black-and-gold iron gates. Cypress trees framed the walkway adorned by a red Persian carpet. Four steps led up to the carved oak door, and two ornamental peacocks adorned the upper step—the step leading into the shrine.

Inside the shrine I followed the line of pilgrims, some of whom sat cross-legged on the floor to pray, while others stood in line and waited their turn to bow their heads at the sacred threshold. The scent of roses intoxicated me. A pure silence, gorgeous and satisfying, filled me. I remained quiet, too, and when it was my turn to bow my head, I uttered no words, no prayers, but simply felt an inexplicable sense of clarity and calm.

If only I could have stayed with that sense of quietude. When I found a place to sit, I pulled out a slip of paper from my purse. The night before, I had condensed my journal writing into a list. I didn't want to forget a single prayer. Who knew if I'd ever travel to Haifa again, if I'd ever have the opportunity to pray in these holy shrines once more?

For the next hour I prayed to be forgiven for all that I had chosen to do that was not virtuous in my life of almost thirty years. I prayed for the healing of my family members and for God to help me forgive them. I prayed for my writing, asking God to work through me. I hoped to write a book on my healing efforts. I asked God to give me the courage to write about my sufferings and ongoing spiritual transformation, to enable me to serve others who needed the belief that surviving violence is possible. I asked God for assistance in completing graduate school and for guidance in pursuing a career. I prayed that my relationship with David would evolve, and that God would help us create a healthy and happy marriage and family. I prayed for help to break the cycle of violence and practice healthier behaviors that would aid me in marriage.

As I prayed for assistance in breaking the cycle, despair and fear flooded me. Was I ready for marriage? Did I know David well enough? Had I healed enough? Had I had enough therapy? Would I harm the children I might have? Had I fully overcome the eating disorder? Were these fears and worries a warning from God that I was not yet capable of marriage and raising children? Would I ever be ready?

I took in a deep breath and waited for an answer. I breathed in and out. And then that steady voice surfaced, the voice of my dreams that enabled me to flee across country, to search for truth, the voice that could be trusted, the voice most connected to God. The voice was sober.

The voice was stern. The voice caught my attention. *You've done a lot of work, but marriage will challenge you. You are barely ready. The work ahead is serious and vital and will not be easy. Don't fool yourself with all the fantasies. Prepare yourself. Trust in Me.*

The sense of sternness humbled and disappointed me. I had expected a positive experience in the most holy shrine. I had wanted to be filled with joy and confidence and knowing. Instead, I felt insecure and concerned. I worried that that voice—the voice I interpreted as the voice of God— was reprimanding me.

A few weeks later, back in Tucson, while meditating one morning, I remembered the perceptive words of two individuals I had worked with years earlier at the Bahá'í National Center. Dr. Geoffrey Marks, my immediate supervisor, guided and supported me as I learned my responsibilities as a secretary in the Department of Community Administration. On one occasion we were talking about some mishap in a particular Bahá'í community. I can't remember my actual response to the mishap, but Geoff looked at me and said, "Kim, it must be agonizing for you to face gruesome reality when you are so idealistic." He said this in the most loving and gentle way. I had never had someone point out my tendency toward idealism and the pain I suffered when reality didn't match the ideals I envisioned.

On another occasion I was lamenting how I had fallen short in some Bahá'í obligation. Dr. Magdalene Carney, at that time a member of the National Spiritual Assembly, the national governing body of the Bahá'ís of the United States, shook her head. "Girl," she said to me, her Southern accent emerging, "You whip yourself up with this Faith. You read a passage and whip, whip, figure out how you are doing something wrong. Don't you realize this Faith is here to uplift you?"

"I guess not," I responded, feeling astonished that she had detected a behavior I was oblivious to.

"We bring in all kinds of luggage to the Faith. Do you really need that luggage of hurting yourself?"

Remembering such caring and honest feedback, I recognized that I had entered the shrine expecting positive confirmation about the dreams I held for my future. When my experience didn't match those expectations, I felt hurt and interpreted what occurred in prayer in a negative way. Perhaps I could lighten up. That was an option. Why not accept that, yes, marriage would bring new challenges? I could look at those challenges as opportunities for that lifelong growth to which I was already committed, and I could celebrate the accomplishments I had achieved so far. I had worked hard in many areas of my life. In the process of healing from the past, I had already overcome much and was continuing to overcome many of my weaknesses and disorders. I had committed to a spiritual path, and I was trying to live my life according to those teachings. Returning to school, I had worked toward and received a bachelor's degree. Then I had been offered and accepted a teaching fellowship and admission into graduate school. I would soon earn a master of fine arts degree in creative writing. While accomplishing all this, I had learned how to live responsibly on my own. Still, during the remainder of my pilgrimage and upon return to Tucson, I wrestled with the question: Was I ready to face the next set of challenges that would come with living with someone else in marriage?

Ceremony

David and I had spent enough time together to discover each other's strengths and weaknesses. We had endured more than a few conflicts. Like most couples, we both had suffered and struggled through our own particular challenges—for me it was an abusive childhood, for David a failed first marriage. We carried that baggage around, struggling to discard it and trying to become aware of how present situations triggered unhealthy patterns of behavior from the past. After months of exploring our relationship over the phone and in letters, we decided to marry. We both wanted to believe that we had learned from the past, that we had developed particular muscles to help us endure the unknown and inevitable challenges ahead, and that we were educated and humble enough to seek out professional help when help might be needed. We shared the love and practice of a common faith, and we believed that the guidance in the Bahá'í teachings and our mutual commitment to work on transforming our weaknesses into strengths would help us create the happy, functional marriage and family life we both desired.

Six weeks before my graduation David flew to Arizona during his spring break. I wanted David and my friends to have a chance to meet each other. I wanted him to see the desert, the mountains, my tiny and wonderful apartment, the university, and the Bahá'í Center. This was the place where I had learned to build a home for myself, a place I would carry in my heart in the years ahead.

I picked David up from the airport in Phoenix rather than Tucson so we could save a few hundred dollars. The jet had landed, and I stood in the waiting area looking at the stream of faces exiting the plane. There he was! He saw me, and the glow and excitement in his eyes, the bounce in his step, took me by surprise. In that instant, I felt overwhelmed and afraid. Then I was in his arms, and a warmth and tenderness spread, a sense that this was right. I resolved not to let my fears devour my dreams.

We drove back to Tucson the slow way—through the White Mountains. I wanted to share my favorite places—the small towns like Show-Low and Globe, the Salt River Canyon where I had gone rafting and tubing, the diversity and beauty of vegetation at different altitudes, and the peaks and folds of the mountains that would appear in my dreams for years when I found myself missing the desert—my soul's home.

Though I taught and went to classes the next week, I introduced David to several close friends. We met with them in coffeehouses, for dinner at favorite restaurants, and on the trails at Sabino Canyon and Mount Lemmon. One night we had dinner at my apartment, and David shared a few haikus he had written for me with some friends. I felt special and loved and thought, *So this is how it's supposed to feel—like this.*

The day before David left, a unity celebration was held at the Tucson Bahá'í center to honor our upcoming marriage. The center filled with friends from various Bahá'í communities in southern Arizona, the university, the ashram where I took yoga, and Bentley's House of Coffee and Tea. Even my therapist attended. Once everyone was seated, the program began. Gail and Stephanie read opening prayers focused on the theme of unity. Nancy read Dr. Martin Luther King Jr.'s "I Have a Dream" speech. Karen, dressed in a flowing white dress, performed a dance. My office partner and friend from the MFA program, Val, read a new poem she had just written. Roger, Wayne, and Keyvan sang a song in Swahili since they had all lived in Africa for several years. Their fabulous clicks of the tongue and efforts to get us to join in had everyone laughing. The spirit and creativity filled me up. I thanked everyone and introduced David. He shared a few words of gratitude in that amazing way of his and had everyone laughing. I felt pleased that my friends could get a glimpse of David's qualities as we enjoyed a few more hours together eating and interacting.

Two months later I received my master of fine arts degree and moved from Tucson to Benton Harbor, Michigan. The wedding was scheduled for July 28, 1990, at the Bahá'í House of Worship in Wilmette, Illinois. Friends and family were traveling to join us from as near as seven blocks away from the House of Worship and from as far away as Tucson. Though Mom had helped with many of the details of the wedding, we still had work to do.

A few weeks before the wedding, David and I traveled to Louhelen Conference and Retreat Center. My friend Steve Powers was at the University of Michigan for the summer, having received a research fellowship. We decided to meet at Louhelen so he could spend some time with David and me. Even though he was going to attend the wedding, we knew it would be difficult to find time during the ceremony for sustained and quality interaction with so many people there to celebrate. After the three of us caught up, Steve and I decided to go for a walk down Kitchen Road, which would take us into the countryside near Louhelen. Cornfields, cow pastures, bushes thick with berries, and mosquitoes surrounded us. Dogs barked, and roosters and hens cackled and carried on. The road wound and went on without the busy traffic of State Road disrupting our peace.

Steve, a thoughtful man and generous listener, shared how happy he and Gail were about my upcoming marriage. He shared memories of when I had lived with their family. I, too, shared a few memories from that time. I acknowledged that he and Gail had both helped deepen my understanding and application of the Bahá'í teachings. They modeled to me healthy ways of interacting, even while enduring some challenges with their adolescent and young adult children. They weren't, to my relief, the perfect family. They taught me there was no such thing as that. They were a family committed to consulting their way through decision-making and typical family problems.

Steve had a very humble nature. As I offered my praises, he would turn the conversation around to focus it on me and David, David's children, and the life we would build together. As we walked and talked, I felt loved and cared for. On our way back, I recognized that perhaps God was working through another. I wouldn't have that father-daughter walk with my own dad. We wouldn't have the conversation that perhaps some daughters are blessed to have with their father before marriage. I was given the gift of a sacred interaction with Steve about marriage and life and moving into the unknown. I was given the gift of his love and belief in me. He was a role model, a healthy father figure. Kindness and strength of spirit radiated from him toward me, and I was able to receive the gift with gratitude, even though Steve was not my actual father.

On the afternoon of July 28, 1990, about a hundred guests sat in Foundation Hall in the Bahá'í House of Worship. A rendition of Pachelbel's Canon, our wedding march, announced the start of the ceremony David and I had created together. Participants—members of our families, and friends—walked down the aisle and took their positions at the head of the room onstage.

Carol opened the ceremony as a preacher might but without the collar or robe. Wearing a bright royal blue blazer and skirt, Carol stood at center-stage and welcomed everyone to the special occasion of our wedding. Of the seventy or so guests who attended, maybe a dozen were Bahá'ís and had experienced the diversity of Bahá'í wedding ceremonies. For so many of our guests, this was their first such experience. David and I had asked Carol to offer opening comments on the Bahá'í wedding ceremony to help our guests better understand what they were observing.

"In the Bahá'í Faith, a young couple considering marriage is instructed to fully explore each other's character and to take time during their courtship to work together and place themselves in situations where they learn about each other's strengths and weaknesses," Carol began. "Marriage is considered a vital and sacred institution, 'a fortress for well-being and salvation.' Because of the sacred nature of marriage, Bahá'ís are encouraged to take the responsibility of preparing for it seriously and to practice chastity to protect them in the process of making such a major life decision.

"I had the privilege of being a part of this process. Kim lived with me while she and David were investigating each other's character. And while investigation might sound like a scientific term void of romance, I can assure you that Kim and David were filled with the marvelous mystery, exhilaration, and energy common in most courtships. Kim returned to my home at night aglow and excited about her evolving relationship with David."

Continuing to share standards of Bahá'í marriage, Carol explained that we fulfilled the obligation of obtaining parental consent and that the reason for that particular law was to bring two families together in unity. She didn't know that I had written to the Universal House of Justice, the international governing body of the Bahá'í Faith, asking to be exempted from that particular law because of the abuse I had sustained from my dad. My study of Bahá'í law indicated to me that following this law was a sacred responsibility and a privilege of both children and parents. Did my dad's abusive ways warrant his participating in such an important part of my life's choices? The Universal House of Justice responded by empathizing with my situation and saying that, since my dad was supportive of the relationship, I should include him in the process, which could enable him and the family to experience the healing bounties of participating in this practice.

My dad, however, refused to write a letter of consent. "Kim, you've been on your own for the last fifteen years or so doing exactly what you wanted to do. Now you want me to be involved. This is crazy, if you ask me," he said.

One of my former coworkers and acquaintances at the Bahá'í National Center proceeded to call my dad to see how he felt about our marriage. "I'm paying for the wedding, coming to the wedding. What more do you want?" That was consent enough to fulfill this Bahá'í duty.

I have learned since then that the decision of whether to grant each request to appeal that law is based on individual circumstances. There have been situations of abuse in which parents forfeit their right of parenthood because of their behaviors, and their sons or daughters do not have to obtain their blessing to marry.

Carol finished her introduction by sharing a few requirements of the Bahá'í wedding ceremony. She explained that the one vow that we were required to recite is "We will all, verily, abide by the Will of God."[9] After David and I stated our vows, we would be officially married.

The ceremony proceeded with music and readings. David and I repeated the required vow, and a few pairs of hands started clapping, then a few more, then each and every family member or friend joined in.

Years later, I ponder the clapping I have witnessed at so many weddings. Does it mean *Hooray, you did it, you're married, you've said your vows?* Or is the clapping more like the cheer of a parent watching a child on the soccer field? Are the witnesses and guests cheering on the couple in that moment of launching the most great effort of bringing two different lives together to create a healthy, functional, sacred home and family? For marriage is, after all, two lives coming together to begin an endurance challenge far more intense than any marathon. I'd like to consider that David and I came together on July 28, 1990, inebriated with the wine of the love of God and each other, and that we valued and celebrated our family members' and friends' support and belief in us. I love pondering in the years since that day that all of our hard labor to make our marriage a lasting and peaceful one will help to improve the health of our world, for certainly we can't create world peace without establishing loving and unified families.

That day, years ago, I wasn't analyzing. I was smiling and crying as I received the clapping of our family and friends as well as their love and good wishes over the next few hours at the reception. We enjoyed the celebration at the Wilmette Golf Club and then our honeymoon in Saugatuck, Michigan. We entered the early days and months of our marriage where we struggled and celebrated as we discovered and worked on who we were as a couple and blended family.

The months stretched out into years. While most days were filled with the details of juggling the various mundane elements of our lives, opportunities existed to continue to grow spiritual and emotional muscles

---

9. Bahá'u'lláh, *The Kitáb-i-Aqdas,* (Wilmette, IL: Bahá'í Publishing Trust, 1993), pp. 105–6.

we didn't even know we possessed. The challenges we had feared that almost prevented us from marrying did arise. Because we married each other rather than those fears, however, we were given numerous opportunities to continue on the path of personal transformation.

Options

I walked into the family room from the carport after a weekend away. I had just returned from Memphis, where I had attended Laurie's wedding. Laurie, a friend from Tucson, had participated years earlier in creating the lists of qualities my friends and I wanted in our future spouses. All three of us—Shawn, Laurie, and I—were now married.

Surveying the scene before me, I thought perhaps I should have added cleanliness to my list. The house was a mess. A pile of laundry lay on the sofa. A couple of jackets were slung over chairs. Dirty dishes were scattered across the kitchen counter. Newspapers lay strewn across the floor and the dining room table, along with mail—some of it opened, some unopened.

"Hey, can't anybody pick up around here?" I called out, setting down my suitcase. "It would be nice to return home to a clean house."

David entered the room to greet me but, seeing the state I was in, frowned. "David, I'm not a maid. I didn't get married to become a maid. I can't live like this. It's a mess around here," I fumed.

I sensed David was pulling away. Neither of us realized at the time that that was a trigger for me, just as my outburst was a trigger for him. I did not pause to consider the emotions erupting inside me. I continued to fume. I stomped out of the room, wanting to throw things. I wanted order, but there was no order. No dust-free coffee table or desktop. No mopped kitchen or bathroom floor. No dishes washed and towel dried and put away in their places. No mirrors Windexed. While some of my reaction had to do with the lack of cleanliness and order, most of it did not.

David followed me into the living room. "Kim, we were busy all weekend. I had two meetings, and David had obligations. We didn't have time," David explained. The younger David was our thirteen-year-old legal foster son and David's nephew.

We stood face-to-face, but I couldn't look at him. Even though he was standing there, even though he was responding to me in a matter-of-fact way, I felt anxious and out of control. "You just don't care about me!" I screamed.

"That's not true. And do you have to shout? I'm sorry about the house, but can't we work this out in a more productive way?"

Shame worked its way into my heart. It was hard even to breathe. I wanted to run. I wanted out, out of this shame, out of acting like an adolescent, out of my life. I spun around and, without saying a word, stormed into the basement. I leaned against the hard cement wall, slid down, and just sat there.

The image of my dad came to me, that man who behaved appropriately and impressively in public and like a lunatic in private. Was that me? All weekend I had laughed and interacted with friends at Laurie's wedding. I was admired and liked because of what showed for the rest of the world—my public self. I was just like him, wasn't I? I hated that about my dad—how he interacted respectfully with people not as important or as close to him as his own family.

There in the dark, I cried, feeling powerless, desperate, and alone. I can't remember how long the tears went on, how long I hid myself away, how long before David retrieved me. He knew I was striving to avoid repeating the behaviors of the past. He also responded to my setbacks with concern, with his own set of emotions, and with the same determination to communicate in a civilized way. His successes were born from an entirely different upbringing.

Back upstairs we sat on the sofa. David held me. He acknowledged my disappointment in returning to a messy house. He explained that both he and young David had lived like bachelors before I came along. An organized and immaculate house hadn't been a priority for them. They cleaned when they needed to clean—before company, here and there. He was willing to make adjustments. He hoped that I, too, would be willing to try to adjust the way I communicated, and he wondered if counseling might help me in that regard.

That evening I thought back to all the years of therapy I had been through. How many counselors had I seen? There was Richard, Lois, Dr. Sing, Laura, Ishwara, and others whose names I couldn't remember. There had been years and years of therapists—group therapy, individual counseling, hospital programs. I was tired of all this healing. When I said good-bye to a therapist, I liked believing in the possibility of *the end*. But the part of me that was getting healthier knew that transformation was not an event but an ongoing process. I had also vowed that no matter what it took, I would strive not to repeat the destructive behaviors and traditions from the past. I believed that my part in advancing civilization was to avoid blindly imitating the traditions of my forebears. To achieve this, I had to become conscious of how the past had affected me. I was committed to not repeating what was not worthy of being repeated. I just hadn't realized how hard it would be to keep that commitment.

While living on my own in Tucson, maintaining this promise had been easier. My schedule was my schedule, and it wasn't affected by anyone else's routine. I selected my own décor. I cleaned when and how I saw fit. My messes were tolerable because I knew why I couldn't get to vacuuming or picking up during a busy time. When I felt frustrated or disappointed in relationships with others, I avoided feeling the anger or the hurt by medicating myself with food. When I discovered and allowed myself to experience the anger I felt about my past, I did so with a detached and impartial professional. I paid a therapist to teach me how to endure and more effectively communicate feelings that scared me because I had only seen them expressed in violent ways.

Now I was married. I was even a foster mom to David's nephew and a stepmom to David's daughter. We were in the process of learning how to live together, learning who we were to each other. We enjoyed our similarities and struggled some of the time to appreciate our diversity. The way we handled our differences caused conflict. I didn't want to continue yelling and shouting. I had to learn new ways to deal with my anger. I had to learn how to express my desires in ways that could be heard. I had to learn how to compromise.

The next morning I woke up, and after praying I meditated on numerous passages from scripture. In the book of Timothy it is written, "I have not given you a spirit of fear." With God's assistance I had sought out help and overcome many of my fears. I could not stop now. I had faith in God. I had years of proof that God's strength and mercy were available to me. All I had to do was ask for guidance, and it would be given. Bahá'u'lláh wrote, "The healer of all thine ills is remembrance of Me, forget it not." Perhaps remembering God more than dwelling on my past could prove productive. Perhaps, as stated in the Bahá'í writings, seeking out the best physicians and doctors for my ailments would empower me.

I decided to meet with a social worker and attend Al-Anon and Adult Children of Alcoholics—both twelve-step meetings. I drove over to the local ALANO club once or twice a week and sat at the long cafeteria-style tables with dozens of other individuals who, like me, were striving to heal themselves. Here I shared frustrations over my behavior or the behavior of others. I shared the details that led to my screaming and yelling and how I felt such shame about these incidents. Listening to other men and women who had been showing up to these tables for years and had more successes in their healing process, I began to realize I had choices. The people at the tables didn't respond to my plight by prescribing a solution. They shared their stories of frustration in their own homes and some of the new ways they were learning to respond to these frustrations. I acquired an array of options from listening to their stories. I could let go of and revise my perfectionist standards by including the family in a discussion about the house. I could explore with my therapist why I was having such an intense reaction to a messy house. I could leave the house and go for a walk or go to a coffeehouse or library—somewhere more organized and clean. I could write out my anger over what I perceived was my family's lack of caring, and perhaps I would discover my emotional reaction had more to do with me and less to do with them. I could pull myself together and share in a more collected manner that I would appreciate some help with the house and that I wondered who would like to do what. I could clean a small area of the house and plop myself down with a novel, ignoring the rest of the mess. I left the meetings and returned home feeling confident that

I could construct a new road rather than continue down the road of my past.

Once a week I also visited with Sara, my new therapist during this time. With Sara, I scrutinized how my extreme reaction to the messy house related to my childhood. When I was a child, if the house was not in order, Dad went berserk and I learned at a very young age to clean, clean, clean. If the floor was mopped, the dishes washed and put away, the furniture dusted and waxed, the floors vacuumed, Dad would not yell and hit—so I came to believe.

I needed to revise that early programming. A clean and orderly house was desirable, but the quality of flexibility while raising children and juggling work and parenting was an even more important trait. I needed to relax the standards I had inherited. While I was at Laurie's wedding, David had been at home with his nephew David, a freshman in high school, whom we were raising. Both had been involved in numerous activities throughout the weekend, and finding time to do household chores had not been a priority. This didn't mean, though, that they couldn't find ways to cooperate. Sara had me practice some of the alternative ways of soliciting their help that I had learned about at the Al-Anon meetings. I rehearsed and began to develop some new communication skills.

Expressing myself in more constructive and positive ways did not occur right away. As with many good things, practice and more practice brought about desired results. The house continued to get messy, which triggered fear and physical reactions in me. I strived to pause and ask myself: What do I need? Is the house really that messy? How might I communicate my desire for help? The process was tedious but better than alienating my family and repeating a toned-down version of the eruptions I had experienced as a child.

I also continued the more difficult journey of trying to befriend the part of me that I labeled ruthless, destructive, and abusive. This shadow self that I would have preferred to extinguish—the thief in me, the binger, the screamer, the one filled with more shame than I could bear— leaked out the more I tried to control or rid myself of what I deemed wrong, worthless, or insignificant. In all the great world faiths, we are asked to love our enemy, befriend the stranger, heal the sick, and offer hope to the hopeless. How could I live up to this exhortation if I couldn't offer this same consolation to the part of me that was broken, the part I considered sick, pathetic, an enemy? Though I spent several years in therapy not wanting to examine my shadow self, though still today there are moments when I would rather plaster on the smile and the makeup and pretend all is well to avoid those places within, I catch myself. The stranger in me needs love if I am to love the stranger on the street corner in a ragged coat who might be drunk. The part of me I have considered unlovable will never be able to heal and to love until she is embraced.

Firstborn

When the doctor shared the lab results, I wanted to hold a megaphone and shout out to the whole world that I was pregnant. I had dreamed of this day, and now I was living through the moments I had known in my imagination. How could I abide by the suggestion to wait a few months before sharing the news? Since some women miscarry during the first trimester, many doctors urge them to wait before sharing with others the news of a pregnancy. I couldn't fathom miscarriage and couldn't resist making phone calls to relatives, informing my colleagues at Lake Michigan College, and saying "Guess what?" to our neighbors. I was so excited that I wanted to tell strangers, everyone and anyone who crossed or didn't cross my path. I wanted to buy maternity clothes, a baby crib, diapers. I examined my slow-to-expand waistline and still-flat abdomen wondering when, when would I be ready for the maternity blouses and pants I had purchased?

During the first month of pregnancy in early October 1993, I sat down one day and wrote a sentimental but heartfelt letter to our unborn child.

Dear little mystery, soul evolving in me, our son or daughter, our child,
I am so grateful and excited about your presence in our life. I have been dreaming of you since I was a child, and I have been

praying for you since before your conception. You are so desired, so loved. As you evolve in me, I am continuing to grow and prepare myself for your birth. It is now early autumn in Michigan. I drive two days a week to teach off-campus at a high school in South Haven. The leaves are brilliant, gold, fiery orange, deep red. The intense blue skies and the intense sunlight remind me of Tucson. Not a cloud lately. Not a cloud. How I feel about your presence, so clear.

I continue on in my commitment to grow and heal. I will someday share with you details about my own upbringing, about the wrestling I have had to do and continue to do to overcome some obstacles that seemed insurmountable at times. But I hope to model to you faith in the power of God. "As ye have faith so shall your powers and blessings be" is a passage I strive to translate into action. Sometimes I have worried that I will fall short and fail in the parenting process. I apologize ahead of time. I hope that someday when you are mature and wiser from having lived years, you will know in the deepest part of your being that I strove with all my heart and soul to raise you as best as I was able, seeking assistance throughout your journey through childhood. I want to avoid repeating the behaviors I learned that were not so healthy. I want to forge new territory. And you, dear child, I will give you permission someday to do better than I was able to do. I will tell you, "repeat the best of what you learned and saw from us and do better in the areas where we fell short." That's how civilization will advance. That's how we will create healthier families in the future.

I love you, dear soul. I love you with all of my being. I pray for you, for me, for your dear father. I pray that we will grow together in faith, in service to the Lord. I am eager to welcome you to this world that will become better through your presence.

With more love than I ever knew I possessed,
Your mom

The nausea and fatigue of the first trimester paled in comparison to the anticipation of the life growing in me. I devoured several books on pregnancy, including *What to Expect When You Are Expecting*. I examined and reexamined the photographs in the book *A Child Is Born*. The picture of the embryo at four weeks resembled a curled milky seahorse with a wobbly oval-shaped head. The trunk looked like a curved version of a lizard's spine. I learned and pondered that at four weeks the heart of the developing embryo resided in the mouth. I was thrilled by that image. Imagine how the world would change if the heart influenced more of our words. When I heard the baby's heartbeat, that hollow drum-like *swoosh, swoosh, swoosh,* I wanted to take the doctor's stethoscope home so I could listen to the music of my baby's heart. Instead, at the end of many days, I lay in bed, lifting my blouse, waiting to see movement. When my abdomen started rolling, I watched, enthralled by the kicks and jabs, the tumbling. To stay in shape and prepare for the hard work of labor, I worked out to a Kathy Smith video for pregnancy and took Lamaze classes. Judy, one of David's colleagues, offered to coach me through labor. I accepted, certain that Judy's knowledge and positive spirit would help.

One afternoon, in the privacy of our yard, I stood tall in a two-piece bathing suit and smiled and squinted into the full sun as David readied the camera. My womb was nine months full, and I wanted documentation of the miracle. Yes, I was showing off the amazing feat of my body accommodating an almost fully evolved fetus.

A few hours later, back inside, I dropped down on my knees to relieve my spine of the pressure and pain I felt with the extra weight. Though I had only gained thirty-five pounds, Dr. Manning was right. Most women, he had said, find the last couple of months of pregnancy difficult, but for those who have had back surgery like mine, the last couple of months could be excruciating. "Bring it on," I cried out, referring to labor and delivery. Over the next couple of weeks "Bring it on" became my mantra.

A week before the due date, my doctor decided to induce labor because the back pain was intensifying. Even though I had hopes and expectations, I realized through all the labor and delivery stories of friends and family members that the birth process can humble those with elaborate goals because it has a course of its own. So it was with me. While I had planned on a night of deep breathing and perhaps a few moans and grunts, I carried on, even screamed, and revised my drug-free plans by accepting a couple of shots to help me endure the process.

At one point, David began to massage my back. "Don't touch me," I snapped. Then David began to say a prayer. "Hon, just don't do that," I ordered. I didn't want to hear anything, didn't want to feel anything. I just wanted to curl up and go to sleep and skip the whole labor, and I managed to do just that for a while between contractions. Then the next wave of pain hit, then the tidal wave, then the tsunami. "David, get the doctor! Hurry! Get the doctor! The baby's coming! She's coming!"

David ran out into the hallway and came back alone. "They said there's no way. You're not dilated enough."

"I know my body. I know . . ." I couldn't finish. I screamed, and just then a ball of water shot through me. My water didn't just break. It exploded. Water was everywhere.

"Thank God I'm not a woman," David said—a comment I teased him about later when I could laugh about the situation.

After my water broke, we called Judy. She arrived within half an hour and took charge. She flung open the closed blinds, letting in the light of the new day and the view beyond the dark closed-in room. She breathed with me during the contractions. She praised and guided me the way I had seen coaches operate on football and baseball fields. When my body was ready to begin pushing, she asked, "How many pushes, Kim? How many pushes before you deliver?"

I said "five" for no particular reason.

"Five it is," she said. When it was time to push, Judy ordered me to breathe out and push with my entire being.

Our daughter was born on that fifth push.

Within seconds, the midwife set the baby on my chest. Our eyes latched in a powerful bond. "Welcome to the world," I cried.

Then David and I looked at each other and said, "Aleah" at the same time. We had selected two names and wanted to wait until the baby was born to see what she was like. "Aleah Taraneh Douglas," we shared over the phone with all of our loved ones. We boasted about her weight and height, her dark hair and deep blue eyes, her tiny fingers and toes. We prayed over her, oohed and ahhhed, enjoyed visits from young David and my stepdaughter, Jenai, who held her new sister. Flowers were delivered, including a dozen white roses from my dad.

On the day of my firstborn's birth, June 15, 1993, Dad sent me, his firstborn child, a dozen roses. I felt both happy and sad, hopeful yet unsure. We were creatures of habit. I sent birthday and Father's Day cards to Dad, and he sent birthday and holiday cards to me. He would be coming to visit to meet his granddaughter. He was trying. And yet there was a distance I couldn't convince myself to ignore, a distance I felt in a most tangible way. The roses withered within a couple of days. I turned my attention toward what filled me with joy and energy—my new daughter.

That first night, after visiting hours, David returned to the hospital with a bag full of surprises for me and the baby. He had developed the two rolls of film containing pictures we had taken right after Aleah's birth and throughout the day. We reflected on and admired the accomplishment of labor and delivery, the miracle of bringing a life into the world. David also purchased five-by-seven and eight-by-ten plastic cards with black-and-white contrasting images on them and a black, white, and red rattle for Aleah's visual stimulation. We placed the cards and rattle in her crib and took turns holding her. David sang a prayer. We celebrated every movement, every blink. I touched every finger, every toe, and traced her tiny ears. And even though breastfeeding hurt at first, I didn't mind. I had read enough to know that learning the art of breastfeeding is a process for both mother and child and had full faith we'd both catch on.

When we returned home the next day, David had set up the portable crib we had received as a gift in the living room. Inside the crib, leaning against the walls were additional homemade posters that David had made for Aleah. Black and white and red shapes against the white poster board would stimulate her brain and prevent boredom, David said. He carried Aleah throughout the house pointing out paintings and objects, explaining to her what everything was. He held Aleah and read to her. He sang prayers. Within months, David would place her in a carrier and perform his tai chi exercises with her on his back.

Our neighbor provided us with a scale, and of course every day we weighed Aleah. I wanted to make sure she was getting enough of my milk. I couldn't see how much or how little Aleah was drinking. I loved that I was not mixing and heating formula or cleaning bottles. I loved how easy it was for her to latch on, and even though I couldn't witness the exact amount of milk she was taking in, I moved the levers on the scale and celebrated each ounce, each pound she gained. I also treasured the support of La Leche League on those days that I felt as if my sole purpose in life had become to provide milk for Aleah yet she was frustrated because she wanted more than was available. She fussed, and I felt discouraged until another more experienced mom shared that my milk supply would build up the more she suckled during her growth periods. I persevered, and after a day or so of some frustration, we moved on to the next day feeling more content.

David and I decided to place Aleah's crib in our room during the first few months of her life. Before long Aleah remained in our bed for and after her middle-of-the-night feeding. In many countries, this is normal behavior. I have sisters-in-law from the Philippines who slept in their parents' beds during their infancy and toddlerhood. They continued this practice with their own children and received criticism from their American friends and relatives. David and I believe in diversity, believe in allowing couples the dignity of making their own choices. Our choice to open our bedroom and bed to our children was given full consideration. I knew I needed a good night's sleep to function well in all of my various roles. Getting up to breastfeed would make it hard to return to sleep. Allowing our daughter to just latch on as needed would enable us to sleep through the nighttime feedings. We also believed the security our children felt in being close to us was a good thing. David, a counselor in the school system, had overheard parents complaining when their preteens and teens started acting and becoming so independent of them, yet he observed that we often push them in their infancy and toddler days to become independent and not need us. They are young for such a brief time, and dependency on us for security and physical proximity is healthy for the development of their brains and human emotions.

Parenting 101

One afternoon while attending for the first time a playgroup held at a local church, I froze when Aleah, at the ripe age of one, reached out her tiny hand and grabbed a stuffed animal from another toddler. The other toddler's mom, whose name I did not yet know, watched and waited for me to do something. I gathered what little sense I had and explained to Aleah that the puppy dog didn't belong to her and we had to return the animal. Aleah pulled the dog to her chest and pouted. I managed to free the dog from her grip and return it to the little girl, who was almost in tears. Aleah cried. I tried to distract her with some of our own toys, but her bottom lip continued to tremble and she turned on her heels and looked away from my efforts.

That night, still feeling anxious, I pulled a few parenting books off the shelf and consulted with David. Until then I had spent most of my time breastfeeding, changing diapers, singing songs, reading stories, taking hundreds of pictures of every little movement and every new sign of development—smiles, reaching for objects, turning over, crawling, standing, grabbing eyeglasses, eating Cheerios, swinging in the infant swing at the park. Now we were entering a new stage. Aleah was testing limits and asserting some independence. Less-than-perfect behaviors were emerging. We, as her parents, had to help her learn about boundaries and also provide her new opportunities to become more independent.

David thought I had handled the situation well at the church. "But Aleah was so unhappy," I responded.

"Well, yes," David said.

"Yes?"

"There will be plenty of times ahead when she doesn't like not getting her way. Just wait until she tells you that she hates you."

"David, how can you say that?"

"It's been known to happen, even before the teen years," David chuckled.

I had spent an entire year providing everything that Aleah needed and often what she wanted in such a full and complete way—physically, emotionally, and spiritually. I changed her diapers, bathed her, clothed her, breastfed her, hugged and cuddled her, kissed her every toe and finger and her little belly. I sang prayers to her, read her books, played classical music on the stereo. I got down on all fours and my belly to witness her first turns and attempts to lift her own body onto all fours. I crawled with her when she crawled. When she cried out, I was there in an instant. I didn't entertain delayed gratification that first year. I couldn't. She was a baby, and the rewards were so great—those giggles and smiles, the sighs, the raw joy she exuded.

But now I had to distinguish her needs from her wants. I had to teach her how to share, delay her gratification, and express herself with the vocabulary she was rapidly acquiring. I had to consider how I was going to discipline her when discipline was needed.

The word *discipline* still agitated me, even after a friend shared that the word discipline came from the word *disciple*. "You know, Kim—Christ and His disciples?" No matter how inspiring and logical the tips and ideas from David and my friends were, I still worried. I wanted a menu to follow. I wanted to know what to do in a given situation.

So I began my study of various parenting techniques by taking a class at Lake Michigan College, where I taught. I sat in the first row, notebook open, pen scrawling as many words that came out of the mouth of the instructor as I could manage. I read each assigned chapter and highlighted main ideas and examples. If I worked hard enough, I would master this challenge, I believed. I would graduate into sensible and masterful parenting. I would feel confident and assured of my progress. I sorted through dozens of phrases printed on varied shades of construction paper cut into circles and laminated. I loved those circles—orange, lavender, yellow, red, green. I could hold them, finger them like rosary beads, repeat the phrases written on them that couldn't be smudged or ripped away because they were laminated. I practiced saying these phrases and loved how positive they were. *You can use all of your senses when you explore. You can be powerful and ask for help at the same time. You can trust your intuition to help you decide what to do. You can do things as many times as you need to. You can think before you say yes and no and learn from your mistakes. I love who you are. You can learn what is pretend and what is real.* These phrases, designed for particular ages, provided me with concrete verbiage in those situations where I felt bewildered or stuck. There were even affirmations for adults. I loved many of the phrases directed at me: *Through the years you can expand your commitments to your own growth, to your family, your friends, your community, and to all humankind. You can be responsible for your contributions to each of your commitments. You can be uniquely yourself and honor the uniqueness of others. Your needs are important.* This was all part of building self-esteem, definitely a family affair.

I was on a mission to break the cycle of violence. Sometimes I wish that I could go back to myself in that time and say, "Relax, Kim. Relax some.

You don't have to be so driven. Breathe a little. Notice the moment you are missing because of the ultra-intensity of living out your intentions. You might try letting God in."

I was more than committed. I studied my notes, reread the highlighted portions of the book, which was like reading the entire book because every sentence seemed important, and I also studied my husband. David's professional skills as an educator and elementary school counselor served our family well. Those skills on top of years of child-rearing in his first marriage gave him an advantage in the area of parenting, and I didn't mind. I watched and learned.

I admired how David taught Aleah manners. When she could sit in the high chair and began eating Cheerios and baby food, he would offer a spoonful and say the words he wanted her to learn. "May I please have some peaches," he would say while giving her a spoonful of peaches, and then "Thank you for the peaches." After doing this, he would then nudge Aleah to say "Please," and she would follow with a "fank ooohh, Daddy."

David handled the challenges of bedtime and sharing just as well. After Aleah's bath, he asked, "Do you want me to read you one or two stories before I turn off the light?" Wasn't that clever? And it worked. Aleah went to bed having had some say in the matter: two stories. He employed the same tactics of offering choices when it came to the big challenge of sharing. When we hosted play dates at our house, David asked Aleah before our guests arrived what toys she didn't want to share and which ones were OK to share, again giving her a sense of power and control. I envied the ease with which David parented.

Surrendering

I sat at the dining room table and gazed out the window at the view. Visible layers of snow coated the various tree limbs and branches. Flurries blew in the arctic air. Golden leaves still clung to the tree in front of the house. I felt soothed by the pounding of drums accented by bird and flute calls. "Spiritlands," by John Huling, played on the CD player. I opened a spiral notebook and felt pleased to face an empty page. During the past couple of months, I resented the pace and the dozens of other activities taking me away from the empty page. Sometimes I wondered if I would ever find time to write again, but I only had to look at the filled crate in my closet. I was writing, not as much as when I was single, and not as much as before children, but I had filled dozens of spiral notebooks with hundreds and hundreds of pages of soul work.

"Mommy, Mommy," Aleah called from her room. She knew not to leave her room. Quiet time was sacred and mandatory. Though Aleah had outgrown her naps, I had not outgrown the need for stillness, a break, those moments when I was more than Aleah's mom.

"Mo-o-o-mmm-y," Aleah tried again.

"What is it, Sweetheart?" I asked, caving in. I couldn't hear her response above the flutes and other instruments. I had a hunch she just wanted to hear my voice. I reminded her that quiet time was over when the timer went off.

"OK, Mummy," she responded.

I retrieved from the bookshelf *The Blue Jay's Dance*, by Louise Erdrich. I reread the first few pages. I pondered her idea that one's "fat ambitions fall into a dreamlike before" when we experience the humbling and all-consuming nature of parenting. My ambitions included sending my writing out more consistently to try to get published in order to avoid the perish part of the "publish or perish" phenomenon pressuring those of us in academia. But I seldom sent my work out. My more important goal of parenting with intention, parenting without resorting to violence, learning how to interact with my spouse in ways I hadn't seen in my family of origin, required most of my energy, if not all of it.

Even that particular day, before Aleah's nap, I felt edgy and tired, having juggled housecleaning with playing Candy Land, reading stories, and pulling out the crayons. Her repeated two-year-old's *no* got to me. The frustrated and angry tone of my own voice let Aleah know she needed to go potty and wash her hands before the nap. "Now, Aleah," I said with more sternness than she was used to.

"Don't talk at me, Mommy," she responded.

The *at* caught my attention. I admired her assertiveness. I *was* talking *at* her. I knew from the "Love and Logic" parenting class that I could have offered some choices. "Aleah, do you want me to help you onto the potty, or do you want to do it yourself?" "Aleah, do you want to go potty before a story or after?" But, tired from the morning and new at developing this parenting habit, I found myself talking *at* my child. And even at the age of two, she sensed her loss of budding independence.

I looked at the empty page and began writing:

I need to write about some jealousy I've been experiencing. I'm struggling to accept that my dreams of accomplishing more as a writer are just that—dreams during these days of mothering a toddler and soon another infant. But despite my efforts to accept my current reality, I feel pangs of envy over a new professor's accomplishments. She is a young talented woman just out of graduate school, publishing and receiving awards. Single, childless, she has time to write. I know envy as a ridiculous, fruitless feeling, yet it hits me, and has throughout the years. I wouldn't want to trade places with my colleague. But I sure wouldn't mind being regarded as she is—the talented writer receiving recognition for her creative work. I think this desire comes from the little girl inside who didn't get enough of the right kind of attention, who is hungering for acknowledgment. I must let that part of me know how much she is worth just living and surviving each day in health. I don't need the Pulitzer for her to be special.

I do, however, hope to publish my work. I hope my work can serve humanity by sharing the message of survival and healing in times when for many it seems impossible. I hope to publish because I need to in order to progress as a college instructor, and I love teaching. Now I'm content with part-time teaching because I want to mother my young ones as fully and capably as I can. These early years are crucial. My presence, my nurturing, and my guiding are necessary for the development of these souls I am so blessed to have in my life. While some of my friends handle the challenge of juggling mothering and their full-time careers, I find that I need additional time for my own healing process.

On that particular day and for the months and immediate years ahead, I felt the pressing need to pay more attention to parenting than to writing and professional goals. Whenever my time to die might come, I wanted to face God knowing that I put forth my best effort in breaking the cycle of violence. So, while I made time to write, I didn't actively pursue the development of my career. That day, in front of me lay a tipped-over plastic yellow shopping cart, plastic people who belonged to a corresponding yellow school bus somewhere else in the house, Legos, a Fisher-Price barn, and a *Love and Logic* parenting book. It all represented an environment I was trying to create for the soul of my daughter to flourish and discover itself.

Now another baby was on the way. I had agonized for over a year about whether or not to try again because juggling the various components of my life—mothering, teaching, writing, Bahá'í community life, maintaining our home, and trying to take care of myself through daily prayer and meditation and physical exercise—was harder than I had anticipated. Another baby? I had questioned. How could I serve another life? I had no energy. My mind couldn't even grasp all the activities we engaged in on a daily, weekly, and monthly basis. When I learned that I was pregnant, however, I was thrilled, and within seven weeks of learning about this pregnancy I had pulled out the packed-away maternity clothes because I was already showing.

The buzzer sounded. Quiet time was over, and Aleah toddled into the living room carrying Barney to the sofa, needing a hug and wanting to sit in my lap before playing. Those wonderful moments of connection and warmth and relationship-building beat jotting down addresses from *Writer's Market* and licking stamps.

The winter subsided, and the warmer days of late March and April were upon us. By mid-April the additional thirty-five pounds I had gained exposed the old injury to my spine. Both the pain of that injury and the baby's position involving my sciatic nerve exhausted me. I could barely walk and felt very discouraged by my lack of energy. I worried that I wouldn't have the stamina to handle a new baby. I didn't want our new infant to sense my tiredness and my blues. Even though I had been striving to replace negative thinking with positive thoughts and optimism, I couldn't fake a positive attitude. I found it impossible to repeat mantras like "I have plenty of time and energy. I have all the support I need. I am joyous." The doctor's advice was bedrest.

During this time I learned to relax some of my high parenting standards and practice the virtue of flexibility. Aleah went to childcare even though I was not working. When she returned from childcare, she spent more time watching videos and PBS than I spent reading her stories. I waved good-bye as David took her out in the backyard to play. I put Aleah to bed earlier than usual and let her listen to stories on tape. I was cranky, and everyone survived my crankiness. Aleah was still curious, spontaneous, and creative. I wasn't damaging her as I feared I could do by making any mistake in the parenting process. I had to get over this notion, a notion embedded in my mind as a result of my commitment to do whatever it took to break the cycle of violence. That worthy commitment lacked balance because of my leanings toward perfectionism. I would learn, as I imagine most parents who also struggle with perfectionism learn, to *let go* of the rigid standards such tendencies create. The focus, the intention to break the cycle of violence no matter what it takes, while worthy and noble, could lead me right into the very perfectionism I was trying to avoid. I could be a drill sergeant with my goals. I knew how to point the finger and reprimand myself for every failure. I knew how to make myself feel unworthy and reprehensible. The last thing I needed was more punishment, more abuse. I needed to *let go and let God* work through me. I needed to relax with the intention and realize I was a work in progress, just like everyone else. I needed to breathe and sit. I needed to *be*. Bahá'u'lláh wrote that the hidden secret is the "letters *b* and *e* joined and knit together." I loved that passage. My soul sensed the release from my own tendencies when I pondered and asked God to help me practice that particular teaching.

At about 2:00 a.m. on the morning of May 7, 1996, I slipped out of bed because I couldn't sleep. I went into the living room and flipped through a magazine and then fell asleep on the sofa. At about 4:00 a.m., my water broke. I raced to the bathroom thinking I had had an accident and then realized this was no accident. I woke David and we called the doctor. Since my first labor had lasted about fourteen hours, I told the doctor I would remain at home until my contractions progressed. I didn't feel like hanging around a hospital room for that long. David, however, asked me to reconsider. He wanted to make sure both the baby and I were OK and felt that it would be better to have monitors gauging our progress. I agreed, and if we hadn't left for the hospital then I might have delivered our second daughter in the living room or the car. My labor was a swift two hours. By the time we arrived at the hospital I had dilated to eight centimeters. "Do you think the baby will be born by lunch?" I asked the nurse. "Honey, this baby will be born before breakfast," the nurse responded. Within an hour Anisa Gabrielle Douglas weighed in at eight pounds and three ounces.

There were so many levels to my joy. I felt thrilled that I had experienced a labor and delivery without being induced and without drugs to relieve the pain. I felt blessed to have another daughter, a sister for Aleah and Jenai. I felt grateful that I had not allowed my own mind, my own sense of limitations, my own rigid will to prevent me from experiencing the birth of another child. I could have continued thinking, "There is no time, there is no energy, there is no space, there is not enough money." I could have battled against the idea of expanding our family and bringing forth another soul. I could have let my own mind imprison me. I might never have known the pure joy I felt holding and welcoming Anisa into our lives.

I will always remember when Aleah came to meet her new sister. David sat her down on a chair and placed the baby in her arms, remaining right there for support. "There's your sister. There she is."

Aleah looked down at the infant in her lap, her eyes widening, her mouth dropping open. This sister was no doll. This sister blinked, cooed, curled her tiny fingers around Aleah's own small fingers. This sister breathed and wiggled. We photographed Aleah's expressions of surprise and amazement as she held Anisa, and we used one of the pictures for the birth announcement.

While those early moments were tender and filled with love, Aleah would also experience the challenge of a new sister who cried and took attention away from her. This sister's presence in the upcoming weeks, months, and years would challenge her to realize she now shared the small universe of her home with another child who also had needs, wants, moods, and a strong will.

I would experience a similar challenge, the ongoing challenge of setting the notebook and pen aside to tend to our new daughter. Sometimes I struggled with the frustration of having to do so, not always realizing that I was engaged in soul work of a different order, of taking myself away from centerstage, of experiencing the humbling and awesome moments of having another soul depend on me to have its needs met, of creating the fodder that would expand me and affect the writing I would get to in the unknown days ahead. Sometimes I didn't realize that because I was so focused on enduring or surviving a particular moment of stress. But in other moments, when I was practicing that hidden secret, the letters *b* and *e* knit together, I could perceive in that wonderful detached state that we were a growing family—growing in size and evolving in spirit. We would live into the unknown, taking one day at a time, sometimes one moment at a time. We would learn from one another, develop virtues because of one another, and discover both the pain and the beauty of what it is to love.

Nurture and Revise

About seven months after the birth of Anisa, I signed up for another parenting class. Both of the girls had tantrums that distressed and confounded me. I didn't know what to do. What if they hurt themselves? How was I going to quiet them down? I just wanted peace. Wasn't that my dream, a peaceful family? Where were those Hawaiian vacations I had fantasized about with the white sandy beaches and my Prince Charming of a husband with his arm around my slim, bikini-clad body, the two children all smiles and bonneted? I knew from all those college classes that I, too, had been influenced by Hollywood, the media, and the unrealistic images that served to make so many of us feel inadequate. That little version of walking Hawaiian beaches, however, seemed rather desirable in those moments when I stood looking at my two children, feeling clueless about how to proceed.

In the past I had given the girls what they wanted to quiet them down. This reinforced negative behavior. They were learning that they could scream and cry and receive what they wanted. Anisa was just a baby, so I figured that she was carrying on because of some need. She was too little to be manipulative. Aleah was older, so I tried to talk her out of screaming. Of course that didn't work because I was trying to reason with her when she was in a state of pure emotion. What to do? I didn't want to scream but sometimes found myself raising my voice, sometimes shouting, and sometimes heading in the awful direction of what felt like my past—screaming. Most of the time, I managed to stop myself, or David intervened. Sometimes I took time out and walked next door and sat on my neighbor's lawn chair to calm down. She welcomed me. A mother of three, she knew about feeling driven to the edge.

I hoped that the nurturing program would help me figure out how to deal with tantrums. The program introduced me to the technique of ignoring not the child but the undesirable behavior. "Pay attention to what you want, ignore what you don't" was one of the slogans of the program, followed by an entire class on the careful steps of implementing and following this technique. Thrilled to have an actual strategy, I decided to try it out. I could see that when I responded to Aleah's outbursts, she accomplished her goal, which was to receive my full attention. She then proceeded to try to convince me to feed her a cookie or a lollipop or to turn on music. If I didn't, she turned up the volume and screeched. To turn this behavior around as directed in class, I informed Aleah ahead of time during a more peaceful moment that I would no longer pay attention to tantrums. Instead, I would be more than happy to help her through a difficulty when she used big-girl words to communicate.

Of course Aleah tested that promise within the day. She woke up that afternoon from a brief nap. "Mommy, Mommy, get me right now!" she howled.

Though I wanted to repeat my warning that I was going to ignore her, I didn't. I continued reading a story to Anisa, who of course looked up, disturbed by Aleah's cries. I took Anisa downstairs, away from the clamor. Every now and then I climbed a few stairs. Aleah was still screaming and sobbing. A part of me wanted to go and comfort her, but I resisted the tendency. Another part of me wanted to try to reason with Aleah, but I had to remind myself that she was beyond reason at the moment and when I had tried to engage her during these kinds of moments in the past, I had become so frustrated that I lost my sense of rationale. I remained in the basement with Anisa and put on a musical video to shut out Aleah's screams.

About an hour later, Aleah stood at the top of the stairs and said, "Mommy, I want you to come here." I climbed the steps to see my red-faced, puffy-eyed daughter with tears and snot all over her face, saying, "Will you hold me please?"

"Absolutely, I am so happy to hold you. And I am so proud of you for deciding to use words to tell me what you want." I climbed the steps and picked up my eager daughter, and we returned downstairs to sit on the sofa for hugs and some quiet recovery time. I praised Aleah again for her budding maturity and her decision to use words.

The very next day, right after Aleah's nap, another tantrum occurred. It lasted only twenty minutes—still very long in my estimation—but it was shorter than the tantrum of the day before, convincing me of the power of this technique. Instead of screaming, Aleah used words and asked me to come to her. I repeated my praises, and we enjoyed hugs and cuddling on the rocking chair while Anisa napped through both the storm and its quiet aftermath. The next day, I witnessed Aleah's evolving self-control. Again, after her nap she came out into the living room and started to scream but caught herself and said, "Will you hold me, Mommy?"

"Absolutely, I would love to hold my big girl who uses words to get what she wants." Aleah smiled, owning her accomplishment, and then climbed into my lap.

We still experienced some of Aleah's tantrums after that, but they didn't occur daily and they didn't last more than a few minutes.

Anisa's temper tantrums startled me even more. By the time she was thirteen months, she threw herself on the floor, kicked her legs, flung her arms, and screeched. Her strong will and frolicking temper overwhelmed me. I didn't remember Aleah showing that much resistance to me or as much focus on doing precisely what she wanted at that age. Once, when I carried Anisa out of the bathroom as she headed for the open toilet to swirl her fists in that compelling bowl of water, she kicked her feet against me and howled. I set her down on the floor and let her have it out there. She bellowed and flopped about like a creature out of its habitat.

I grappled for solutions, but the emotional impact sometimes voided any sense of rationale. I couldn't stand the screaming. Screaming increased my anxiety. To do anything, just anything to stop the screaming was what I wanted as a child, and that same inclination flared up in me when the girls screamed. I reminded myself that giving the girls what they wanted to appease their tempers was not the way to go. It felt just as wrong to raise my voice or shout at them. I didn't want my girls to someday draw posters of themselves that looked anything like the one I had drawn of myself in one of the Nurturing Program classes.

During that particular class each participant was given a large piece of poster board. We were to draw an outline of our own bodies and then draw all the places in color where we had received nurturing touches, and then place gray x's where we had been hurt or violated in some way. The image I drew contained dozens and dozens of x's reflecting the numerous broken bones, the emotional wounds, and the chaos of my childhood. Yes, I had bright colors reflecting the impact of my Grandpa Max and Grandma Esther, of my mom's efforts to compensate for the pain, and of Aunt Lorel's artistic influence. But the gray x's dominated.

"What about your own children?" Pat Crum, the instructor who has since become a friend, asked. "What would their posters look like, their images, their wounds?" We were asked to imagine what our children would draw, what they would share. This was one of many activities that increased our levels of empathy. Our children were human beings, souls, and not our possessions to toss around or mistreat. I knew from this class and from scripture that our children were a sacred trust and that my work as a parent was more important than any other task. I'd much rather imagine my children's posters x-free, though I knew I would inflict some x's because I'm human and a work-in-progress. But with God's help, my own efforts, and grace, I wanted to imagine colorful posters with aqua, lavender, and rose prevailing over however many gray x's my own children might someday draw.

I proceeded to try to figure out how to ignore with empathy the behaviors I didn't like. And I had to do so with my youngest daughter, who still didn't possess the tool of language. She was just leaving babyhood.

I knew better than to ignore a baby. Crying is a means of expression for a baby. Ignoring her would be comparable to abuse, I thought.

At Anisa's one-year checkup, Dr. Johnson asked if I had any concerns.

"Oh, yes, I do. There's a lot of screaming and tantruming, and she is only a baby," I said, sighing and looking down at my mellow child, whose big brown eyes roamed the room, scrutinizing the doctor. "Am I doing something wrong?" I asked, still quick to believe that I was inadequate in some way, that I was not meeting some of her basic needs.

"What do you do when she tantrums?" Dr. Johnson asked.

"What do I do?" I repeated, trying to still my mind, to remember when so much chaos could ensue in a day. "I sometimes try to explain to her what's going on. I try to stay calm and hope that I am conveying through my tone that everything is going to be OK. And, well, yesterday, I just walked out of the room. I didn't know what to do and I felt agitated. I didn't want to do something I'd regret, so I left to collect myself."

Dr. Johnson went on to elaborate on the tool of ignoring, affirming what I had learned through the nurturing program. "We don't want our children to get the idea that this is how they can get attention or get what they want. If we pay attention, we'll get more of the undesirable behavior."

"But she's so young. I do this with Aleah. She's older."

"Anisa is smart. She's leaving babyhood. Of course you don't want to ignore cries that have to do with getting her needs met. If she's been fed, diapered, rested, and loved and cared for, and if her cries seem more about tantruming, you can walk away without harming her."

I explained to Dr. Johnson that I was striving not to repeat the abusive behaviors I had experienced in childhood and that I didn't want to harm my children. She knew about my fears of harming them, so I felt relieved by her instructions.

Yet I returned home and Anisa's cries as I changed her diaper evoked both an emotional and physical reaction in me. My chest tightened, and my breath became shallow. As she squirmed and wriggled out of my grip, I pulled her back, held her down, and said, "I know you don't like to have your diaper changed, but I am putting a clean diaper on you and then you may crawl." When I finished, she stopped crying and crawled to her toys. I sat there, staring at the heavy, heavy thick green and swirling leaves outside the window. I felt dizzy with inadequacy and uncertainty.

I couldn't ignore her while changing a filled diaper. I couldn't walk away this time. Was my reaction OK? *Of course,* I told myself. I hadn't hit her. I hadn't shouted. But was I too firm when I held her down? Had I used too much strength? Was I acting like my father?

What tormented me was the worry that I would pass on some of the behaviors that didn't just hurt me but wounded my very soul. I held my squirming baby down, though there had been a few times in the past when I had grabbed Aleah and carried her to time-out. Aleah screamed, "You're hurting my arms! You grabbed me!" I was not just holding her, not just carrying her to time-out, but grabbing her with my own anger at her fury. I learned to stop carrying Aleah to time-out and to let her go to her time-out chair by herself. This was an important change because I was not emotionless during major outbursts. I, too, felt frustrated or angry. I made the decision that day not to touch my children during those emotion-filled moments. Sometimes I even gave myself time-out and announced that decision to them. I used the time to restore myself to equilibrium. We all began to learn that time-out was not a punishment but a tool to center and restore ourselves to balance.

One year, through luck or creativity, I fell upon the method of revision. I had often taught my students that revising their papers allowed them to reexamine the possibilities of their ideas, to deepen them, to expand and explore and question. One day I revised a moment of inadequate, rather terrible parenting. Although I had tried to handle a tough moment through deep breathing, counting to ten, and walking into another room, I still fell short of handling a situation well. "Time-out!" I had shouted, louder than I would have in a rational and centered moment. That increase in volume silenced us all. A vibration hung in the air in that stunning aftermath. What was going on? The girls were fighting over some prized object. *Mine. You never share. I don't have to. I always share. No you don't.* And I had my agenda. I wanted peace. I wanted absolutely no fighting. I wanted no raised voices. "That's one," I said in a neutral voice. *No. Mine. I don't have to. You can't make me.* "That's two," I said in that same neutral voice, hoping they would respond, hoping I wouldn't need to say, "That's three, time-out." The girls persisted.

What happened?

What happened in me that I didn't even say, "That's three, time-out," in a moderate tone, the tone I wanted to model to them? What made me scream "Time-out!"

The girls stopped their arguing. They looked at me as if I were crazed. They headed to their separate chairs, Aleah whispering, "She needs time-out."

Yes, I was the one needing time-out. I sat down trembling because of my voice, my loss of control, my not handling a common situation that millions of parents worldwide face every day with their children—a situation I believed I could handle. I had watched the how-to video, watched other parents, and believed I could utilize this tool. It was so simple that it was almost brainless.

But I had allowed the girls' arguing to get to me. I had not remained detached and calm. I felt angry. I was tired of all this nonsense. Rather than recognizing this and giving myself some time to regroup, I had hollered.

"She needs time-out," my daughters were whispering to themselves. They were right.

The next challenge, after realizing I had not used what I regarded as a simple tool, was to forgive myself, to pick myself up, shrug, take another step, and move on. But I didn't do that, at least not right away. Instead, I went down that other familiar and oppressive road of beating myself up with an internal barrage of negative thoughts: *terrible mother, couldn't do what most parents could do, David's the better parent, hopeless.* The negativity lasted awhile, but when I realized what I was doing, I stopped myself.

After pulling myself together, I apologized to my daughters and asked if I could redo that moment. "Let's pretend you two are still fighting."

They smiled at me when I said that because they had moved beyond their squabbling.

"Let's pretend I've already said, 'That's two.'"

They nodded and waited.

"OK, you two are each still insisting that the Polly Pocket with brown hair is your Polly Pocket." I paused and let silence fill the room for a minute. I whispered to myself so they could hear, "I guess the girls are not going to stop fighting, too bad." Then I raised my voice so the volume was moderate but loud enough to be heard in another room.

"That's three, girls. Time-out."

The girls looked at me.

"Well, let's pretend. We're redoing this," I added.

"OK, Mommy," Anisa said and headed over to the chair by the window.

"Drats," Aleah said. "I hate time-out." She headed over to the stairwell and sat down.

I set the timer for four minutes, and we all waited until the buzzer sounded. Then I announced, "OK, time in."

Both girls came over to me.

"Well, what do you think? Was that better?"

"Much," Aleah said.

Anisa nodded and smiled. "I liked that way better."

"I'm sorry that I didn't do time-out better the first time. Please forgive me."

"We forgive you, Mommy," Anisa said and hugged me.

"It's OK, Mom," Aleah said, also hugging me.

"Now, I have a question. How could you two have handled your problem of not sharing without yelling at each other?" I wanted to ask that question because I didn't want the girls to think that the focus on my mistake would erase their mistakes.

"We could have shared," Aleah said.

"Why was that so hard?" I asked.

"Because that Polly Pocket is mine," Anisa said. "Aleah always takes my things."

"I do not," Aleah said.

"Yes you do."

"Well, I share my things with you."

"Sounds like this is a real problem area. Sometimes I have put toys that you can't share in time-out."

"I hate that, Mom," Aleah said.

"What are some other options?" I asked.

"We could set the timer. Aleah could have Polly for five minutes, and then I could have it for five."

"That sounds good. Any other choices?"

"Well, I could have let Anisa have the doll first, since it's her doll."

We went on for a few minutes sharing ideas, and I was happy that we were able to explore options, express our apologies, and move forward, all having learned something. This process was important for both the girls and for me, as it demonstrated that we were all a *work-in-progress*. I would never be a perfect parent. My children would never be perfect children. We were evolving, and in that evolution we would make numerous mistakes. We needed practices to help us deal with and learn from our mistakes and choices.

I am humbled each and every day when I fall short in modeling the behaviors I'm trying to teach my children. I know I am making progress, though, when instead of beating myself up for my mistakes, I make amends and either ask to redo a moment or work out an alternative approach, knowing that I will have another chance to practice better parenting. I was learning that living my life was all about showing up for the rehearsals. My producers, directors, stage managers, and all those involved in helping me learn how to optimize that performance were the sacred texts of the world's great religions, my teachers, and my family and friends who were close enough to me to offer honest and constructive feedback.

Tatiana

When I entered Joann's kitchen to meet her newly adopted three-year-old daughter, Tatiana dove under the kitchen table, where she froze and stared at the grain of the hardwood floor. A few other families lingered in the kitchen. Others had moved out onto the deck and backyard. We had all come to meet Tatiana and celebrate her arrival, but we also knew from Joann and her husband, Mark, that Tatiana's transition from a Russian orphanage to their home had been excruciating.

Joann and I ran together several mornings a week. During those runs Joann had shared with me that she was pained to witness some of her new daughter's behavior. When Joann changed Tatiana's diapers, she shrieked and screamed for up to an hour afterward. She made no eye contact with anyone in her new home. At meals she stuffed herself as if she might not receive any food again for weeks. For days she held in her bowel movements. When she at last sat and grunted and pushed out her own waste, she screamed like a woman in labor. The doorbell, the phone, and guests in particular terrified her so much that she often dove under the kitchen table.

The family doctor verified what Joann had suspected. Tatiana had experienced repeated sexual abuse, and serious internal damage had been done. This information helped Joann and Mark make sense of Tatiana's bizarre behavior and difficulties connecting with her new family members. Joann continued to face enormous challenges on a daily basis and began to doubt that Tatiana was capable of bonding in any meaningful way.

After remaining under the kitchen table for over half an hour, Tatiana joined the rest of us in the backyard. Mark stood at the grill flipping burgers. Joann chatted with Amy, Todd, and Barb. Several of the children peddled in paddle boats and floated on rafts on the pond. David and I stood knee-deep in the water, keeping an eye on Aleah and Anisa as they paddled around. Tatiana stepped into the water and moved toward us. I looked at her and offered a smile—a mistake. She stomped out of the water and stood glaring. Feeling guilty for the trespass I didn't intend, I turned my gaze toward the willow trees and the shimmering pond reflecting the sun just beginning to lower into the western horizon.

Aleah and Anisa tired of the water and guided us back to the sand, where we plopped down and pulled out the buckets, muffin tins, and other sand molds in order to make goodies for the bakery Aleah thought we should create.

Within moments Tatiana, forgetting herself, joined in. She patted the damp sand into the molds and flipped over the variety of forms. "Star," she said and smiled.

I remained cautious and held in my enthusiasm.

Tatiana continued making dozens of cookies and then pointed to one and said, "eat."

I pretended to gobble up the star-shaped delight, licked my lips, and said, "Yummy."

She giggled and offered me another one and another, laughing each time I made a slurping sound.

Anisa, jealous of the interaction, tugged at my hand and pointed to the trampoline. "Jump," she ordered. "I want to jump."

"Sure," I said, hopping up and heading toward the trampoline, Anisa's small hand in mine.

A few minutes later Tatiana climbed on and grabbed my hand. Our bodies sprung skyward. "We're flying! We're flying!" Anisa shouted.

Aleah climbed on and wanted to play "Ring around the Rosie." We all joined hands and shuffled around and around, singing. Then we collapsed into giggles. Though Tatiana wouldn't make eye contact, her joining us thrilled me. Joann winked at me from across the way, and Mark shook his head in disbelief.

At dinner we sat at one of four picnic tables. Tatiana sat on one side of me, Anisa on the other. Anisa tapped my shoulder, covered her eyes with her palms, and then spread her fingers, creating Vs for her eyes to peer through. "Peek-a-boo," she blurted out with a smile. I imitated her and when I spread my fingers into Vs, pecked her with a kiss and poked her in the tummy. She giggled. Tatiana tapped my arm and covered her eyes. She wanted to play. To prevent Anisa from having another attack of jealousy, I said to her, let's play peek-a-boo with Tatiana. She nodded and placed her hands up to her eyes, spread her fingers apart and chanted peek-a-boo. Tatiana and I giggled and followed the gestures. Enjoying the pleasure of the moment, I pecked Tatiana with a kiss. She screamed and threw herself onto the cement. I closed my eyes and shook my head. Darn. How could I have so easily forgotten? If I had been thinking, I never would have kissed Tatiana. She was willing to hold my hand, willing to play bakery, "Ring around the Rosie," and peek-a-boo when she initiated the gesture or activities. The kiss was a violation and no doubt triggered a memory of the abuse.

I knew about such triggers and still struggled with them myself. There had been times when I spotted one of David's socks on the floor and felt nervous and fearful. Who would have thought a simple sock could cause anxiety like that? I would ask my therapist. She would encourage me to remember what had occurred in the past to evoke that reaction. That sock took me back to my father's socks, socks worn over the foot that kicked me. "I hate socks," I had cried to my therapist. "I hate them."

Socks represented bruises and broken collarbones. Socks represented my very sick father.

No matter how I tried, my reactions to certain objects, expressions, or moments caught me off guard and canceled out all efforts to reason with myself. When David looked concerned or angry, I worried that I had done something wrong again, something that could cause him to shout or hit me, though he had never shouted or hit me. I would point out to myself that every single human being on occasion looks concerned, upset, or angry. This logic didn't relieve me either. Then I would spiral further into a negative self-evaluation. What was wrong with me that I couldn't just grow up and get over the trauma? Why hadn't I graduated from having these kinds of reactions after all the years of therapy? Would the effects of the abuse ever end?

Watching Tatiana helped me to better understand and to exercise some patience with myself. When I reacted to a situation with more emotion than the situation called for, I felt disappointed in myself and guilty. I tired of trying to analyze or empathize with my own outbursts and rages. I was embarrassed by these outbursts and sometimes feared that I would lose family and friends when the wounded part of me showed up. Tatiana was an actual child who embodied the effects of ongoing abuse. I felt for her—compassion, concern, and sadness. I also hoped that she would heal and enjoy her childhood. Through Joann and Mark's incredible determination, boundless love, and wisdom in seeking professional help, Tatiana began to recover from her early childhood horrors. Couldn't I offer myself the same care and concern?

One afternoon, a few weeks after our visit to meet Tatiana, I shared a story in Aleah's second-grade class about Merrick Johnson, a remarkable young girl residing in Alaska. Merrick was the youngest person ever to climb Mount McKinley. She was only twelve years old when she accomplished that feat. A few years before reaching her goal, she asked her mom if she would support her in the effort. Merrick's mom not only agreed to support her but joined her. Together they trained for a couple of years, and during their practice and their eventual journey up those daunting peaks, they both relied on the mantra "I can do it, I can do it, I am doing it." The day I shared that story in the second grade classroom, I had the children repeat the words. They chanted with glee. Anisa, too, used that chant that same year when at the age of three she faced the challenge of peddling uphill on her new bike sporting training wheels. She begged me to hold the handlebars and pull her up the hill. Instead, I reminded her of Merrick's special words, words we could use to help us along. Those words enabled Anisa to pedal to the top of the hill.

I thought of Joann and her heroic efforts to bond with Tatiana and help her heal. She and Tatiana were like Mrs. Johnson and Merrick preparing to climb Mount McKinley. Ongoing effort was required. Knowing the terrain that lay ahead would be helpful in meeting the challenges. So many virtues were required to continue on that mutual journey—love, commitment, determination, patience, and faith, to name only a few.

I needed a Joann inside me. I needed a Mrs. Johnson. I couldn't afford to pass off the ongoing work of healing the child I once was, the child who was still a part of me. I needed to mother her. I needed to sit as Joann sat with Tatiana, holding her even when she resisted, even when she kicked and screamed and shouted "no." I needed for the child inside me to learn like Tatiana did that she could be touched, cared for, and loved, and that the way she had been treated in the past would not be repeated.

Even though I had many friends who had engaged in what they referred to as "inner-child work," I had resisted that kind of engagement with myself. I made excuses—I didn't have time, I was too busy mothering, I had a career. I wasn't about to buy a doll, for goodness sake. My kids had dolls and stuffed animals. I was an adult, not a child. I was endeavoring to divorce myself from the child within me that I labeled wild and untamed, rather than wounded and in need of love.

Over the years I continued to admire Joann's faithful and loving determination to raise and help heal Tatiana. As a result of Joann's and Mark's dedicated parenting, Tatiana evolved from an emotionally broken toddler to a self-assured and confident teenager. Tatiana's presence in my life accessed the part of me that deserved a deeper respect, the part of me I had buried and had to resurrect to survive.

Knitting Needles

One night after dinner Aleah sat with yarn and needles in her lap and a booklet of directions in her hands.

"Would you like some help getting started?" I asked.

"Yep," she answered. "This is kind of frustrating."

"Let's see if I can remember how to do this," I said, taking the yarn. Let's wind the yarn into a ball. Aunt Mildred taught me to do that first. She said that it was much easier to knit if the yarn was in a ball."

"Really?" Aleah said. "Your aunt Mildred taught you a lot, didn't she?"

I nodded. I became close to my aunt Mildred during my freshman year in high school when she moved from Milwaukee to an area close to where we lived in Glenview. I suspected she knew about our problems either from Mom or other family members. She always welcomed me into her home any time of the day or night. A mother of four daughters, she was more than familiar with the peculiarities of raising girls.

Mildred taught me to sew and knit. I spent hours at her house working at the sewing machine making clothes for myself. This allowed me a way to avoid being at home. Dad didn't seem to mind if I spent time at a relative's house learning something constructive, something domestic.

I hadn't yet explained to Aleah just how much of a refuge Aunt Mildred's home was. She knew I had experienced challenges as a child, but she didn't yet know the extent of those challenges. It delighted her to know I had a special aunt who had taught me crafts that I was now teaching her.

After winding the yarn, I cast onto a knitting needle several stitches. I didn't even need to examine the directions. I knit the first row, the moves returning to me. I handed the needles to Aleah and showed her how to hold them, how to maneuver the needles around the yarn, and how to transfer the stitches to the alternate needle. "Don't worry if you make mistakes. That's part of the process," I explained.

Aleah bent her head toward the needles and yarn and began. She lost a few stitches, but I showed her how she could re-needle them. I was pleased that when she made mistakes or had a difficult moment, she was able to exercise patience and had the willingness to try again. Before long, she was knitting away, thrilled to learn a new activity.

Later that night, Anisa expressed her desire to also learn to knit. Aleah, within seconds, wailed that Anisa could not learn to knit, that she was too young, and that this was *her* activity. Anisa began to cry, and house war number zillion between the girls erupted. David explained to Aleah that Anisa deserved an opportunity to learn, just as Aleah had had that opportunity.

"No, Anisa always spoils everything!" Aleah screamed, stomping out of the room and up the stairs to her bedroom where her tirade persisted.

After Aleah quieted down I headed upstairs. "So, Aleah, what's going on?" I asked.

"If you want to know the truth," she said, "I don't want Anisa, who is in first grade, to pass me up. I'm in fourth grade. She's trying to read the same books I read. She's reading Nancy Drew books. And she's not supposed to get as smart as me. Then I'll just be a stupid nothing. There's a voice in my head that says 'Anisa's a genius and you're a stupid nothing.'"

O dear God, help me, I thought. The emotional intensity behind Aleah's words challenged me to listen and empathize. There had been occasions when such intensity triggered me, and there I was—on the same rollercoaster, taking the same plunges. This never resulted in a positive experience unless I realized somewhere along the ascents and descents that we were all plummeting. Then I gave myself a time-out to regain my equilibrium.

Sitting there with Aleah, I felt glad that my first thought was to ask God for help rather than thinking, "I can't stand this. I can't take this fighting and yelling. Those children are going to drive me nuts." I had had those thoughts before, and I had learned in some of my first parenting classes that blaming our children rather than taking responsibility for our own emotions was ineffective and would teach our children to do the same thing—blame others for their emotions rather than learn to regulate and control them.

Asking God for help with my emotions and how to respond to my children when I was in a difficult emotional place was a much better first step. It allowed me to pause and reflect on some of the various options and skills I had learned in parenting and Bahá'í classes. Besides, I was the adult. My children were children, though I all too often expected them to behave like little adults. David always said, "It takes eighteen, sometimes eighteen-plus years to socialize children."

I asked David to join Aleah and me so that Aleah could explain to her dad why she didn't want Anisa to learn to knit. Aleah, still animated and upset, repeated what she had shared with me. We listened. We sighed. Then David shared with Aleah that he tried to let her experience all the crafts and wonders of the world. He couldn't favor one child over the other, and as a parent he wanted to expose all of his children to the variety of crafts and activities available. Aleah grumbled some more and cried, still worried that Anisa might become smarter than she was.

I decided to try out a new emotional theory that I had just learned at Louhelen Bahá'í School at a conference on preventing domestic violence. Since domestic conflict occurs to some degree in every household, learning how to express ourselves and control our actions can keep conflict to a minimum. Keyvan Geula, a therapist from California, shared her ideas on controlling our actions by exploring and choosing alternative thoughts to guide our emotions, intentions, and behavior. Initially, all of us perceive people, places, things, and events through the senses. Then we have an initial thought about our perceptions. That thought influences our emotions. From there we develop some kind of intention and then act in a way to achieve that intention.

Since I had brought home an illustrated poster of this five-step process, I asked Aleah if we might apply this situation to the theory. She shrugged, not appearing too interested, but when I brought in the poster with the illustration of a five-pointed star, each point corresponding to a step, she leaned forward.

"So, Aleah, tell me if I have this right." I put my finger on the first point of the star, which was labeled *perception*. "You perceived or noticed that Anisa wanted to learn to knit just like you are learning." Then I pointed to the second point of the star, labeled *thought*. "Your first thought was 'Oh no, not again. My little sister always wants to do what I do and she is getting too smart and I'm going to be a nobody.'" Then I pointed to the third point, labeled *emotions/feelings*. "Because of this thought, you started feeling worried and upset." Then I pointed to the fourth point, *desire or intention*. "You wanted to prevent Anisa from touching the yarn." Then I pointed to the last point of the star, *action*. "You then screamed and demanded that Anisa not touch the yarn." I paused a moment. "Did I get this right, Aleah? Am I perceiving what happened accurately?"

"Maybe," she mumbled, looking away from the poster.

"I wonder what would happen if you came up with some other thoughts? All of us have thoughts about what we see or hear that aren't always positive, and those thoughts can upset us. But we can change our thoughts, and that can change our emotions and our behavior and can produce better results. How about it? Would you like to try out some other thoughts?"

Aleah looked at me as if I were crazy and insisted her only thought was that Anisa was ruining her life.

"You're not allowing any other possible thoughts in. May I offer you some?" I asked.

She looked at me with suspicion but nodded.

"How about when you see Anisa wanting to learn, thinking maybe that the whole family could do a project together. Maybe we could make a family quilt with each of us knitting a square."

Aleah looked up, pondering. "That might be OK," she started, "but we always start something, do it for a few days, and then stop."

"You're right about that," I said. David and I often found ourselves consumed with busyness—going to work, taking the girls to their various activities, facilitating homework and music practice, heading to Bahá'í and civic activities—and some nights just getting the girls to bed seemed like an expedition up Mount Everest. We needed to think about our obligations and activity level before suggesting ideas so that we modeled trustworthiness and the ability to follow through with plans.

Aleah seemed pleased that we owned up to this. Since the clock read 9:30, however, I suggested we say a few good-night prayers and continue our conversation the next day. Everyone agreed, but prayer time was filled with the leftover negativity. Both girls made mad eyes at each other. Anisa said her prayers, aiming for an academy award for prayer-saying, trying to win our favor. Aleah stuck out her tongue at Anisa and managed to string a few words together in her worst voice.

Tucking Aleah in, I suggested that maybe we should visit a counselor to get some ideas on how to deal with the jealousy issues.

"No, I don't want to see a counselor. I won't go," she said.

Surprised by her negative response, I asked why.

"I don't need one. I just don't want Anisa to knit." She was back on the same track.

I sighed. Maybe if I shared some of my own struggles it would help her out. "I've struggled with jealousy, too," I started.

"You have?"

I nodded.

"What happened?"

"When Uncle Mike announced he was getting married, I felt as if God had forgotten me. Here was my brother getting married, and he was younger than I was. I didn't even have a boyfriend."

"But now you have Daddy."

"That's true, but back then I didn't even know Daddy, and I didn't realize that I was jealous of something I didn't want."

"What do you mean?"

"Well, Uncle Mike didn't have a happy marriage. He was married and divorced and remarried and divorced, and hopefully now he's going to remain happily married."

We sat in silence for a moment.

"Aleah, both you and Anisa deserve to discover and develop your gifts and talents. Anisa might someday become an artist. You might become a doctor. Does that mean one of you is better than the other? No, not at all. If one of you gets married and the other doesn't, would that mean one of you has a better life? Not at all. As a family we need to support each other and help each other become who we are meant to be. We need to encourage each other to develop our unique gifts and talents."

Aleah insisted that she could support Anisa later, but she still didn't want her ever to knit.

Figuring I was making no headway, I kissed Aleah good-night and headed off to try to unwind. But my concern grew. Aleah was acting out her jealousy, and the intensity of her behavior had to be curbed. Screams, shoves, and relentless commentary were behaviors that would not serve her as she grew.

That night I started down that all too familiar road of blaming myself. Was the girls' negative behavior my fault? Were they demonstrating behavior I had modeled in my worst moments as a wife and mother? God knows how I had struggled and what progress I had made. Would I be paying for my mistakes forever by watching my children make the same ones?

I went to bed that night feeling disheartened. Maybe I needed to get back into counseling to figure out how to continue on this tough road of parenting. Maybe the girls needed counseling. I didn't know. I turned out the light and uttered a prayer or two and fell asleep.

The next morning Aleah announced to Anisa at breakfast that she had changed her mind and thought Anisa should learn to knit. "I had another thought yesterday, but I was too proud to admit it. I thought someday when I'm teaching my children to learn to knit, I could tell them this is something I used to do with my little sister."

"When can I learn? When can I learn?" Anisa asked, and the two girls started planning their knitting activities.

I took the time that morning to compliment Aleah. "I'm so glad you tried out another thought, Aleah. That's a positive step. I'm proud of you. Did the thought change how you feel?"

"I don't know," she said, smiling. Her smile was enough of an answer for me.

The relief I felt was enormous, and I realized that even though the results of trying out what I would refer to as the "Five-Star Method," were not instantaneous, change did occur. Here was one more method to add to my growing toolkit for those parenting moments when I felt bewildered and in need of help.

Uppercut

I stood on the turf of an indoor soccer field with seven other women and readied myself for an hour of kicks and jabs, uppercuts, and elbows. Our instructor, an iron woman named Tammy, stood in front, modeling to us the warm-up moves. We mirrored her motions. We stretched to the unreachable ceiling. We rotated our right shoulders, then our left. Then, reaching our arms straight down, we squatted. Swinging our arms back up toward the ceiling, we rose to a straight-legged position.

After the warm-ups, we circulated around seven stations for the strength-training segment. At each station we spent two minutes performing one challenging task. Traditional pushups, band strengthening exercises, jump-roping, jogging in place, boxing, and weight training were among the required activities that had us women sweating, grunting, and groaning.

Despite the grueling demands, I loved starting my day accomplishing something measurable, something that allowed me to feel awakened and powerful. I loved strengthening my body, a body I had wanted to escape for much of my life. Physical exercises—dance, yoga, kickboxing, and hiking—enabled me to feel comfortable inhabiting my own body. I was no longer an object for someone else to violate. I was learning how to treat my body with respect, and I no longer wanted to harm myself.

Following the strength-training circuit, we performed a series of kickboxing moves. Some mornings we wore boxing gloves and pounded cylindrical bags. Other mornings, gloveless, we pounded a bag we imagined in the air in front of us. This morning's sequence involved a series of four front jabs with the right arm, four uppercuts, and then three front jabs followed by a left hook. We repeated the sequence for several minutes and then switched arms. I loved the swings and jabs, pivoting my body so that the power from the center of my being was thrust forward. The blows against the bag were solid and sound. I kept at it through various sequences to the grand finale—a longer, continuous set of punches. This, at the end, after so much energy had been expended, challenged me. I wanted to quit, but everyone else kept at it, and I drew on the group spirit to keep going.

My therapist asked me if kickboxing was a way to release the rage I felt toward my father and the past. The question didn't surprise me as much as it did when my first few therapists asked me questions about anger, hurt, and fear. Back then I didn't allow myself to feel angry. I was taught to smile. I was taught to be *a good girl*. I was taught to be forgiving and to overlook the shortcomings of others. I wondered about these odd therapists who seemed attached to dredging up unpleasant emotions. But the more I continued to unearth what I had buried—so many moments, so many snapshots—the more I realized I was examining horror, trauma, and abuse. I felt shock at first. That shock turned into anger that I cut into tiny portion sizes because anger scared me. Anger's name was Dad. I was not going to be like him, so I could not possess this emotion. Instead, I intellectualized anger: *Yes, it's upsetting that what happened happened,* I would admit to my first few therapists and return home after sessions and binge to avoid facing what I was beginning to feel.

But one therapist, Dr. Sing, with whom I worked while living in Tucson, would work with me on the condition that I sign a contract promising I would not use my drug of choice, food, while we worked together. As a result of abiding by that contract, the anger I had buried through clever intellectualizing emerged and felt like an actual hurricane. I started slamming cabinets instead of downing Twinkies. I ran several miles without feeling tired or relieved instead of crunching Cheetos. Sometimes I caught myself grinding my teeth.

Dr. Sing and I scheduled a session to be held at a small private gymnasium down the road from his office. He thought I might benefit by releasing some of that pent-up and powerful anger in an actual therapy session. I put on a boxing glove but couldn't bring myself to swing at the punching bag with him there. I was too self-conscious. Even though I could have run ten miles, seething as I was that day, my head intervened. *Immature,* it said. *Punching out your anger? Come on! Get over yourself!* I left the gymnasium shrugging and apologizing, but Dr. Sing asked, "Why are you apologizing? When you're ready, you will know." He handed me the key. "Maybe you need to do this alone and then we can talk about it."

The rage over years of being violated crept up each week as I met with Dr. Sing. I felt raw, examining the memories I had kept buried. Uncovering them took me closer to my core, which felt swollen and bruised.

During my work with Dr. Sing, I received a surprise letter from my dad. He wanted to know if I felt sufficient remorse over reporting him to the state several years back. He talked about family loyalty and suggested that even if a family member murdered someone, other members should support that person. My initial response was to scratch a brief note to thank Dad for sharing his thoughts without responding to his actual question. He wrote again and requested a direct response within the week. I wrote back and stated that if the circumstances were the same and I had to do it over again, I would respond in the same way I had before. I later learned that Chuck had reported Dad to the state for punching him in the eye. Dad had hired a lawyer to try to clear his name and his growing file with the state. He needed documentation that I regretted making that earlier report. To this day, I'm glad I did not succumb to his pressure.

Somehow I managed to keep the contract with Dr. Sing and avoided binging on food during this time. I attribute this to sheer willpower and the grace and healing bounty of God. I could have gorged on gallons of ice cream, cookies, and pastries to sweeten my existence. Instead I felt not just anger but hatred toward my dad. And when I got all heady and said to myself, "Hate the behavior, not the person," I felt anger toward myself. I told that part of me to shut up, that I was in therapy and needed to get to these feelings and understand them in order to heal.

I took myself straight to Dr. Sing's gym, unlocked, opened, closed, and relocked the door. I didn't want any witnesses. There, alone in that small gym, I thrust myself into the weighted bag hanging by a chain from the ceiling. I punched and kicked and threw myself at it, and I screamed at the bag as if it were my father. "How could you? How could you beat and break the bones of your own child? How could you torment us?" The questions and statements subsided into moans and cries and single phrases and ended with "Get out, get out of my life, get out of me, out, out of me!" Then I collapsed onto the floor and wept.

Though I bruised and bloodied my knuckles in the process of releasing my rage without the right equipment, I felt cleared. I shared with Dr. Sing at our next appointment that had I continued to hold that energy inside me, I believed it could have killed me. It could have turned into cancer or some disease in which negative cells consume all the good cells. I shared my pride in releasing the storm inside me. "I'm done, aren't I? This is like graduation time, isn't it?" I asked, back in linear mode.

"Well, I'm not quite ready to hand you a diploma," he said, smiling tenderly.

"Why not? I need to start taking responsibility for my own happiness as an adult. I can't just sit here and blame my parents for everything that's gone wrong."

"I think you're behaving very responsibly by engaging in this hard therapeutic work. I don't hear you saying that it's all your parents' fault that you've struggled. I see you learning how to experience your emotions and process your childhood experiences in a safe and therapeutic way. You've unearthed some intense emotions. You may not be done with experiencing these feelings. Sometimes discovering what we've suffered and endured is like peeling an onion."

"There's that metaphor again. There are all kinds of layers, you're going to tell me. You're not the only therapist who's ever reminded me about process," I responded. However brief and unrealistic, I had enjoyed those moments of feeling triumphant and graduated. Dr. Sing's response made sense, though. I was glad that he didn't see me as someone who whined about her bad childhood but rather as someone who was examining it in an effort to not repeat what was unworthy of being repeated and to discover and accept herself.

Years later, though still peeling the onion with a different therapist across the country, I was further along in my recovery. In those pre-dawn kickboxing classes, I did not see my father as I jabbed and kicked. Even when I felt anger because some recent event had reminded me of my past, I felt relieved of it as I swung at the air. I suspected that would continue to happen, and I felt OK about allowing that anger to get released in a physical way that harmed no one. I felt happy, as well, that I no longer had the inclination to punch at some image of my dad. In fact, I found myself one morning jabbing the air and thinking, "No, Dad, this is not for you but for the hidden and powerful forces that played a part in shaping you—patriarchy, sexism, the cultural and global messages that you as a white man had the power, that you owned your wife and children and were responsible for embedding in them the norms you did not question." Driving home from that class, I pitied rather than feared my father. I saw him not as a monster but as a human being like the rest of us—complex and mysterious. He no longer took on the gargantuan proportions that kept me feeling small, afraid, insignificant, and victimized.

Those mornings I threw precise kicks and punches, hitting the bag again and again, drenched in sweat. My half-asleep brain became clearer and more alert, and the release of endorphins energized me. During the cool-down, I watched the other women and wondered how many of us were here for reasons other than keeping fit. How many had been raped? How many had been victimized by domestic violence or child abuse? How many of us were trying to reclaim our bodies, to find our strength, to free ourselves of the debris of the past, or at least to manage that debris? I knew I was not alone. The alarming statistics and years of getting to know other women had revealed to me that survivors walk down every street, occupy every business, and inhabit every corner of the globe.

Part 5: Grace

No Contact

One warm October afternoon in 1998, my dad sat smoking on the deck of my home, blowing smoke rings toward the tall oaks in the yard. This was the third day of an already too long visit. I didn't mind having Mom around, but Dad? I remained inside breastfeeding Anisa and watching him watch the oaks and the sky, his rings of smoke rising up and dissipating into the air.

How could he? How could he lie?

He had chuckled the night before when David put Aleah in time-out and said that he remembered putting me in time-out when I misbehaved as a child. Every time we disciplined the children, either through reasoning with them or utilizing time-out, Dad remembered doing exactly the same thing with me. I was tired of how his memories of the past differed from mine. I was tired of the denial. I was tired of having Dad refer to me as a "mental case" whenever I mentioned the past. The lack of acknowledgment hurt.

A few weeks after Mom and Dad went home, Anisa fell off the sofa and broke her wrist. While the X-ray technician at the hospital processed the film, I stood by my daughter as she gasped and cried, and I struggled with my helplessness over her injury. I wondered how it was possible. How could my dad break my leg, break my collarbones, blacken my eyes, punch me in the stomach, and toss me across a room? How could anyone do that to their own children? And how, how could Mom stand by and watch and continue to stay with him?

I considered my reactions to these latest events with my therapist and made the difficult decision to not have further contact with my Dad. I wrote a letter:

Dad,

This letter may come as a surprise to you, as I have been talking on the phone to you, visiting, and having some interaction with you over the past several years. Now I'm writing to say that I don't want to have contact with you for now because of issues regarding the past. I have tried to act like the past is over and done with, but unresolved feelings and memories still exist for me. Having young children and parenting them makes it even more unbelievable for me that the past happened as it did. I just can't fathom treating my young children the way I was treated by you. Recently, I drove by the house on Colfax Street and stopped and parked the car. What happened there was tragic.

A part of me doesn't even want to send this letter. When I have brought up the past before, your response has been to deny the severity of what happened and to suggest I have problems and that I'm not getting on with my life but dwelling on the past.

I'm assuming that's the same response I'd receive now, and I'm not interested in the same kind of dialogue we had several years ago. I might be willing to try and sort through these issues with a professional counselor or mediator present. I'm content, though, not to talk, not to have contact. Please do not try and convince me to change my mind or put me down for making this choice. Please do not communicate through Mom any upset over this communication.

I realize this may sound cold. I am reluctant to have hope that you would want to talk through these serious matters with the help and expertise of a professional. You have never been inclined in that direction before, and I'm suspecting your attitudes about such help are unchanged.

I do pray for you, that you are happy and content. I am grateful that you and Mom conceived me. I am grateful that, despite the horrific violence of the past, I was influenced by your strengths—a sense of inquiry, a love for books and the written word, and a sense of nonconformity and independence of thought. Despite that, to have an honest and respectful relationship with you would require an acknowledgment and sorting through of what I clearly remember, an acknowledgment of what the emotional cost was then and is now, and a sincere and complete apology for what happened. I hope that you are able to respect my wishes.

Kim

The decision I made to send this request upset the family's equilibrium. We had all learned how to walk around the past when we gathered for the holidays or visits. We pretended it did not happen the way it did. We ate turkey and ham and gave each other Christmas presents. We talked about our jobs, household projects, and world events. We did not even hint at the past.

Mom wrote me a rather philosophical appeal about forgiveness and happiness stating that Dad had changed. I wrote back to her. The letter began with newsy updates about the girls, and then I got to the point:

I wanted to respond to some comments you made in your note. You mentioned that I would not experience happiness until I could see that Dad had changed and forgive him. I can understand your perspective since a religious and philosophical truth often is expressed—until you forgive you are not free.

I do have a different perspective. I do experience great joy and happiness and I also experience times of pain and unhappiness, frustration and anger, like most people. While I have forgiven what happened in the past, primarily on an intellectual level, I won't forget what happened. I don't dwell on the past—I'm too busy living. But there are consequences I experience here and there that relate to the past. Most researchers and professionals state that if a child is abused, especially during the formative years, there will be lifelong effects. I've experienced some of these effects, and I'm doing my best to heal and move forward. Denying what happened, denying my feelings as a result of what happened, creates internal havoc for me. My intent since marriage and having children in continuing on in therapy is to make certain I break the cycle of abuse and to make certain my children get what they deserve—a violence-free, healthy childhood. I did not have that kind of childhood. I remember the violence. I remember the screaming and yelling. I remember the beatings. And I remember living in a state of constant fear.

Our needs, as children, did not come first. I believe Dad's violence made certain that his needs came first and that he didn't realize, and perhaps still doesn't realize, what he did was wrong. I think he blamed everyone else for his problems. I have not known Dad to seek such help for his problems, to sincerely try to uproot his tendency toward violence. I have known instead that he hired a lawyer to try and clear his name from state records. This is not a sign of taking responsibility for his actions or showing remorse for his behavior.

I'm baffled that you and Dad seem to infer that something is wrong with me when it appears I'm the one in the family who has sought years of professional help and faced the painful issues of violence in our lives. I'm not trying to boast in saying this. Healing has required years of hard work. I would much rather have spent that time building my career, serving the Bahá'í community, and engaging myself in other types of activities.

When you question my motives or my making the decision to not see Dad, it brings to mind some very difficult questions: How could you watch your own children being thrown across rooms, getting broken bones and bruises, being called names, being beaten for minor infractions and such senseless things as getting sick? How could you stand by and allow this to go on? How could you protect Dad and not us—your babies, your children? How can you now ask me why I don't want to maintain contact with someone who terrorized and terrified me? If any other human being did what Dad did to me, it would be considered a crime, and I would not be expected to visit the criminal in jail and initiate reconciliation. How can you say Dad has changed? If he has changed, why has he not pleaded for forgiveness, offered compensation for the enormous amount of money therapy has cost me, and acknowledged the cost in time—time I can't get back? Why has he not sought out professional help, family counseling? There are no signs that I can see that he has changed.

Mom, I feel intense pain and sadness that my relationship with you is so conditional upon my perspective of the past matching that of what seems to be the family's perspective. I feel sadness that you didn't protect me when I was little and helpless and deserved protection, safety, acceptance, and love. I feel sadness that we may live out this life not resolving these incredible trials openly and honestly and with the professional help our kind of situation requires.

Finally, I want to say that I care about you enough to be this honest. I hope you read this letter not as an indictment but as an attempt to share what is in my heart and soul, what is my perspective of the past and present . . . a different perspective than anyone else's in the family. I acknowledge that my perspective is limited, that I don't see all the complexities as our All-Knowing God might, yet that doesn't make my view wrong, just limited.

I wish we could somehow see each other, but I suppose that is impossible. I imagine that you either don't want to because of my not wanting to have contact with Dad, or that you are not allowed to have such contact. I don't know. As I said, I do pray for all of us and trust that the limitations each of us brings to our family relationship will not exist in the next realm, that through God's grace we will know unity.

Love, Kim

It didn't take long for my brothers to learn about the letters I had sent. Though they couldn't understand why I would do such a thing, though my mom was hurt, though Dad wrote David dozens of e-mails trying to persuade him to take charge of his wife, though my dad showed up in my dreams several nights each week and I consulted with my therapist trying to figure out if I had done the right thing, the no-contact policy would last over two years.

Confronting and setting a boundary with my dad helped me on many levels. Since getting married, I had been struggling not to dump onto David the fallout of the past. Some of my frustrations and upsets in marriage were intensified because of my past. David, like all of us, had his own issues that he was striving to overcome, and I endured a little fallout from some of those issues. But I had learned enough from twelve-step programs and the Bahá'í writings to know that David was responsible for his growth and I was responsible for mine. We would better inspire each other to continue on the lofty road of self-transformation by being an example, not through coercion and pressure. When I took out on David what was meant for my Dad, I worked hard in therapy to connect present occurrences with past events and distinguish them. I often discovered a simple solution to a current problem after I expressed, often for the first time, the grief related to the events I thought were over because they had occurred in the past. My past lived on in me—in my dreams, in my reactions, in my language, and in my habits. I had to serve as my own historian. Therapists helped me do that and fulfill Bahá'u'lláh's exhortation not to blindly repeat the traditions of our ancestors. Without examining those traditions, behaviors, and beliefs, and without making choices about what to repeat and what to discard, I was unconsciously bringing some of the debris from the past into the present.

Many of my therapists helped me engage with my dad through the imagination. I wrote letters to him that I didn't send. I visualized him sitting in a chair across from me, listening to me describe what I felt, what I had endured at his hand. In the safety of an office, under the watchful and trained eyes of social workers and psychologists, I peeled more and more layers of that onion, more and more layers from my past. When I confronted my dad, I had had some practice that prepared me for the bold gesture of cutting off contact. Though I didn't realize it at the time, standing up to my dad helped to preserve my marriage and helped me to see David as David, rather than viewing him through the veil of my father and my past. Standing up to my dad also helped me start to forgive him.

Puzzle Pieces

For the next two years, instead of spending time with Mom and Dad during our summer vacation or the holidays, my family and I traveled elsewhere. We made plans in 2001 to spend Thanksgiving with my brother Mike and his family.

Mike called me a few days before Thanksgiving to inform me that Mom and Dad had decided to join us.

"Why am I getting this information through you?" I asked Mike.

"I don't know, Kim. They weren't planning on going anywhere for Thanksgiving. They just decided to come yesterday. Maybe they should have called you, but you don't really want that. I don't think Dad knows what to do. He just wants another chance."

David and I consulted and decided to proceed with our plans. I knew Mom was torn up over not seeing us. I knew Dad controlled her and that he would not allow her to visit us without him. I also came to accept that Dad and I were just not going to have the kind of conversations I wanted to have about the past. Perhaps he wasn't capable. I didn't know, but I decided to accept that he was incapable. I also made the decision that if Dad were to mistreat us in any way, then I would resume the no-contact policy. Fortunately I didn't have to do that.

Because Thanksgiving went so well, David and I accepted an invitation to spend a week of our next summer vacation with my parents. On the long drive to northern Wisconsin from our home in Michigan, we stopped in northern Illinois for a couple of days to visit Mike and his family. While there, we thought it would be wonderful if my niece, Nicole, who was the same age as Anisa, could join us. I called Mom to inquire, and she responded favorably. But a few hours into our journey, the cell phone rang. My brother Mike was on the other end. "I'm not sure what to do, Kim. Dad's furious about Nikki's going with you."

"Why?"

"You know how he is. He sent me an e-mail. Listen to this: 'Dear Mike, Once again you interfered with family plans. Your Mom and I have planned a nice visit with your sister, David, and the girls. Are we allowed to proceed with this visit? No. Little Nikki needs to be indulged once again. Can't you and Pet ever lay down the law and let your daughter know that she can't get everything she wants? No. Why not? Because you are not a man, Mike. You have not once in the course of your marriage exercised authority. The consequence—Nikki comes with David and Kim and makes it impossible for us to continue with our plans of boating, going out for dinners, and other activities. Thank you, Mike, for ruining our plans.'"

Same old Dad, I thought. He couldn't handle any situation where he didn't have complete control, where plans were not predetermined, hours and minutes precisely charted.

David, less reactive to the situation than I was, viewed the situation diplomatically. "Your Dad is upset because he wasn't consulted and had counted on a particular kind of visit," he said. I admired how David related to my dad. He simply tried to understand his particular viewpoint. David's detachment and counseling skills made our visits more pleasant. But I wasn't able to feel the same detachment and mirror back my dad's response without my own experiences and history interfering. The mean-spirited tone of that letter filled me with dread. Did I have the strength and courage to face Dad knowing that he was seething over Nikki's accompanying us? I could feel myself, that authentic part of me that breathed and thrived and coped away from my dad, that part of me that I had hoped I could begin to feel more comfortable revealing with my parents, retreating.

When we arrived, Dad was visibly agitated but managed to curb his emotions, I believed, because David was present. He desired David's respect, and he knew that David expressed himself with dignity and tact, without resorting to demeaning others who thought differently. While I regarded David as capable of responding with respect to Dad's views about Nikki, I felt insecure about my own reaction. I didn't feel capable of viewing my father as a man with a particular response to a particular situation. I viewed him through the lens of my prior experiences with him. I envied the freedom David possessed. He was able to see Dad as just a man with a view and a strong reaction to the situation. My programming had me fearing Dad and struggling not to allow those fears to consume me.

After some initial tension, and due to David's skill at reflective listening, Dad relaxed and seemed to let go of the situation. Though he never admitted it on that particular trip, I believe he even realized there were some advantages of having Nikki join us. The girls occupied themselves in fun and creative ways, and this allowed us adults some time to interact.

While my dad treated my family and me with courtesy and respect, he still mistreated Mom. I hated the way he talked to her. "Carole, can't you fix anything better than this for breakfast? We have guests, for God's sake." "Carole, you sound like an idiot on the phone talking to Marlease. Can't you explain anything clearly?" An hour didn't pass that I didn't resist getting pulled under into the muck of that old tone lodged in my cells, my memories. I breathed, and breathed some more. I reasoned that

Mom was an adult. She had made the decision to stay with Dad all these years. I couldn't do the work for her that I had to learn to do myself. I decided I would walk out of the room when Dad talked like that, not in a noticeable way, not in a way that indicated I was making a comment or judgment, but in a more subdued way, as if I were going to use the restroom or retrieve a novel.

One afternoon during this visit, Dad was grumbling about something or other. I continued to read, tuning him out. Anisa, however, walked right up to him and said in a singsong manner, "Graaaandpa-a-a." She kneaded his neck the way she sometimes kneaded mine. "Grandpa, don't be so crabby." Anisa exhibited no fears. She didn't endeavor to tune him out or decide to walk away. She was beautiful in her spontaneity, beautiful in her ability to express in such a forthright manner her response to her grandpa's grumpiness. She did not carry the heavy load, the same baggage as Mom and I. And Dad, her grandpa, responded with love. "Yes, I shouldn't be so crabby, little Anisa. You're quite the angel, aren't you?"

And for a while he remained calm.

During that visit, Dad took a couple of days away to travel to a tournament with his bridge partner, Duane. The two of them, champions throughout the state, often ventured out of state for three-day tournaments. This particular trip involved traveling a couple of hours away. I felt the same relief I had felt as a child when Dad went to work on the weekends. I could breathe a little easier. He was gone.

When he returned we supported the Lions Club annual fundraiser, where Dad volunteered to cook hamburgers. Once again I could see what I saw as a child. In public he impressed others. Over the years his acquaintances, colleagues, and some neighbors praised him and offered congratulations of sorts. "How lucky you are to be raised by a man like him," they would say. If only Dad's public nature better matched his private behavior.

Dad's accomplishments and some of his behaviors were admirable. He was once airman of the year; a chemistry major at Purdue; a philosopher who admired the work of Loren Eiseley, Paul Tillich, and Rachel Carson. A conscientious citizen, he worried about population, starvation, and war. A trusted and loyal friend, he played on a baseball team and served as a bridge partner and won tournaments. He helped out the Lions Club by accepting the nomination to be its secretary. He loved fishing and boating. He enjoyed cruises and trips to Florida. On occasion he encouraged us children, explaining to us over dinner that we should honor our dreams, thoughts, and desires because that's what made us unique. A student of world religions, he encouraged us to love people of all faiths and to understand that the great religions had a lot in common. Professionally, he worked as a systems analyst for his dad's company until it went under due to the advent of computers. He found another position and within a short time served that company. A proud homeowner, he took on the roles of Mr. Fix-it and remodeler. He retired early to accomplish his dream of writing a book on the connections and tensions between science and religion. He became a grandparent, a better grandfather than father. He took his grandchildren on boat rides and told them stories. He sent them good luck notes for recitals and basic training. He hugged them, and they hugged him back without any of the reserve his own children felt.

One morning I sat on an old wooden chair that my mom had recently painted white and gazed at the calm waters. Loons cried their strange deep cry that sounded like a whimper emerging from a deep lost place. The blue sky overhead did not appear as vast infinite space but as puzzle-pieces between the branches and limbs of pine and fir, birch and maple. The waters down the hill, less than a quarter of a mile from where I sat, glistened. The sun, still low in the horizon from my vantage point, warmed me, hinting at the heat to come.

A view such as this, I thought, was fuel for my artistic soul. To gaze at such calm, such beauty—to wake far, far from my childhood war and Dad's invasive military mentality—encouraged me. Ironically, I was far from the physical reality of my childhood—miles from that locale. I was years away as well. But this was the view my parents had available to them every morning.

That familiar reserve crept up in me when Dad wandered outside and joined me there, on the patio, where I sat soaking in the beauty. I preferred relating with Dad when David and the girls were around because they provided a buffer to our interaction. I sometimes thought, *If Dad weren't my father, I wouldn't choose his company,* but here he was, my dad, and I was acting the part of his daughter. I didn't feel close to him, however. I didn't feel close the way I sensed my own daughters felt with David. Their spontaneity, giggles, hugs, and even their anger revealed that they could be themselves with the man they called "Dad."

Dad sat down across from me and lit up a cigarette. "Glad you and David could come," he said.

"Me, too," I responded, wishing I could relax.

"You probably don't remember way back to California, do you?" Dad asked.

"A little," I said, wondering why he was bringing up California and thinking that I remembered more than he'd be comfortable hearing about. However, I was no longer choosing to discuss with him how our memories varied.

"You were just a little nothing, and it was not good that I was away from home so much. The Air Force controlled my life. Officer school took me away for days. Even before that, I fought a lot of fires. You were just a baby and I'd go off for days fighting fires. It had an effect on me. It was grueling."

"I bet it was," I said, trying to engage with him.

"Imagine, now that you're an adult, going out into those mountains . . . you remember Mount Arrowhead, of course. Well, imagine going out with the unbearable sun searing down, and then facing a scorching and uncontrollable fire. One time—I'll never forget it—a helicopter went down, and my assignment was to bring back the bodies. Here I was, just a punk of a kid. I'm assigned what even men couldn't handle. I went out there for the charred remains of two men."

"That must have been hard," I said, stunned by the images he was creating.

"I maneuvered myself into that copter, tried to pull them out, and what happens? Their bodies just came apart—they were ash and bones sifting through my hands. It impacted me. It was terrible." Dad paused and looked up to the trees.

I didn't know what to say but continued to listen.

"Then I'd have to go home after that. I couldn't even be with you and your mom, really, so disturbed by all that hell."

As Dad talked, I began wondering if the subtext to his sharing was "The reason I abused you was because of all the military hell I went through." I felt for him, felt the horror of his duties. Tears filled his eyes. He continued to tell me about the abuses he experienced from some of his officers, how he was sent away to officer's training school the very day his own parents came to visit, how he believed that his commanding officer deliberately telephoned on the day they arrived to see how he would react.

"Would I be man enough to accept his orders without complaint? I figured that question was lingering in his mind. But I mentioned that my parents had just arrived, that they drove all the way from Chicago to visit for Christmas, which . . ." Dad looked at me and continued, "was only a few days off. 'Perhaps, Officer, Sir, I could leave the day after Christmas. Wouldn't classes be starting then anyway?' I was fool enough to ask. 'These are your orders. You leave tonight. But then, we don't have to make you an officer. We can keep you right where you're at.'" Dad acted out the exchange with his officer, creating a distinct and commanding voice for the officer in charge of him. "That was it. I told Ma and Dad I was leaving. I went off to school the next morning." Dad sighed and looked off toward the trees.

"Then, that same year, I went to a bar one night. A few of us would meet there, have a beer. I'm sitting right next to Johnson, who's not saying much. He puts his hand in his jacket, pulls out a revolver, and bang!" Dad held up an imaginary gun to his own head and dropped his arm. "Shot himself right there in front of me." Dad fell silent.

A seriousness filled me, the awareness that, yes, I didn't know as a child what my dad had endured, that these were horrific situations. Later, when my mom read a draft of this manuscript, she said, "The helicopter incident never happened, Kim. That didn't happen."

But that day Dad continued, "Those were some hellish times. Your mom pretty much handled everything at home. My life was pretty much out of my hands." Dad stood up.

I felt awkward, though I managed to say, "Sounds really tough, Dad, what you went through." I even thanked him for sharing with me as he began to head back inside.

Still, for me, there was another conversation we weren't having. While he was sharing what had hurt him, he did not take responsibility for how he had hurt me. I stared at the pieces of sky, pieces that didn't seem to fit together anymore. The leaves and limbs crisscrossed in thousands of different ways, intersecting one another, parallel to one another, cutting the sky into more and more pieces.

Months after that interaction I recalled a scene from a memoir titled *Because I Remember Terror, Father, I Remember You.* Sue Silverman, an acquaintance and writer who lives north of me, received the Associated Writing Program award for nonfiction the year her book came out. Her memoir chronicles the sexual abuse she sustained during her childhood. One of the scenes in the book reminded me of the interaction I had had with my dad. During a hospitalization Sue experienced, her dad confided in her that he had been sexually abused by an uncle when he was younger. Initially, Sue pitied her dad, but when she later met with her therapist, the therapist grew upset that her dad was not taking responsibility for violating Sue and that her dad chose to share this information with Sue when she was journeying into the pain of the past, pain that was so great she needed hospitalization and close care to examine it.

I also thought about all the other men in the military who had to perform emotionally challenging tasks. Did they go home and break their children's bones? Did they beat their wives? Some, no doubt, did. Was my dad among that group that chose to take out his frustrations, his anger toward others, on his own family? Some days I believed that. Other days, I wondered. Was there something else that caused or contributed to his violent behavior? Was he capable of controlling himself? He acted appropriately in public. He charmed others. Why couldn't he choose to behave that way at home? Exhausted and stressed as he might have been when he returned home, he had had options other than taking it out on his own family. He could have begun by seeking professional help. He could have done whatever it took to avoid resorting to violence, couldn't he?

Corridors

Dad gasped in a breath and snorted back out a breath. Wires and tubes connected his body to machines. His heart rate, temperature, blood pressure, and respiration were all being recorded. Contracted against his ribs, his left arm and hand sat paralyzed. His mouth slanted downward, some of that slant caused by the intracranial bleed and some of it, I believed, by some misery and mystery I would never grasp. I went over to him and touched his hand, kissed his cheek, and said, "Dad, I'm here. It's Kim. Hang in there. We're at your side." I took hold of his right hand and looked at this man, my dad, a man who had made many horrific choices and was now suffering a horrible affliction. Though I had prayed throughout my life for his death and I would pray again in the next few days for God to take him, to relieve him of his misery and give Mom some years of freedom, I prayed again. This time I prayed for my own strength and the dignity to treat my dad the way God would want a suffering man to be treated.

For the past two years, Dad had agonized and obsessed over the possible consequences of the surgery that would clear his clogged arteries—a procedure recommended by more than one physician. Day after day he sat at his computer, searching the internet, checking out Web sites such as Mayoclinic.com, and writing down a list of questions to ask. These questions surprised his physicians, who were more accustomed to patients who trusted that trained doctors wouldn't recommend a procedure unless it was in the patient's best interest.

Dad asked them, "What happens when you clear these arteries? Isn't it going to be as if you're suddenly turning on a faucet full blast and the blood starts rushing to the veins and arteries in my brain? How will those veins, not used to this kind of flow, accommodate the new pressure?" The doctors assured Dad that 95 percent of the time the brain accommodates the new flow just fine, but yes, there was a 5 percent chance that a subsequent stroke or bleed could occur. These answers, as well as stories his friends shared about having the surgery and playing golf within the next week, encouraged my dad, though he continued to read and reread everything he could find about the procedure.

The day after the surgery, the doctor released Dad from the hospital knowing that he would be nearby at the home of Gloria Thell. Gloria, a good friend whose summer home was right next door to Mom and Dad's home in Minong, worked as a translator for the Korean community at the hospital and the doctor knew her. Though released, Dad felt a little nauseous and his head bothered him, but his blood pressure was normal. The doctors involved in the procedure didn't seem concerned by these symptoms.

The day following his release, Mom and Dad drove the three hours back to Minong. That night after dinner, Dad complained that his hands felt numb. He stood up to retrieve the blood pressure kit but felt dizzy and sat back down. Mom rushed for the kit and connected Dad to the monitor. The readings were not good. When the left side of his face drooped, Mom dialed 911. Within minutes, the paramedic, who happened to be a friend from their small town, arrived to transport Dad by ambulance to the clinic. From there he was flown by helicopter back to Minneapolis.

By the time I arrived a few days later, doctors had already warned Mom that Dad might not survive and that if he did, his life would never be the same. Extensive brain damage had occurred. His left side was paralyzed. The effects of this damage would require extensive care in a nursing home. At the age of seventy, my dad was facing death. Even if he didn't die, paralysis, brain damage, and subsequent nursing home care would effectively end the life he knew. As I looked at him I thought, *Take him, God. This is not how he would want to live. Please, just take him, relieve him of this misery.*

For the next few days I prayed both in the hospital chapel and at Gloria's home, where Mom and I stayed. I said the Long Healing Prayer and prayers from my own heart. I asked God to take him from this suffering that I believed he couldn't handle and added, "Please, dear Lord, I beg of you, let Dad experience peace, and forgive him." I added as a sort of postscript, "If it be Your Will." As much as I preferred considering that my prayers came from an utmost state of purity, the past and my complicated relationship with Dad no doubt inclined me toward asking for what was *my* will rather than God's.

Four days after I arrived, Dad opened his eyes and began moving the side of his body not harmed by the stroke. At first he lifted his right hand and pointed and shook his finger—one single index finger. Dad waged all of his power into that small two-and-a-half-inch finger, and I jumped. Imagine fearing a finger, a finger that had a mostly paralyzed body operating it. The doctors didn't jump. The nurses didn't startle. But there it was—the old nauseated breathlessness, the fear. I was forty-seven, not seven. I was an adult, not a child. This, even though I had stood up to my dad and told him, "no more contact, no more abuse, not without a full acknowledgment of the past."

Standing in the hospital room in Minneapolis, I considered how Dad had suffered from an intracranial bleed. His left side was paralyzed as a result. He was coming out of a three-day coma. He was shaking a finger at us, uttering unintelligible sentiments that I heard as "I'm going to get you, I'm going to get you . . ." and I jumped. What was that all about? Was I programmed at a cellular level to fear him? Why did I react in such a visceral way?

The following day he held up more than one finger. He lifted his whole hand in what appeared to be a fist. Both Mom and I jumped backward. Then we looked at each other, shook our heads, rolled our eyes, and laughed. Not the mirthful kind of laugh associated with watching truly funny movies, but an odd kind of laugh. It was a laugh of recognition that we could just as easily be crying but we had already shed enough tears. It was a tragic laugh that reflected our powerlessness. Our life experiences with Dad had us programmed to respond to him in fear, even though we knew he no longer possessed the physical capability to harm us.

Then Dad snapped two fingers together, and garbled words emerged from his mouth that none of us could decipher. After a while I discerned the word "gauze."

"Do you want gauze, Dad?"

He nodded. Then he snapped his fingers as if making an order. As a child I had seen him snap his fingers together and say, "Water, now," to my mother. Now that he was out of his coma he was exemplifying some of the same old behaviors. He still wanted to be waited on.

Mike, the nurse, looked on. What did he think? I wondered. I pushed through my embarrassment, laughed at my dad, and said, "Guess what, Dad? It's a new day. You can't snap your fingers and expect to be waited on."

But he snapped them again.

"Ron, if I did that at home, my wife would throw something at me," Mike said.

"I'll be glad to get you gauze if you can ask me respectfully," I added.

"Please, get me some gauze," he said, surprising me.

"Hey, Dad, that brain is reprogrammable, isn't it?" I laughed. Then I added more seriously, "I'd be glad to get you gauze."

And I did.

He tried to spit out the phlegm lodged in his throat and chest but was so weak that his cough resembled a whisper. None of the phlegm clogging his throat was released. Finally Mike suctioned some of the fluids that had accumulated during the past three days of unconsciousness.

For the next several days Dad slept and woke and experienced full body spasms. His heart rate, blood pressure, and oxygen levels were monitored. Numbers rose. Meds were intravenously given to him. Some of them worked, some of them didn't. Allergic reactions caused a high fever and deep sleep. New medications were tried—medications to keep him alive.

Would he want this? Would he want a body that could not move? Would he want a brain that had been damaged and could not remember what was said just a few moments ago? Would he want to move into a nursing home where he would be one of the youngest residents? Did these questions even matter?

Dad spent two weeks barely surviving but did not pass from this realm, even though we all prayed God would just take him. I continued to wrestle with myself. Had I any right to pray for his passing? I had done so when I was a helpless child, but I was no longer a child. Were these prayers about making my own life easier? Did I just want him removed so that I could enjoy a relationship with my mom that he wasn't trying to control?

Dad didn't pass, and I would discover the wisdom in this in the coming years.

Visits and Phone Calls

A woman sat slobbering soup onto her blouse. The upper torso of the woman across from her flopped forward. A man stared at the space in front of him. Another man spoon-fed his wife and chatted about the weather. A nurse with a spoonful of something soft struggled to pry open the sealed lips of a woman who moaned. I sat across from my dad, who focused on the door leading out of the dining room.

"Don't you want to try to eat, Dad?"

"This slop? Take a look at the gruel, Kim. Would you eat it?"

I didn't answer. The food didn't look that appealing. But then Dad was in the dining hall for those who had serious and special needs. He still had trouble swallowing, and he could choke on solid food. There was no need for me to repeat what the nurses had already told him.

"Just look at these people. They're a bunch of beauties," Dad mocked.

I looked around. "Yes, they are," I countered.

"Kim, look a little closer."

"Dad, these people are beautiful. Right now, they're struggling because of a stroke, Alzheimer's, or other ailments. All these people have lived long and full lives. This is a small segment of their lives."

"So they're beautiful," he said, shifting in his wheelchair. "Go get the nurse. I can't stay here. I need to go back to my room."

Rather than say, "No, you've got to try to eat," I agreed so that Jessie, the nurse, could be the one to give those orders. I explained to Jessie that I thought my dad was experiencing culture shock. Ten to fifteen years younger than most of the other residents, he didn't want to identify with them, I believed. I didn't want to appear unsupportive of him so I asked Jessie to serve as commanding officer. He agreed and explained to Dad that he needed to try and eat.

"Red, I'm in pain. I need to lie down." Dad had given nicknames to all the staff. Jessie was called Red, probably because of his red hair.

"Ron, you can't go to bed. You have to spend some time sitting each day. Otherwise, your heart and circulatory system are going to shut down."

"Red, it's not that. Look, my daughter's visiting and we need a little privacy as a family. Can't we have that? Can't we return to my room?"

"I'll compromise, Ron. I'll wheel you to the conference room and you can eat and visit there."

In the conference room, Dad complained about Mom. "She doesn't visit. When she does, she doesn't listen at all. I tell you, Kim, your mother doesn't care. She doesn't care at all that I'm in here."

"So you don't feel cared for by Mom?" I asked, mirroring back to him what he had said. Rather than argue, I figured this method of reflective listening might serve Dad better.

"That's right. I want you to tell her she needs to visit more often and to get me a cell phone."

I knew Mom would not allow Dad to have a cell phone. The one time she had left her cell phone with him, Dad had made twenty calls back to back, demanding that she transfer him to the hospital.

Just then Mom followed Judy, the speech therapist, into the room, relieving me of the need to respond to Dad's concerns.

"OK, Ron, I need to have you eat for me. I want to check out how your swallowing is coming along," Judy said.

"You finally decided to show up and support your husband, I see," Dad said to Mom, ignoring Judy. Before either of them could respond, his leg went into a spasm and he broke out in a sweat. "Kim, get me out of here now. Wheel me to my room. I can't take this pain. I can't take it."

"OK, Dad," I said and unlocked the wheelchair.

"Ron, you go ahead and get some rest. We'll deal with swallowing tomorrow," Judy said.

While Mom and Judy remained in the conference room to discuss details of Dad's rehab, I returned Dad to his room. He wanted me to help him into bed, but because of the condition of my own back, I couldn't.

"Get the nurse. Go get the nurse now," he said.

"Dad, the nurses are helping those in the dining hall. There are sixty patients and only a handful of nurses, which means you have to wait. They know you want to get into bed."

But within minutes Dad repeated the command and I left the room as Mom had learned to do, pretending to follow his directives. I walked the hallway and returned saying they would be there soon. For the next ten minutes, Dad badgered me to get the nurses. Finally, two women arrived, wheeled Dad near the bed, lifted him so that he stood on his one good leg and then turned him while they held him in an upright, standing position, and set him on the bed. They then had to lift his legs and straighten him. It was quite an ordeal.

When Mom returned from talking with the speech therapist, Dad asked, "Where in the hell were you, Carole?" Before she could answer he interjected, "I'm here in bed sick, needing you, and you just do whatever you want. You don't give a damn."

"Dad, Mom was talking to the speech therapist," I said.

"Yeah, but you just don't know, Kim. She doesn't come for days. She doesn't care that this happened."

"Dad, that's not true. She's very concerned," I said, though I realized Mom had pulled away from Dad. Who could blame her? Dad's mistreatment of her persisted, now in public. Mom had telephoned me almost daily during the first several months after Dad's stroke. When he was at St. Mary's in Duluth for rehabilitation, she had confided that Dad swore and yelled at her in front of the nurses and doctors. One of the doctors pulled her aside and asked if Dad's behavior was new or old. She was honest and shared that it was old behavior.

"The doctor said to me, 'No person has the right to treat anyone the way your husband is treating you, stroke or no stroke,'" Mom confided.

The doctor had gone on to explain to Mom that he couldn't allow her in the room with Dad when he treated her that way. When Mom shared the doctor's response, I felt an odd combination of grief and joy. Grief that my dad continued to communicate in a violent way, and joy that this was the first doctor of many who intervened when Dad mistreated Mom. She needed that kind of feedback, needed to hear from professionals that she did not deserve to be treated the way Dad treated her. It might seem obvious to others, but my mom had been so put down by him over the years that she doubted herself and sometimes believed what Dad said about her.

After Dad was settled in bed and received some of his medication, he calmed down. Even though he was acting up, I wondered about his wheelchair, a pathetic piece of machinery. I asked Mom if insurance wouldn't cover something more comfortable. She said the physical therapist claimed that this particular chair was high caliber. I encouraged her to talk with the physical therapist again to see if they could at least order a chair that allowed Dad to recline the back in a few different positions to relieve pressure from his spine.

Dad shared a room with no one because, according to Mom, he was too disruptive. All night long he pushed the call button for the nurses, and if they didn't arrive within seconds, he pushed the call button again and then started hollering. The other residents complained about him. "Who could handle sharing a room with him?" Mom asked. Eventually they placed a man who had lost most of his hearing with Dad.

There were moments when Dad seemed OK. He talked about politics, the war, or global warming. He asked questions about David and the girls. He asked about Angie, Chuck's wife, who suffered from kidney failure and would die within the year. He expressed concern for his own sister, whose husband had passed. Sometimes he joked around with the nursing home staff in that old public way that had endeared him to others. When I had to say good-bye he said he wished that I could visit more often, that he wished I lived closer, and that he loved me.

The long weekend visit came to an end. Mom and I drove to Superior, Wisconsin, that night and stayed at the Comfort Inn for the convenience. I was scheduled to fly out of the airport in Duluth on an early morning flight to head back home. Superior was minutes away from that airport, and Mom preferred to skip the predawn drive because of the risk of hitting a deer.

In the motel room, I pulled back the quilt, lay one pillow on top of another, and collapsed onto the bed. The cable TV station played "When Harry Met Sally," and Mom went outside to smoke a cigarette. The cell phone played its tune and I answered, "Hello."

"You've just won a million bucks," my brother Chuck joked.

"How you doing, Chuckie?"

"Hangin' in," he said. He wanted an address from Mom, but since she wasn't around he refocused the conversation to Dad. "Angie thinks he wants to die. He's not tryin' because he wants to die. She's seen it when she worked in the nursing home. Those patients who didn't try died within a year."

"Maybe so," I said.

"You know, Kim, I'm surprised at my lack of responsiveness to this ordeal. I'm not as upset as I always imagined I might be. Dad's been a hell of a person. I know I've always put you down for talking about the past, and I really got mad when you wouldn't see him for a while, but I'm starting to understand that."

Initially Chuck was heartbroken over Dad's stroke, and he had always come to Dad's defense in the past. But now he seemed to be able to look at the past more directly and honestly. He had no one to protect, no one to fear. Since Dad couldn't harm any of us, we were all a bit freer now to have more genuine reactions to the behaviors that hurt us.

Chuck went on to share a story that further astonished me. The night before, he had heard the neighbors across the street having a heated argument. "It brought back the past," Chuck said, "hearing that man scream. He sounded just like Dad used to sound—swearing and carrying on." After a while, Chuck decided to intervene and headed across the road and rang the doorbell. The shouting subsided and the man came to the door. He asked Chuck what he wanted. "I want to tell you this," Chuck started. "I want to tell you I hear every damn word you're saying to your wife, and you need to cut it out. First I thought I should call the police, but then I thought, hell no, I'll head on over and give you a piece of my mind. I grew up in a home where my dad was a lunatic, yelling, screaming, hitting for years. I know you've got kids. You want to permanently damage them? Then keep it up. But if I hear you again, I'm heading over and you'll have to deal with me. You got it?"

I laughed as Chuck shared this because only Chuck, with his outgoing, sometimes rather gruff personality, could carry this off. I asked him how the man responded.

"He wasn't all that thrilled, but he shut up."

I still smile when I think of Chuck stomping across the street and confronting his neighbor. But just like Chuck had responded to me when I reported Dad to the state, the woman across the street gave Chuck a dirty look when she saw him next and later continued to avoid him.

That night and the next morning, Mom confided that she had begun to open up with her closer friends about the past. I praised her for that. I imagined the isolation she had to have felt during all those years of keeping the violence a secret. I knew from my own experiences and the experiences of friends who had also survived violence that opening up and sharing the story was a step toward health and wholeness.

Mom's willingness to share her reflections helped me as well. While she had apologized off and on over the years, shared her guilt for not getting help, and cried over the effects of the violence we endured, she had not shared some other details that I learned that weekend. One of the more haunting details related to a phone call she had received from a therapist when Dad was ordered by the courts to seek family counseling. The therapist called Mom one afternoon and asked whether or not Dad was home. She said that he was not. The therapist said, "I have to tell you that I seldom make this kind of call, but I felt the need to. I'm very concerned about your safety and the safety of your children. I'm concerned for your life."

Why didn't Mom leave after that?

Terror, I guess. Fear was the catch-22 of the situation. There was a fear of death either way. If we stayed, Dad might kill us. If we left, Mom feared he would hunt us down and kill us. Too bad the therapist didn't provide Mom with more particular details on a way out, information on a shelter, or names of professionals who could actually help.

Hearing Mom and Chuck and, later on, my brother Mike all express their thoughts and feelings about how the violence affected them affirmed my perceptions and my healing process. While I had spent years acknowledging the past, striving to work through it with the help of therapists, on occasion, usually after a family visit or a talk with a family member on the phone, a part of me wondered if maybe the rest of the family was right, maybe things were better and I was making too much out of what had happened. Now none of us were minimizing what had happened. At last, we could share openly and honestly.

Updates

Aleah asked me when I arrived home after my dad's initial hospitalization if Grandpa had apologized to me for what he had done.

No. No apology.

I had hoped. I thought, just maybe, that during Dad's brush with death, maybe in those moments of utter powerlessness he would reflect and feel inspired to want to make things right. I waited, but nothing . . . no acknowledgment. Maybe there was too much brain damage, too much trauma preventing any kind of self-examination. Maybe it was mental illness. In his more lucid moments he still said things like "We have a wonderful family, don't we?"

While I didn't receive any acknowledgment from Dad, I observed that Mom, finally freed from his tyranny, was beginning to make decisions about his care and money and was beginning to exercise some of the power she had been denied for the fifty years of her marriage. Along with the newly acquired power, she possessed a lot of fear. She was afraid the federal government would show up on her doorstep if she made any financial mistakes. I felt annoyed by all of her fears, but I understood that fear was a habit from living with Dad and that it wouldn't just disappear. She spent hours calculating, worrying, consulting with lawyers, and writing letters about the bills coming in. She paid bills a year in advance. She realized all the savings Dad had forced her to agree with—hundreds of thousands of dollars—would go toward his care.

Some old anger and resentments resurfaced. I remembered how Dad had boasted over the years that he had paid for my entire college education, when in reality I didn't receive a penny from him and owed over twenty thousand dollars when I received my master of fine arts degree from the University of Arizona. This, along with all the years of therapy, equaled a nice share of his empty nest egg. David and I struggled to save. We spent a good portion of our earnings investing in our children and their future. My dad had not done that even when we were younger. But he promised that someday when he died, he would be leaving us a nice sum. That sum would now go into his end-of-life care.

One evening I received a call from Mom with a disturbing update. The head nurse had telephoned her to say that she had spotted Dad in the dining hall holding a spoon with his good hand. He was focused on the wall, and she realized he was trying to stick the spoon into the socket. She went to him and asked him what he was doing. "I know precisely what I am doing," he responded. "I've worked in data processing for years, and I know precisely what I'm doing." She told him that she had to take the spoon from him, that what he was doing was very dangerous. He repeated that he knew what he was doing and that he had worked in data processing.

Stunned, I sat in silence as my mom continued to talk about all the brain damage the stroke had caused and that Dad no longer knew what he was doing. I disagreed with that interpretation. I thought that perhaps, as he said, he knew what he was doing and that he was getting tired of constant pain, constant spasms, and living in a nursing home. He wanted to die.

During this time I struggled with a number of activities. I was well into the demands of teaching during the fall semester at Hope College. David and I shared the chauffeuring tasks and bustled around town getting the girls to their extracurricular activities—piano, violin, Girl Scouts, and horseback riding. Dinner, homework, household tasks, and faith obligations were all a part of our typical routine.

On top of all of this, we were dealing with some major happenings. David and I had been invited to Dublin, Ireland, to serve as keynote speakers for a cross-cultural family conference sponsored by the National Spiritual Assembly of the Bahá'ís of Ireland in response to a governmental request to commemorate the tenth anniversary of the United Nations International Year of the Family in mid-October 2004. We had plenty to do to prepare for international travel and finish up our speeches. Right after returning from Dublin, we would participate in and celebrate Jenai's marriage to Sean Jennings. Aleah and Anisa were going to be junior bridesmaids, and their excitement was boundless. I felt touched that I had been asked to read a poem as part of the ceremony. We were also waiting to receive a new addition to our family—a puppy. Chloe, born in August to our friend Sara's beagle, was joining us right after Jenai's wedding.

Life was overflowing with some great activities and some disturbing ones. I received frequent phone calls from Mom updating me on Dad's condition and behavior. Though his behavior had been acceptable when I visited, he was becoming more unruly and was continuing to disturb everyone around him. For years, most of the family had denied or minimized Dad's behavior. Suddenly it was the topic of every discussion.

All this stress and an incredibly busy daily pace were a recipe for my own downfall, especially in terms of my parenting skills. I had noticed that I was shouting at the children and David. I disliked that I was projecting onto the children the pressure that was building up inside me. They were not to blame for my shouting. I was. Shouting, yelling—what good was that? What would that achieve except a momentary relief of all the pressure inside me?

I knew I needed to find the time to get back into therapy. I had managed a few years without the weekly visits, but I needed that trained eye, those particular questions that helped me to explore my options. I needed to deal with all the changes that were continuing to occur in my family of origin. I was juggling many important activities and believed that none of them could be dropped to alleviate the pressure. I needed help to figure out how to cultivate the stamina and strength to handle what was in front of me and to deal with all the stress. I reconnected with my therapist and made our weekly sessions a priority.

One afternoon I received a phone call that probably shouldn't have surprised me as much as it did. Dad was being sent to a behavioral health hospital in Minneapolis because the nursing home could no longer deal with his difficult behavior. He would receive extensive testing and evaluation from a top psychiatrist. He might be there for some time. The nursing home would not take him back if they couldn't handle him.

Throughout my life I had cried out to God asking, "What is wrong with my dad?" Perhaps now we would discover some answers.

Within two weeks Dad was returned to the nursing home. The evaluation was complete. The list of mental illnesses was long—bipolar disorder, mood disorder, paranoia, and possible schizophrenia. The vascular dementia also compounded his problems. Medications that could have helped him most of his life were now prescribed.

For the next several months Mom called to report how well Dad was doing on the new medications. He was quiet throughout the night. He was no longer trying to run over other residents in his wheelchair. He had stopped slamming the wardrobe door in his bedroom or throwing pillows out into the hallway. He controlled his use of the call button. He cooperated with the staff. He participated in activities. He didn't mistreat Mom. When we visited the following summer, he played checkers with us, enjoyed a picnic held on the grounds of the nursing home, and talked about the other residents as if they were friends, even pointing out some of their idiosyncrasies in a kind way. He lamented, once again, that David and I lived so far away. He enjoyed our visits. He sometimes felt bored. He still wanted to return home.

I felt the incredible tragedy of our lives that week. I agonized over all the what-ifs. What if Dad had somehow received the help he needed way back when? What if he had been medicated when we were young? What if his parents had insisted he get a psychiatric evaluation rather than a physical when they learned of his violent behavior the first time Mom separated from him? What if Mom's priests had understood that we were in such an unsafe situation and had intervened to get our family the help we needed? How might all of our lives have been different?

Welcome to Normal

Aleah wanted nothing to do with the fish fry Grandma wanted to support during our summer visit of 2006. If I had dared to assert, at thirteen, that I hated fish in response to family plans to support a fish fry fundraiser, Dad would have pummeled me. Aleah, at thirteen, had no trouble expressing her likes, dislikes, loves and hates, gratitudes, and angers. And she let us all know that she couldn't understand why she was to help do yard work before Grandma treated Anisa and her to miniature golf at Captain Dan's—one of a handful of restaurants in the tiny town of Minong, Wisconsin, population 531.

After some prodding, Aleah and Anisa headed out to the yard and grabbed fistfuls of torn branches and limbs from a recent storm so severe that wind gusts and lightning strikes had downed hundreds of trees and Minong's fate that night made the state news. Mom was still cleaning up from that storm, and the girls' help was little to ask after a week of Grandma's treating them to several dinners at various restaurants, horseback riding, and shopping sprees. However, her reasonable request was not met with the same reasonable understanding and response. The lure of miniature golf, however, had the power to cure the girls' sore muscles, their frowns, and their audible sighs. Revived, they tossed sticks into the larger woods for at least a few moments. Then there were more frowns, more sighs.

I wish I could have thought, *Welcome to normal.* Instead I felt embarrassed by the lack of appreciation the girls expressed to Mom. Perhaps, though, their way of showing appreciation was different than what I was expecting—a little helpful work. Perhaps their *thank-yous* at the time seemed enough to their preadolescent and adolescent minds. But their lack of cooperation and willingness bothered me nonetheless. According to my idealistic notions, the girls should have been singing as they picked up sticks.

Mom placed forty dollars on the kitchen counter, two piles of twenty dollars each, one for each girl to spend on miniature golf and dinner at Minong Summer Days. Anisa came in first, and Grandma showed her the piles, which caught her attention. Then Aleah traipsed in looking as if the less than ten minutes of work had just about killed her. She, too, spotted the money, and Anisa explained, "It's all our money for tonight."

"Hmmmm," Aleah said and headed back out to pick up sticks with Anisa following her. The required thirty to forty minutes of work shrank down to about fifteen minutes. The money, their reward, was distributed even though they had not completed their tasks, which didn't please me.

We made it to Captain Dan's. The girls putted balls around on a course of smooth greens with miniature waterfalls as backdrops. Mom, David, and I enjoyed a drink. Mom took off to check out the activities a couple of blocks away at Minong Summer Days while I pulled out my laptop and caught up on e-mail. David browsed through a book on tai chi.

After the girls finished, we headed over to the actual site of Minong Days. Anisa pointed out an amusement park-like ride and said, "Wow, this might be cool for Minong." But that initial enthusiasm waned when they realized the rides were designed for toddlers. Thank goodness barbecued ribs were available from one of the many vendors. Both girls love ribs and scarfed them down. Townspeople and tourists milled around, selecting their choice of Indian tacos, hamburgers, ribs, and the healthier but less popular smoothies. Others aimed the cameras slung around their necks to snap a photo of a loved one. Cheers and whistles from the nearby softball diamond mingled with the strums of a guitar, the band leader warming up. Young girls in heels and tight-fitting dresses stood chewing gum and flipping their hair back.

We found a picnic table, and within minutes Aleah nudged me and whispered, "When are we leaving? This is the lamest carnival I've seen."

I encouraged Aleah to strive for patience. "Grandma is hosting us at one of the few activities that she has selected this week, and this is our last night in Minong."

Aleah turned back to her ribs and gnawed on a bone.

Mom spotted Linda, one of her closest friends, and asked me to go over with her to say hello. "Linda hasn't seen you since your last visit."

We brought Linda back to the table to see David and the girls. I felt grateful that Mom had such a caring and down-to-earth friend. She had shared with me that Linda had called her every morning during the past winter to check on her. "I think she's checking to see if I'm alive," Mom said, laughing. She had confided in her the details of the past, shredding the illusions most of the people believed of Mom and Dad.

David and I escorted the girls over to the local ice-cream and gift shop, hoping to relieve their boredom. They could sit in the booths, enjoy an ice-cream cone, and read magazines. While David browsed through the gift shop and kept an eye on the girls, I returned to visit with Mom and Linda. Instead of visiting, though, I found Mom dancing with an elderly woman. Grinning, she gyrated, twirled, and swung her arms to the music. Linda greeted me and leaned over to talk directly in my ear to be heard over the music. "Isn't this great? I've never seen this side of your mother until now. She's blossoming."

"She's free," I told Linda, leaning in toward her ear.

"You had a rough time, all of you, I understand."

I nodded. We both watched Mom, in sync with the music, smiling. I felt as if I were looking at a woman I didn't know. Her blue jeans and embroidered V-neck shirt accented with a wide leather belt made her look ten to fifteen years younger than her almost seventy years. She wore new wire-rimmed glasses that framed her blue eyes that glowed with a new-found joy. Before me was a fun-loving, vibrant woman, finally free from the oppression of living with Dad.

Mom and I met up with David and the girls at the ice-cream gift shop and spent some last moments at the end of our visit browsing and selecting a few mementos. Mom chatted with the owner, filling her in on Dad's progress since the visit to the behavioral health hospital, and then she headed outside to have a cigarette. I prayed this was a habit she would break so she could live those extra years she so deserved.

We spent the last couple of hours before bed back at Mom's house, taking pictures with the digital camera. After taking several of Mom and the girls, I asked Aleah to take some pictures of David, Mom, and me. She pointed the camera and snapped several shots and then examined them. "No, this one is terrible of Mom. You blinked. Dad, this one is bad. You're not even smiling. Smile, please. Bad one of Grandma. Another terrible one of all of you." Mom couldn't control herself. She laughed and laughed at Aleah, at our inability to get some good photos. After several dozen shots, Aleah saved three that were only OK but better than nothing.

Aleah then pulled out old photo albums of Mom as a baby, toddler, school girl, and high school student. Her spirit, that joy and vibrancy, shone through. I paused on the photo of her leaning into her dad, a man she loved for his tender, relaxed ways. Sadly, the next pages of her wedding photos indicated a clear departure from the nurturing atmosphere of her childhood into the murky world of her marriage and Dad's mental illness.

But Mom shared with me on this visit that she had packed away her wedding photos. "You and your brothers can have them, if you want, when I pass. Do whatever you want with them. I'm just not going to live the lie anymore."

I had noted how Mom was engaged in redecorating the house and making it her own. She had removed numerous photos. Instead of her wedding portrait, a photograph of a bird perched on a high branch in a pine tree rested on the table. Instead of the photo of Mom and Dad on a cruise years back, a photograph of Mom and her new friend Les sat on the nightstand next to Mom's new double-bed in a room other than the one she had shared with Dad for so many years.

Mom had met her new friend Les at the nursing home. Les visited his wife every day. A victim of Alzheimer's, she had been unresponsive for seven years. I had seen her when I visited Dad. She was a beautiful woman with silver hair and a perfect complexion, but her vacant eyes looked out and appeared to take in nothing. She occasionally moaned. Nurses lifted her from her bed to her wheelchair and back to her bed.

Les wheeled her out to the deck during good weather. While she sat, he talked to her about the view.

A few months after Dad was situated in the nursing home, while Mom was visiting during his lunch hour, Dad started ranting at her. He swore at her. He hollered, "If I could get out of this chair, I'd kill you."

Mom left the room and walked outside to calm herself.

Les followed and asked if she was OK.

She nodded.

"I've never seen anyone treat someone the way your husband just treated you. No one deserves that," he said.

What began between Mom and Les that day was a wonderful friendship and a gift to my mom. To have a man pay attention to her in a positive way, to have a man compliment her and praise her for her efforts, her generosity, and her looks, boosted her self-esteem and spirits.

That positive regard, coupled with less stress at home, affected Mom in many ways. She began to follow the advice of her close friends Marlease, Linda, and Gloria and bought new clothes, styled her hair, wore night cream, and cut down on smoking. Marlease and Fran Bogner and Jean Richards, neighbors who continue to support her in meaningful ways, encouraged her to follow the advice of her attorney and make home improvements. She painted the inside of the house herself and hired painters to do the outside. Roofers finished off the roof that was only half done under Dad's regime. Now the tough winter snows would slide off the metal roof on the east side of the house as well as the west. Steps were put in down to the lake to replace the ancient crumbled cement steps as old as the house. An electric garage door was installed so that, after all these years, Mom wouldn't have to trudge through the rain or snow to open it manually. Inside, Mom purchased new cabinets for the bathroom. She purchased new bedroom furniture for her new bedroom. She made a guest bedroom out of Dad's study in the basement. She bought a new washer and dryer. And the new installation of central air conditioning would relieve her on those hot and humid summer days.

Perhaps to some it may seem she went overboard with the spending, but I know our history. I know how Dad controlled the money and didn't allow much for personal care and the household. So I was amused and happy when on the first day of my visit, Mom showed me her new wardrobe. Blouses, skirts, pantsuits, sweaters, blazers, and nylons filled her closets and drawers. She had a drawer for black underwear, a drawer for white underwear, and a drawer for nylons. Dozens of pairs of shoes filled her closets. She showed off several pairs of high heels, laughing that she had so many choices for the nights when she might venture off with friends for dinner or to a nightclub. She purchased a few pairs of walking shoes to trek around her property, boots to trek through the snow, and boots to show off her slender legs.

Grace

On March 29, 2007, I flew from Grand Rapids, Michigan, to Duluth, Minnesota. Mom and her friend Jean Richards picked me up and we headed straight to the nursing home. Dad was not expected to make it through the week. Within an hour I sat on the chair next to Dad's bed. He lay still, quieted, made comfortable by the morphine suppositories nurses inserted every few hours. No more IV, no more feeding tube, only oxygen and a clean white sheet and cotton blanket.

"I'm here, Dad." I said, taking his hand. No squeeze or body movement indicated he sensed my presence, but I chose to believe he could hear me since hearing is one of the last body functions to go as the physical system slows and shuts down.

Mom left so that I could spend some time alone with Dad. I held his hand and noted the disconnect over which I felt so powerless. Even as Dad was passing from this realm, my physiological response was rooted in the past. Though I didn't feel afraid, I acknowledged the oddness of touching him. Our physical relationship was never affectionate the way David's was with the girls.

"Dad, I hope you don't mind, but I'd like to sing a prayer," I said, then closed my eyes and to the tune of *Amazing Grace* chanted a short healing prayer. When I sang the passage, "Thy mercy to me is my healing and my succor in both this world and the world to come,"[10] I realized the significance of the phrase "in this world and the world to come," and acknowledged the threshold on which we stood.

I sat, keeping watch. Dad's body remained motionless. His thin arms rested at his sides, both as paralyzed as the stroke-impacted left side of his body. His breathing was only somewhat labored. "Dad, Mike and Chuck will be here soon. They're driving up. Pet's coming, too. They're about four hours away." In case Dad had less time than I was intuiting, I wanted to let him know the time frame. I had heard that sometimes people hung on until their loved ones arrived to say good-bye.

Here, in the room that had housed Dad for almost three years, there was Vaseline Intensive Care lotion on the nightstand along with mouth swabs, a cup of water for the swabs, and a portable radio and CD player that Dad did not listen to. The bulletin board Mom had hung was now half-stripped of the family photos identifying Dad in terms of his family. The framed fifty-year anniversary certificate of his graduation from Purdue, Dad's alma mater, remained attached to a nail on the dreary beige wall. On another wall hung a picture frame containing several photos I had sent as a Christmas gift. We had taken the photos during a visit with him. While playing checkers, we had noted how much calmer Dad seemed. The medication prescribed by a psychiatrist was effectively arranging his brain's chemistry to work for him rather than against him and, thus, everyone else.

Almost thirty years earlier I had stuffed dozens of slides and photos capturing posed moments from childhood into a brown paper lunch bag before my trip out west. It was proof. I needed proof that we were sometimes happy as a family, that we sometimes loved and knew joy. The photos captured moments at the zoo, in front of the Christmas tree, out in front of the Maple. In some we were posed and offered our serious smiles. In others we acted zany—sticking out our tongues, pointing to a Christmas ornament hung around an earlobe, or kicking our legs as if doing a cheer. I could share these with others as proof of some stability. The partial truth could boost my self-esteem to a degree back then. A more complete and genuine positive regard for myself I constructed,

---

10. Bahá'u'lláh, in *Bahá'í Prayers,* (Wilmette, IL: Bahá'í Publishing Trust, 2002), p. 96.

however, through years of digging inside for the truth and exposing what I remembered to myself and to those I trusted.

While I had spent years excavating the pain I had denied, I spent the remainder of that afternoon with my dad sharing some positive memories. I have shared with some of my friends and confidants these moments, final and moving for me. Some friends have shared that they couldn't do what I did and that they were not sure about my choices and gestures. They believed my father didn't deserve this kind of send-off.

Perhaps for others who have suffered, endured, and struggled to survive from childhood violence, a farewell such as the one I offered my father could never occur. I consider it a result of God's grace and years of challenging, sometimes excruciating, inner work that I was able to feel gratitude in those moments while I sat next to my dad. I chose to be there, not out of obligation, not out of expectation, not out of some external pressure to do what didn't match my own sensibilities, yearnings, and desires. I was there because I had been able to stand up to him, this man, my father, who was so ill he broke my bones and called me names no one should ever be called. I was there because I needed closure.

"Dad," I said, "I know you have not necessarily believed that there's something after this life. But I believe that you are getting ready to begin your eternal life and that you will be free of all the ailments that have afflicted you. I want you to know, Dad, that I love you and I have completely forgiven you. I wish you only peace." I kissed his forehead. A single tear formed in his right eye. That tear—smaller than a dime, maybe the size of a pearl—remained in the corner of Dad's eye. It did not fall or slip down his cheek—the cheek I wished I had felt comfortable enough, safe enough as a child to rest my own cheek against rather than obediently tap with a kiss until he said I was old enough and no longer needed to kiss him good-night.

I initially told others that the tear did slide down his cheek. I needed the significance of a falling tear. Some part of me still craved from him some hint of recognition and authentic acknowledgment of the tragedy we had barely survived. The possible meanings of a falling tear could fill a page in a dictionary, but what I needed was some representation of Dad's remorse, grief, or regret for the crimes he had committed against my mom, my brothers, and me.

I shared this adaptation of what occurred for several days until I reflected upon the significance of the tear that doesn't fall. That tear—small as a gem, pooled in the inner corner of Dad's right eye, where it remained in place—did not run down his cheeks and vanish and could not be wiped away and therefore erased. The inner corner of his eye held the clear pool of his grief, our grief, the surprise of my love that emerged without reservation, freed from the old pain and anger. That tiny pool contained the complex universe of our lives.

Dad held on throughout that afternoon and into the early evening. When, finally, my brothers and sister-in-law arrived that night, we all gathered around his bed. Chuck joked around in his usual fashion. "Dad, you're looking all right. You're resting well. Everything's taken care of," he offered. Mike was quiet, struggling for the words his tender and sensitive heart felt. I was philosophical and direct, as I had been all afternoon. Later Mike said that he wished that he had said something. "I don't know what's wrong with me. I just stood there. How did you talk to him like that?"

I mumbled an answer to my brother about being an English major and said that after all the years of studying and teaching, words came easily to me. But I would wonder over the next several days, how did I forgive the man I had feared? How could love exist after all we had endured? Why did I tremble uncontrollably when I called Dad's sister, my aunt, later that night and cried out, "Dad's dead"? How could I insist on a memorial when Mom was ready to uphold Dad's wishes for not having one? How was I able to greet his friends and receive their memories and praises and accept them, realizing their perceptions were as real and legitimate as mine?

The answer that came to me again was grace. While it's true that I have worked hard for many years, each step of the way I sensed assistance that comes from beyond my perceptions. I sensed the grace of God working through others who have listened, shared, counseled, and loved. I sensed grace when I sought spiritual guidance through the world's great scriptures, particularly the scriptures to which I most often turn—the Bahá'í writings. I sensed that grace came to me through my dreams.

That night, within an hour of our returning to Mom's house, the phone rang. We had left Dad, thinking he would hold on for a day or two more because he appeared stable and quiet. But that was not to be.

— — —

The day after Dad died, I, along with my mom and brothers, arrived at the funeral home and behaved as many do in such moments. We consulted the undertaker on the arrangements—no wake or showing, a memorial instead. Dad's ashes would be interred at the veteran's cemetery as he had wanted. We decided on the wall, above ground, rather than a burial below ground. We selected the date. The military funeral would consist of a military chaplain offering a few words, the folding and presentation of the American flag, and the sounding of taps by uniformed members of the armed forces, his colleagues offering the final honors for his service to his country. The complexities of our individual lives and our collective life as a family remained hidden behind the social conventions and expectations of this occasion.

After our consultation, the undertaker led us into the parlor. He left the four of us standing before the casket. We stood in silence for a few moments. Then Mike commented that Dad looked pretty good.

"Not a gray hair on that head," I said.

"But look at those sideburns," Chuck said. "Dad, you should have used some L'Oreal hair dye."

Our laughter at Chuck's remark subsided, and each of us fell into our own separate quietness. Mom moved back to the periphery of the room, detached and no doubt relieved that the many details she had been taking care of since Dad was placed in the nursing home were almost behind her. Chuck leaned over the casket and choked back tears. Mike stood before the casket one last time, nodded his head, and then left the room.

While the three of them went out to smoke, I remained at the casket and took a long last look at Dad's body, emptied of the complexity of who he was in this life. All that remained was the emptied cage, almost like a prison cell, scheduled for cremation. His eyes were closed, his mouth in somewhat of a smile. This face was the same preoccupied face that had barely regarded me, especially during those early years when I craved his recognition. I remembered a photo taken in 1959. Dad wore the Air Force uniform—ironed slacks, a short-sleeved shirt, and a hat. Glasses framed the eyes that bore straight ahead into the lens, as expected. I stood wearing a cotton dress, anklets, and white-tied shoes, my head reaching Dad's knees, tipped up toward the face that looked away. We both stood on the gravel driveway next to the old Chevy he drove to and from the base where he spent most of his waking hours exerting such effort that he earned Airman of the Year awards.

Here was the body of the man I had known longer than any other. Here was the body of the man I had called Dad. He had influenced me in profound ways—both positive and negative. He loved and wounded me. He guided and abandoned me. He taught me some things that I would accept and some that I would reject. He was a man I feared. He was a man I sometimes loathed. He was a man who I believed should have begged my forgiveness. I came to accept, however, that I was powerless over him, that I needed to pray to understand and to forgive him, while setting that firm boundary of not allowing him to violate me as he had for so many years.

That afternoon back at Mom's home, Mom and I spent a few quiet moments together. "I want to say something, Kim, and don't stop me like you have before," she began. "Don't say, 'It's OK.' Just let me speak." She looked in my eyes. "I want you to know that I will go to my grave knowing and regretting that I stayed and didn't protect you children. You always want to spare me and say, 'It's OK. That time period didn't have the kind of resources they have today for women.' But I know women who left such situations. I have met women who didn't stay, who didn't allow their kids to endure what I allowed you and your brothers to suffer. It cost all of you. I know many of your challenges and problems relate to the past, and I live with that. I live with the regret that I didn't do anything, and I am so sorry."

I stood there and received my mom's words. I felt sober and sad. I wished that none of us had had to endure what we endured. We as a family needed institutions, agencies, and the individuals representing them to help us. We needed the Centers for Women in Transition, the Child Protective Services, and the justice system. We needed trained and sensitive members of religious institutions to ably respond and advocate for us. We needed the educational and health care systems to serve our fragile and broken family. We needed healing, and we needed justice. We were too broken, too weakened, too sick to mend ourselves or even to see where we needed such mending. As a family we were paralyzed by our fears and the effects of violence.

The memorial was held a week later at the beautiful lakefront home of Jean Richards, a dear family friend who offered to host the gathering. That afternoon the wind swept the rain across Lake Pokegama, still frozen from the long winter. Jean's home provided a comfortable place for family and friends to come together and pay tribute to Dad's contributions, Dad's life. Turkey, ham, vegetable and bread platters, casseroles, and desserts filled the island and countertops. We spread out throughout the main floor into the dining and living rooms and the den, where a wet bar offered a variety of drinks. The view of the lake, the gray sky, the pines and the bare trees that would soon be filled with buds became a conversation piece. The view comforted and pulled us from the details of mixed nuts, cocktail napkins, and club soda toward creation, the natural world, and the complexities of our human existence.

I met friends of Dad from his bridge group, the Lions Club, and the community at large. "Your Dad was the most gentle soul I've ever known, so caring and kind." "Ron's brilliance kept us working hard at bridge." "He served and gave of himself." "Such a tender man."

I had heard similar sentiments before as a child and teen, and as a teen I had responded by saying, "Every family has its problems." Back then I couldn't stand that Dad behaved one way for the public and another for his family. I had not yet matured, not yet acknowledged that I, too, could be one way in public and another way with those closest to me. I had also come to understand that Dad had been diagnosed with various mental challenges, had not learned appropriate ways to handle conflict and differences of opinion, and had internalized traditional and oppressive messages about his role as a man. Not that his violence toward us was legal or justified because of these reasons, not that any person's violence should be accepted because of these reasons, just that knowing for me cleared some of the inner chaos of my own past and allowed me to receive different perceptions of Dad at his memorial and, once again, realize he was more than the sum of my experiences with him.

After mingling and after the latecomers arrived, we gathered. Mom had asked David to speak. My parents loved David for his dignity, strength of character, sense of fairness and justice, and his sense of humor. David welcomed everyone and shared his memories of Dad—how they met, how Dad wrestled initially with the reality that his daughter had fallen in love and wanted to marry someone who was biracial, and how he accepted and welcomed David into the family.

Words came easily to me. I shared what years of hard work and the grace of God allowed me to share, those moments with Dad before his passing. I also added that my relationship with him was complex and challenging and that I was grateful, however, that I had managed to offer that kind of good-bye. "At one time, way back when, I ran away and left home, angry with my dad, hurt by him. At another, I didn't see him for a few years. I no longer debate with myself whether that was right or wrong. It just was." I paused and caught my breath. "I tell my own children, repeat what's worthy of being repeated, and where your dad and I have fallen short or failed, you have our permission, our blessing, our encouragement to strive to not repeat that.

"I have worked hard to not repeat what I believe my dad now knows from the great beyond should not be repeated. And I also want to acknowledge, as I did with him that final afternoon, what he gave me that I hope will go down through the generations: an independent mind that thinks and questions and does not blindly accept information and traditions, the love of a good debate, a love of nature and great writers and thinkers, concern for the world and the problems that face humanity, appreciation for the world's great religions, respect for the environment, and a hard work ethic.

"One afternoon when I was perhaps in fifth grade, Dad asked me, 'What do you have that no one else has?' I thought and thought and didn't know. 'Your dreams. Your imagination,' he said. Though it took me a number of years to allow myself to dream and to revere my imagination, I remember that moment, that gift."

～　～　～

The next day we said our last formal good-bye at the veterans' cemetery. As I learned when I refused to see Dad for a few years, absence can be a powerful presence. During those three years I dreamed of Dad, I thought of him, and I agonized over my decision. I was angry at him. I hated him. I couldn't understand him. I grieved over the life we had had together, so much pain and hurt. And all along, he was my dad, the man who biologically fathered me and yet lacked the capacities to raise me well. Still, he was my dad. I yearned for the kind of father-daughter relationship I never had. That yearning, that deep hunger, I filled in destructive ways at first. But, through seeking professional help and allowing myself to grieve, I began to allow others to provide what my dad was unable to give. I found refuge in nature and music and yoga. I brought in the justice system, knowing that I was too close to the situation to handle the variables. I learned to set boundaries. I came to understand that healing is a process, one that is lifelong and without graduation dates. I also came to experience something more than survival—thriving. I could thrive in this life.

A few weeks after Dad's passing, I dreamed that he sat in the backseat of the car. A peaceful and rare silence enveloped him. His skin radiated health, his eyes a joy I had not observed until this moment. Without any physiological or self-inflicted ailments, his soul shone through the body housing it.

Epilogue: Reflections

Eight months after Dad's passing, my brother Chuck was arrested. A mug shot appeared on the second page of the newspaper in his community. The headline summarized that he was arrested for threatening to kill his girlfriend and two others. The ten-inch article reported that Chuck and his girlfriend had been out drinking at a bar and began arguing. They returned home and continued fighting. She left and returned with two friends to retrieve her belongings. Chuck came out on the front porch waving a gun and threatening to kill them. The two friends took off, but Chuck's girlfriend, fearless, went inside. He threatened her again and she called the police. As she was dialing, he pistol-whipped her and shoved her to the ground. He did not resist arrest when the police arrived and was later released on bond.

After Mom, Mike, and I got over the initial shock of what had occurred, Mike telephoned and asked me what I thought about the whole situation. I didn't hold back in my response. "I think what I've always thought, that no one can survive a childhood like ours without getting professional help. Many years back, both you and Chuck ridiculed me and even suggested that if I was the crazy one, I should go ahead and get some help, but that you were fine. I've spent years of painstaking work trying to overcome the effects of the past, and I still struggle. You and Chuck have chosen not to get help. Chuck acts a lot like Dad. He has a violent temper, and now this has happened. You're an alcoholic, and both David and I are afraid. You don't look healthy. We're worried that if you keep on drinking, you won't be with us much longer."

There was a long silence.

"You're right, Kim. It's not like Chuck didn't hear Dad threatening to kill Mom all the time. And you're also right about the drinking. I have a problem."

Within a month Mike checked himself into a rehabilitation center in Jacksonville, Florida, to detoxify and begin to get at the root causes of his alcoholism, which he now believes just might relate to our childhood. His disease was so advanced just before he checked in for treatment that he couldn't hold a glass of water in the morning without dropping it. His whole body shook. He needed three to four shots of straight alcohol just to calm the shakes.

Both of my brothers have had newspaper articles written about their infractions—Chuck having threatened to kill his girlfriend, and Mike having been arrested for one DWI after another. The reader of such an article could make a judgment about my brothers, just as I have made snapshot judgments when I read articles about people I don't know committing a wrongdoing or a crime, but I know my brothers. I know they are more than the crimes they have committed. I believe the root causes of their adult problems stem from the childhood we shared. I witnessed Mike as a young boy being thrown against a radiator, punched and shoved, sworn at and ridiculed. I observed Chuck receiving similar but somewhat less severe treatment, maybe because he learned to identify with my Dad to ward off the kinds of beatings Mike and I received. I hope that these two men, my brothers, will seek out and receive the help they need to heal from the effects of violence and to make amends with the individuals they have harmed. My love and compassion for them does not mean that I believe they should be spared from the justice system. Should they not get the help they need to overcome their challenges, and should they cause harm to others, I would be the first one to want justice delivered. Perhaps if the laws had been stronger when we were children, our Dad would have been removed from the home, perhaps even arrested. Perhaps if the laws had been stronger, more options would have been available to Mom, and she would have been able to protect us without fearing for her life and ours.

In our most recent phone call, Chuck said, "Put this in your book, Kim," referring to his own arrest. "Look what happened. People need to know this. The kind of shit we went through just gets repeated. I'm not trying to blame Dad. I take full responsibility. It's my fault, and I need some major help—maybe some anger classes. If I have to do time, I will. I'll take what's coming to me. I'm not going to be like Dad and blame others. This was my doing."

Chuck also shared that in those moments of rage, he felt totally out of control, which disturbs him. Though court dates have been pushed up, he will serve time and experience the consequences for a moment that fortunately did not lead to an even more horrific outcome.

In the past year in my small town of Holland, Michigan, three women have been murdered by their husbands or live-in boyfriends. Sadly, all of the women had restraining orders that did not prevent their deaths. This is one town, one dot on the world map. How many women and children have been killed by supposed loved ones? How many of the perpetrators were once victims and did not get the help they needed to overcome the effects of the violence inflicted on them?

Chuck and his girlfriend are back together, and she is pregnant. I have urged both of them to seek help so that this new evolving soul does not experience violence. Without help, the likelihood exists that their pasts will come creeping into the more difficult and stressful moments of parenting and will demolish their great intentions. Chuck confided that he would like to parent his child the way David and I parent our daughters. I appreciate the compliment, and I also know that even with all the classes, all the therapy, there are moments I wish I could redo. I often recall the words Hoda Mahmoudi shared at Bosch Bahá'í School: "Getting married and raising a family is the hardest work you will ever do." For those of us who have come out of violent childhoods and intend to do everything in our power to break the cycle of violence, creating a healthy family life is excruciatingly taxing, and, based on my experiences and observations, can only be accomplished with outside help.

The interventions and services of professionals and institutions are crucial to stopping the cycle of violence from affecting another generation. Families such as my own that have been affected by domestic violence need help, even when—and especially when—they may resist it. When families such as my own state that they don't need help, I believe they are coming from a position similar to my own right after I was hit by a car. I thought I would be fine, even though I had sustained spinal compression fractures that left me partially paralyzed. I thought I could somehow heal without surgery and that I would run a 5-K race. There are thousands of books on the power of positive thinking, and I believe that our thoughts can determine the quality of our lives, but I'm not talking about that here. I'm talking about denial. I'm talking about a particular incapacity to see a situation for what it is. I'm talking about how crucial outside professional intervention is for those of us who minimize and deny the painful reality of our situation and need help to get a healthy perspective on it. Without the help of the doctors in Tucson, I might be using a cane or a wheelchair today, still dreaming about running a 5-K rather than actually running one. My denial of the serious nature of my accident matched the tendency of my family to deny the reality of our situation. Without outside help, I never would have been able to examine my childhood. Sick cells, cancerous cells, can't cure themselves. They need the influence of healthy cells. They need treatment to destroy, dismantle, or heal the sick cells. They need treatment to engage the healthy cells and help them flourish and prevail.

Over the years I have had many therapists ask me what I have done to heal as I have. They express surprise that I am able to function as well as I do and that I've managed to overcome as much as I have. They have said that most people who have endured similar sufferings struggle throughout their lives to survive and that some actually don't survive.

In addition to seeking out professional help, there are several other ways I have helped myself to endure the pain of the healing process, to make progress, and to celebrate successes as I continue to evolve. I offer a number of suggestions in the spirit of the twelve-step philosophy—a smorgasbord of ideas for those who are endeavoring to heal and break the cycle of violence. These suggestions come from over thirty years of recovery work, and I certainly did not incorporate all of them at once. I have come upon these ideas little by little over the years, and I believe they have helped me not only to survive violence but also to go on to thrive. This is by no means an exhaustive list, but I hope it provides enough of a healthy start to be of service.

Emotional Health

- Commit to getting counseling and educating yourself on intimate-partner and family violence. Check out the yellow pages, make some calls, interview a few licensed therapists, and choose one with whom you connect—preferably one who has some background and training in family and intimate-partner violence. While I have benefited from many kinds of therapy, I made significant progress when working with therapists who specialized in family violence and eating disorders. A few of the many books that helped me are *Why Does He Do That?* by Lundy Bancroft, *The Macho Paradox,* by Jackson Katz, and *Addiction to Perfection,* by Marion Woodman. Many of these books can be found at your local library. If a lack of finances prevents you from seeking out professional help, check with your physician or a community or mental health agency. Centers for Women in Transition often provide counseling at a discounted rate or free of charge. My recommendation for counseling is so strong that I don't consider it optional. Counseling is essential.

- Seek out twelve-step program support. There are a number of twelve-step programs—Alcoholics Anonymous, Al-Anon, Adult Children of Alcoholics, Overeaters Anonymous, Narcotics Anonymous, Sex and Love Addicts Anonymous, Gamblers Anonymous, Codependents Anonymous, and many more. The program follows twelve spiritual guidelines. Members share their experience, strength, and hope to help one another. I attended twelve-step programs right after my accident and right after getting married. I gained knowledge from the wisdom expressed by the members, and I found that the combination of counseling with a professional and the support of members of twelve-step programs—regular people like me facing similar challenges—was extremely beneficial.

- Develop anger management and conflict resolution skills. For those who grew up in homes where anger was not managed and conflict was not resolved, help is needed to learn skills that were not modeled. We can help ourselves by reading up on these issues, exploring methods with our therapists, taking classes, and most importantly putting into practice what we learn. Becoming aware of what triggers our anger is a vital step toward managing it. I am still working on this, but I use the following tips:

1. When I feel the anger rising and sense I'm on the brink of losing control, I give myself a time-out to calm down. I have an agreement with my husband that if I don't catch myself and stop myself from yelling at the kids, he is to give me a signal or intervene.

2. I separate from whomever I may be angry with and agree to reconvene when I'm in control of my emotions. I am not aware of anyone who is able to resolve conflict in a state of anger.

3. When I mishandle this emotion, I always take responsibility for it. No one is to blame but me, and I need to apologize.

4. I know anger itself is not a bad thing; it's how anger sometimes gets inappropriately expressed that's the problem. I don't stuff my anger down by overeating anymore. I explore my anger with my therapist or in my journal, and I figure out how to communicate what is bothering me. I usually discover that beneath the anger are other emotions—sadness or hurt.

5. I am learning how to pause. To pause is one of the best skills. There is no reason when I feel upset that my emotions need to be communicated right then and there.

6. Read the book *Anger*, by Thich Nhat Hanh.

- Be selective about who you choose to share your experiences with. When I became serious about therapy and started revealing my life story for the first time, I suddenly wanted to talk and talk. I regret that I shared some of the painful details of my life with people who were not sympathetic or trustworthy. Therapists will keep your life story confidential and will work with you in a professional manner. I have a few trusted friends I confide in, and that is it. I know them well and I know I can trust them to keep what I share confidential.

- Recognize that joy and pain coexist. Every day I find something that can irritate or cause me pain. Every day I find something that brings me joy. Because I found a way out of the deep pain of my childhood through therapy and the acknowledgment of the pain, I opened my life up to the discovery of joy. I heard the late Christopher Reeve, an actor known for his film role as Clark Kent/Superman who was paralyzed in a horseback riding accident, share that he allowed himself twenty minutes every morning to grieve and then he turned his attention to appreciating and enjoying the day ahead with his wife and children. We all have something to grieve about, and giving ourselves a limited amount of time to honor and express our grief can help us manage it. I also take some time every day to focus on and express what I'm grateful for. This elevates my spirit and puts some of my daily challenges into perspective. Though I recommend developing this habit, I also acknowledge that when I began to explore more honestly how I had been violated, the pain was overwhelming. There are usually times in the healing process when grief emerges and more painful emotions prevail. Early on in my healing process when I endured those times, I reached out to my therapist, my twelve-step program sponsor in Al-Anon, and the closest of friends. I did my best not to isolate myself. After listening to me, sometimes crying and empathizing with me, my friends would suggest a hike or a movie, which was a way to help me refocus my attention and find relief from the therapeutic and healing work.

Spiritual Health

- Honor your soul. Many of us may already have a religious affiliation or a spiritual practice. The teachings of our religion can serve us while we undergo the challenging process of healing from violence and striving to break the cycle. Continue to connect or reconnect with your religious community. Those who do not have a religious community may want to investigate the option of finding an organized group of believers who will offer spiritual comfort.
- Use your faith to uplift, rather than abuse, yourself. Since so many of us who have been victimized by violence tend to see life through the veil of that violence, we can, as I did, misinterpret scripture or situations. I have met many women like me who interpreted

the scripture from our various faith traditions inaccurately. We remained in abusive situations because of the exhortation to forgive and to love everyone. We took those passages out of context, failed to remember passages about justice, and didn't even consider that the individuals perpetrating the abuse were not following scripture. Strive to soothe your soul with scripture rather than beat yourself up for falling short of the guidance it offers. It is also important not to interpret passages without considering their historical context. Consult with others to better understand scripture as a whole, and involve professionals to help you identify your options if you are in a questionable situation.

- Create time for prayer and meditation. I spent so much of my life relying on myself to fix everything that discovering I could rely on God or a higher power came as a great relief. I didn't have to carry the burden I was carrying. I came to believe what is stated in twelve-step programs, that "God can do for me what I can't do for myself." Starting and ending my day with prayer and meditation makes a difference in my life. Taking this time allows me to remain vigilant to my own inner state rather than to run from it, as I used to do. Meditation has also helped me empty my mind of negative chatter and worries and the items on my never-ending to-do list. When I meditate I focus less on the material world and more on the matters of my heart and soul. I invite God in to help me develop the virtues I need in my various roles as an individual, mother, wife, daughter, sister, friend, community member, and professional. I invite God in to help me develop my soul, and I invite God to help me overcome whatever tendencies from the past are not helping me.

- Practice affirmations. I became conscious that I had internalized the emotional battering from my past. To replace the negativity lodged in my own mind, I continue to read books on positive thinking and affirmations, I enjoy listening to CDs of meditations and affirmations, and I strive to replace my negative thoughts with positive ones. Just recently, my daughter Anisa and I began listening to Marianne Williamson's "Meditations for a Miraculous Life" following our morning prayers and meditation. We love how the uplifting and soulful expressions help us to release stress and frustration and remind us to rely more fully on God in the day ahead.

Physical Health

- Develop a positive relationship with your body. Those who have been physically battered need to claim or reclaim their bodies. Our bodies—the temples of our souls—deserve respect. I didn't know how to respect my body. I had to learn. Though I managed to stop drinking alcohol after I became a Bahá'í, I needed professional help to overcome my food addiction and eating disorder. If you suffer from an addiction of any sort, seek out medical attention.

- Find time to exercise. I schedule exercise into my daily life. Though I was not athletic as a child, I value exercise because it has helped me reconnect with my body, relieve stress, and remain healthy and fit. Again, people ask, "what kind of exercise should I do?" The best answer I have heard is "the one you will do." The diversity of exercise available provides us with many wonderful and fun choices. I like variety, so I have tried out weight training, yoga, tai chi, pilates, aerobics, spinning, and so on.

- Eat well and learn about the power of nutrition. At one time in my life, I thought I would never overcome my addiction to food. When I started learning about other ways to soothe myself and began to feel more comfortable with my emotions, my problems with food went away. I love learning about good nutrition. Hippocrates, the father of medicine, said, "Let food be your medicine and medicine be your food." I feel more energized, alert, and emotionally balanced when I eat plenty of fruits and vegetables, whole grains, and legumes. Explore your options and seek out guidance.

Family Health

- Commit to creating a violence-free home. I promised God long before I left my childhood home that I would not do to my children what had been done to me. This was easier said than accomplished. But that commitment, that promise, motivated me to do whatever it took to learn the skills and get the help I needed to avoid recreating my childhood.

- Avoid blindly repeating the traditions and behaviors of the past. If civilization is to advance, we must examine our personal and collective lives and make some tough decisions. What traditions and behaviors are worthy of being repeated and passed down to the next generation? What traditions and behaviors need to be discarded? I have pondered these questions as they relate to marriage, parenting, and family life, and then made decisions about what to keep and what to discard.

- Educate yourself on marriage, parenting, and family life. I envision a day when public schools will offer courses on marriage, parenting, and family life. We seek out education to develop our professional lives; yet, sadly, too many of us do not receive education on how to develop our personal lives. Until our schools realize the value of including courses on preparing for marriage, parenting, and family life, we need to pursue our own investigation to prepare us for these important aspects of our lives, should we choose them. Check out your local community college, community education, and hospitals for courses on parenting. Churches, mosques, and synagogues often provide courses to help couples prepare for marriage. Check out books from the local library. Check out Web sites and databases on the internet. Some excellent resources on the world wide web are: http://www.acf.hhs.gov/healthymarriage/index.html, http://www.healthymarriageinfo.org/, http://www.marriagetweets.com/, http://www.marriagetransformation.com/, http://www.virtuesproject.com/, http://www.nurturingparenting.com/ and http://www.loveandlogic.com/. Numerous other resources are available. Become a lifelong learner.

- Try out marriage and/or family counseling to deal with difficulties. We take our car to the mechanic when it needs repair, but many of us seldom take our marriages or families to professionals when our relationships are in need of repair. When we can't find ways to deal with problems on our own, it's time to get outside assistance. I am so grateful for the help my family and I have received. I'm also grateful that my children know there are tools that can help them get through difficulties that might arise in their future, that they don't have to struggle alone, and that there are professionals who have been trained and are eager to help.

• Balance *being* and *doing*. In our busy world we can fall into the rush and frenzy of doing, doing, doing. We overschedule ourselves and our children. This kind of pace and busyness puts me at risk for not handling stress well. I need slow moments in my day, time to reflect, to be, to know stillness. I love the saying that people too busy to pray are busier than God wants them to be. I strive for balance and sometimes know that I have failed to achieve it when I am quick to anger, irritable, or when I find myself overeating. I often have to reconsider my schedule and make some healthier decisions.

Though several professionals have acknowledged the progress I have made, I continually strive to undo the effects of the violence and to establish new behaviors. I have enjoyed periods—some a few years in duration—of not visiting a therapist on a regular basis, but I remain vigilant. Now that my daughters have entered adolescence, for example, but I need to parent differently than when they were children. Their emerging independence has challenged me. I have sometimes responded in overly emotional ways to normal situations typical of the adolescent/parent relationship. In addition to making visits again to a therapist for professional guidance, I choose from the tools cited above to help me get through these challenges more effectively than if I were to just "wing it." I keep up my practice of prayer and meditation, relying on God for assistance. I remain committed to self-care. I exercise some of the stress away, eat well, and strive to get enough sleep. I read books to learn about effective ways to parent teens. I talk to friends also parenting teens for support and ideas. I focus on what I love about my daughters and express gratitude to God and to them for their presence in my life. By employing these practices and strategies, I am making efforts to reduce conflict in the home and facilitate unity.

In a statement about the family unit, the Bahá'í International Community writes, "Like the world as a whole, the family is in transition. In every culture, families are disintegrating, fragmenting under pressure of economic and political upheavals and weakening in the face of moral and spiritual confusion. The conditions surrounding the family surround the nation. The happenings in the family are the happenings in the life of the nation. Bahá'ís see these disturbances as signs of humanity's struggle toward a new age in its collective development, an age of maturity."[11] The process of maturing presents challenges and opportunities. While many of us may share the dream of creating healthy and unified families, how many of us are aware that our efforts to realize that dream can affect the health of our world?

Those who have been victimized by violence have choices and serious decisions to make. We can choose to minimize or deny the violence with which we were raised and therefore do nothing. This will more than likely lead to passing down the violence in varying degrees to another generation. We can choose to survive the violence by seeking out professional help to heal and to reduce our risk for repeating the behaviors that caused us harm. We can choose not only to survive but to go on to thrive. We can rely on God and the higher power of our understanding to heal, to build the lives of our dreams, to serve our communities and the world, and to learn new behaviors to create violence-free personal lives and families. Making the effort to break the cycle, though challenging, will influence future generations. My hope for those who have been victimized by violence is that we utilize the available tools and resources to help us put an end to this global social epidemic. The work we do to transform ourselves—an ongoing lifelong process—is significant and has a far-reaching impact. Though the process may seem slow and may include setbacks, each day allows us opportunities to improve on our efforts and practices and refine new behaviors. We must continue to polish the mirrors of our hearts, remain committed to our personal transformation, and continually practice the virtues we are developing. These activities will transform our lives, improve the health of our families, and improve the world, for a family is a nation in miniature, and healthy and unified families will make for a healthier and more peaceful world.

---

11. The Bahá'í International Community, Family in a World Community, (Pamphlet first distributed at the World NGO Forum launching the United Nations International Year of the Family, November, 1993), p. 1.

Baháʼí
PUBLISHING

and the Baháʼí Faith

Baháʼí Publishing produces books based on the teachings of the Baháʼí Faith. Founded over 160 years ago, the Baháʼí Faith has spread to some 235 nations and territories and is now accepted by more than five million people. The word "Baháʼí" means "follower of Baháʼuʼlláh." Baháʼuʼlláh, the founder of the Baháʼí Faith, asserted that He is the Messenger of God for all of humanity in this day. The cornerstone of His teachings is the establishment of the spiritual unity of humankind, which will be achieved by personal transformation and the application of clearly identified spiritual principles. Baháʼís also believe that there is but one religion and that all the Messengers of God—among them Abraham, Zoroaster, Moses, Krishna, Buddha, Jesus, and Muḥammad—have progressively revealed its nature. Together, the world's great religions are expressions of a single, unfolding divine plan. Human beings, not God's Messengers, are the source of religious divisions, prejudices, and hatreds.

The Baháʼí Faith is not a sect or denomination of another religion, nor is it a cult or a social movement. Rather, it is a globally recognized independent world religion founded on new books of scripture revealed by Baháʼuʼlláh.

Baháʼí Publishing is an imprint of the National Spiritual Assembly of the Baháʼís of the United States.

For more information about the Baháʼí Faith,
or to contact Baháʼís near you, visit
http://www.bahai.us/
or call
1-800-22-unite

Other Books Available from Bahá'í Publishing

Creative Dimensions of Suffering
A-M. GHADIRIAN, M.D.
$15.00 U.S. / $17.00 CAN
Trade Paper
ISBN 978-1-931847-60-5

A noted professor and psychiatrist explores the link between suffering, creativity, and spirituality

Creative Dimensions of Suffering draws upon the author's personal knowledge and experience as a psychiatrist, as well as extensive research in literature, to explore the enigmatic and intriguing connection between creativity and suffering. He examines the lives of many artists, writers, poets, and scientists, as well as ordinary individuals, who have risen above their own suffering and left behind a legacy of unique and amazing experiences. Among these are well-known figures such as van Gogh, Tchaikovsky, Beethoven, Helen Keller, and Christopher Reeve. Examining their lives for insight into how they dealt with their adversity through creativity, he also explores how various conditions such as alcoholism, depression, bipolar disorder, and dementia can influence a person's creative impulse and how the interplay of creativity and spirituality can help a person deal with trauma and hardship.

Drawing on principles found in the teachings of the Bahá'í Faith, Dr. Ghadirian considers the meaning of suffering, its place in human society, and how it can lead to a closer, happier relationship with God, as well as a better relationship with oneself and with others. Indeed, many of those who have suffered the most in life have found new meaning through adversity and have emerged victorious. Their encounters with adversity and their victory over it suggest the presence of another force beyond understanding that reinforces the individual during periods of intense suffering.

Illumine My Family

Prayers and Meditations from the Bahá'í Faith
BAHÁ'U'LLÁH, THE BÁB, AND 'ABDU'L-BAHÁ
Compiled by Bahá'í Publishing
$12.00 U.S. / $13.50 CAN
Trade Paper
ISBN 978-1-931847-62-9

A heartwarming collection of prayers for people of all faiths to meet the challenges of everyday life

Illumine My Family is a collection of prayers and meditative passages from the writings of the Bahá'í Faith that will help any family wishing to incorporate spirituality into their daily lives. The passages included offer guidance and prayers on subjects relevant to any family regardless of their background or current circumstances. Subjects covered include marriage, parents, motherhood, children, love, healing, the loss of a loved one, and more. The book has been put together with the hope that it will assist families to grow together and to foster strong relationships with each other and with God.

Life at First Sight

Finding the Divine in the Details
PHYLLIS EDGERLY RING
$15.00 U.S. / $17.00 CAN
Trade Paper
ISBN 978-1-931847-67-4

Phyllis Ring divulges in this collection of personal essays how to "see the spiritual" in everyday moments and everyday life. Like love at first sight, "life at first sight" focuses on instant recognition and irresistible attraction, a sense of something mysteriously familiar and a sense of spiritual connection. The essays show how to develop a new sense of being during daily activities and everyday interactions, as well as through engagement with the natural world. As a jumping off point for spiritual conversation, these compositions offer food for thought on how to lead a more spiritual life.

". . . Captures the web of meaning that unites and sustains all of human life. These sparkling essays remind us that the spiritual side of life is not a luxury or an optional nicety, but utterly crucial. At this moment in history, no message is more vital."—**Larry Dossey, MD, Author of** *The Power of Premonitions and The Extraordinary Healing Power of Ordinary Things*

"These essays are a treasure, especially as they pursue the journey of the human spirit through the perils—and joys—of 'the road not taken.' This is the sort of book that will warm, celebrate, and console the reader on a sour day. The book is lovingly written and beautifully conceived, and dares to approach the practical reality of the spiritual life."—**Dolores Kendrick, Poet Laureate of the District of Columbia and Author of** *Why the Woman Is Singing on the Corner* **and** *Now Is the Thing to Praise*

The Universe Within Us
A Guide to the Purpose of Life
JANE E. HARPER
$15.00 U.S. / $17.00 CAN
Trade Paper
ISBN 978-1-931847-58-2

A provocative look at the purpose of life through a mixture of religion, science, and personal experience

Author Jane E. Harper offers insight into a new way to look at life. *The Universe Within Us* is a mixture of science, religion, and personal experience that offers a new understanding of our place and purpose in the universe—an understanding that leads to the conclusion that every human being possesses a spiritual nature. Harper argues that, traditionally, answers to questions about the purpose of life have long been the domain of priests and clergy, and, more recently, scientists—and often the answers have been less than satisfying. The religious answers often leave the intellect out and defy what the rational mind can accept, while the scientific answers satisfy the intellect at the expense of the heart and soul. Drawing on resources available from the sciences, from the world's sacred scriptures, and from personal observations and experiences, she offers a unique map of the universe and an explanation of life's purpose that is truly satisfying.

To view our complete catalog,
Please visit http://books.bahai.us